THE Complete Coconut Cookbook

200 Gluten-Free, Grain-Free and Nut-Free Vegan Recipes Using Coconut Flour, Oil, Sugar and More

Camilla V. Saulsbury

Robert
ROSE

For complete cataloguing information, see page 311.

Disclaimer
The recipes in this book have been carefully tested by our kitchen and our tasters. To the best
of our knowledge, they are safe and nutritious for ordinary use and users. For those people with
food or other allergies, or who have special food requirements or health issues, please read the
suggested contents of each recipe carefully and determine whether or not they may create a
problem for you. All recipes are used at the risk of the consumer.

We cannot be responsible for any hazards, loss or damage that may occur as a result of any
recipe use.

For those with special needs, allergies, requirements or health problems, in the event of any
doubt, please contact your medical adviser prior to the use of any recipe.

Design and production: Martina Hwang/PageWave Graphics Inc.
Editor: Sue Sumeraj
Recipe editor: Jennifer MacKenzie
Proofreader: Sheila Wawanash
Indexer: Gillian Watts
Photographer: Colin Ericson
Associate photographer: Matt Johannsson
Food stylist: Kathryn Robertson
Prop stylist: Charlene Ericson

Cover image: Gingered Carrot and Coconut Soup (page 158)

Other photographs: Coconut Meat © iStockphoto.com/AnjelaGr; Dried Coconut Meat
© Shutterstock.com/Madlen; Unsweetened Dried, Flaked Coconut © Shutterstock.com/
exopixel; Virgin Coconut Oil © Shutterstock.com/Geo-grafika; Shredded Coconut
© Shutterstock.com/optimarc; Coconut Flour © iStockphoto.com/marekuliasz; Coconut Sugar
© Shutterstock.com/marekuliasz; Full-Fat Coconut Milk © Shutterstock.com/Brent Hofacker.

The publisher gratefully acknowledges the financial support of our publishing program by the
Government of Canada through the Canada Book Fund.

Published by Robert Rose Inc.
120 Eglinton Avenue East, Suite 800, Toronto, Ontario, Canada M4P 1E2
Tel: (416) 322-6552 Fax: (416) 322-6936
www.robertrose.ca

Printed and bound in Canada

2 3 4 5 6 7 8 9 MI 22 21 20 19 18 17 16 15 14

For Sue Sumeraj, Martine Quibell, Jennifer MacKenzie,
Nina McCreath and Marian Jarkovich

Contents

Introduction: Coconuts for Health

Over the past decade, the humble, hairy coconut has become a pinnacle product for everyone and anyone interested in healthy eating and living. The tropical staple is available in supermarkets and health food stores in the form of oil, butter, flour, water and more, and a growing band of supporters — including scientists — are singing its healing and restorative praises.

Coconuts are anything but a fly-by-night fad. The meat, juice, milk and oil of the coconut have nourished people for thousands of years. The coconut palm is often referred to as the "tree of life," and the Sanskrit word for coconut can be roughly translated as "the food that sustains all life." Ayurvedic texts dating back centuries indicate a wide range of folk medicine uses for the coconut, and traditional cultures across Asia have long regarded it as a symbol of fertility.

Justification for this reverence is easily found: coconuts contain ample amounts of nourishment (water, protein, fat, carbohydrates, fiber, vitamins and minerals), the trees themselves offer shade, the leaves are repurposed for cooking and shelter, and the shell and its fiber can be used for rope, cooking fires, currency and flotation devices.

Coconut Oil in North America

Coconut oil, in particular, became a popular option in North American homes and bakeries, as well as food manufacturers, in the first four decades of the 20th century. This was due to a variety of factors, including its low cost, versatility of use, long shelf life and low melting point.

But the tide began to turn against coconut oil in the 1950s with the emergence of research connecting saturated fats and heart health. The first scientific indictment came from a physiologist named Ancel Keys, who in 1953 published "Atherosclerosis: A Problem in Newer Public Health." Keys wrote that while the total death rate in the United States was declining, the number of heart disease–related deaths was steadily climbing. Keys argued that the differential death rates could be attributed to one cause: greater consumption of saturated fat — such as animal fat and coconut oil — in the U.S. compared to other countries. In short, the higher the saturated fat intake, according to national diet surveys, the higher the rate of heart disease. Keys' causal analysis became known as the diet-heart hypothesis.

Ample skepticism and criticism of the many flaws in Keys' research and conclusions quickly followed from the scientific community. In a 1957 paper, renowned biostatistician Jacob Yerushalmy pointed out, for example, that while data from the six countries Keys examined seemed to support the diet-heart hypothesis, statistics were actually available for 22 countries. And when all 22 were analyzed, the apparent link between fat consumption and heart disease disappeared. Other critics noted that Keys had no basis for his causal link hypothesis; at best, they argued, he had merely observed a correlation between saturated fat consumption and heart health. Other factors, such as exercise and/or the consumption of refined sugars and grains, were completely ignored.

Nevertheless, the diet-heart hypothesis took hold, and it was soon heavily promoted by the American Heart Association (AHA), the American Medical Association (AMA) and the media.

At the same time that health officials began warning consumers of the health risks associated with consuming saturated fats, coconut oil was becoming increasingly difficult to purchase in North America. Prior to the Second World War, the Philippines and other South Pacific islands were the primary sources for coconut oil and coconut products. Japanese occupation disrupted this supply chain, and it took many years post-war for coconut commerce between the Pacific and North America to resume. By then, North American food manufacturers had worked to create a viable and very profitable alternative: polyunsaturated oils.

Coconut oil's reputation went from bad to worse in April 1994. That spring, the Center for Science in the Public Interest (CSPI) put out a study claiming that a large movie theater popcorn — popped in coconut oil — delivered as much saturated fat as six Big Macs. CSPI executive director Michael Jacobson went so far as to claim that such popcorn was a nutritional "Godzilla." The announcement caused movie theater popcorn sales to plummet by as much as 50%. Consuming coconut oil became the food equivalent of smoking cigarettes.

The Health Benefits of Coconut Come Full Circle

So how does a nutritional pariah make a complete turnaround?

Simultaneous with the health prescriptions to avoid coconut fat at all costs, clinical evidence of the myriad health benefits of coconut was mounting. Coconut in general, and coconut oil in particular, is packed with nutrients, is an excellent healing agent and kills a wide array of bad bugs that cause infection, illness and disease. Based on the growing research, coconut oil should be considered a functional food that has its place as part of a healthful diet.

Medium-Chain Fatty Acids

Perhaps the most surprising news regarding coconut oil pertains to its composition. While the fat in coconut is about 92% saturated, the most recent studies on coconut fat indicate that not all such fats are created equal. The length of the chains of the carbon atoms in fats determines how our body processes them; the saturated fat in coconut oil is made up of medium-chain fatty acids (MCFAs), which raise blood cholesterol levels only slightly, if at all. Instead of storing the fatty acids, the body transmits them straight to the liver, where they are used immediately for energy.

This explains the findings of a long-term, multidisciplinary study in the 1960s and '70s of the health of people living on the Pacific islands of Tokelau and Pukapuka. Researchers found that, despite eating a high-fat diet (35% to 60% of the islanders' calories were from fat, mostly saturated fat from coconuts), the islanders were virtually free of atherosclerosis, heart disease and colon cancer. Digestive problems were rare, the islanders were lean and healthy, and ailments such as kidney disease and high blood cholesterol were entirely absent.

Antimicrobial Properties

The oil in coconut has another profound benefit: immune system support. About 49% of the MCFAs in coconut oil are lauric acid, while the rest of the fats include 8% caprylic acid, 7% capric acid, 2% stearic acid, 6% oleic acid and 2% linoleic acid. Lauric acid is recognized for its antimicrobial properties. Once ingested, lauric acid transforms into monolaurin, a multipurpose antiviral and antibacterial compound that infiltrates the membranes of lipid-coated bacteria or other microbes such as fungi, protozoa and even viruses. It destabilizes their membranes, causing them to disintegrate, and kills the microbes as a result. Further, the latest research indicates that lauric acid specifically inhibits the growth of *Helicobacter pylori* bacteria (which cause chronic gastritis), boosts metabolism after meals and may promote weight loss.

Weight Loss

Although it may seem counterintuitive that fat intake can produce fat loss, coconut oil can be part of a balanced weight-loss plan. The first explanation supporting the use of coconut oil for weight loss is that it contains 2.6% fewer calories per gram than other fats. This difference of about 100 kcal per pound of fat may appear small but can become significant over time. In a study published in the March 2008 issue of the *American Journal of Clinical Nutrition*, researchers had a group of 49 overweight men and women adopt a calorie-restricted diet, including a daily dose of either coconut oil or olive oil. Both groups lost weight, but the weight loss was more significant in the coconut oil group. The group that consumed coconut oil lost 7 pounds (3.5 kg), while the olive oil group lost only 3 pounds (1.5 kg). These results are in line with other studies showing a reduction in weight and body fat in overweight participants who consumed coconut oil as part of their diet. Other studies have found comparable results. Many participants involved in some of the weight-loss studies using coconut oil also have reported higher satiety and more stable energy levels, which can facilitate weight loss.

Cardiovascular Disease

It will likely surprise many to learn that, despite decades of dire warnings, dietary saturated fats are not associated with cardiovascular disease. According to a March 2010 meta-analysis published in the *American Journal of Clinical Nutrition*, an examination of data from almost 350,000 people who were followed for up to 23 years revealed that there is no relationship between saturated fat intake and the risk of cardiovascular diseases and stroke.

Further support for this lack of connection comes from research that involved a randomized clinical trial of 40 middle-aged Brazilian women with abdominal obesity. Each of the women were given 2 tablespoons (30 mL) of soybean or coconut oil daily for 12 weeks. At the end of the study, both groups lost weight, but only the coconut oil group saw a significant decrease in waist circumference. In the soybean oil group, levels of total and LDL ("bad") cholesterol significantly increased, while HDL ("good") cholesterol levels decreased, worsening their cardiovascular risk profile.

Neurological Conditions

Research shows that coconut oil can also improve glucose metabolism in the brain in Alzheimer's disease, which is sometimes called type 3 diabetes because it is associated with a decline in glucose metabolism in the brain. This is why dietary strategies that promote ketosis (a high rate of burning fat for energy) can help the brain obtain an alternative source of energy. While glucose tends to be the brain's primary energy source on a standard high-carb American diet, ketone bodies can supply more than half of the brain's energy needs when carbohydrates and glucose become scarce.

A Brief History of Coconut Palm Trees

The botanical name of the coconut palm is *Cocos nucifera*, with *nucifera* meaning "nut-bearing." The English word "coconut," first mentioned in print in 1555, comes from the Spanish and Portuguese word *coco*, which means "monkey face." However, the first known written reference to coconuts comes from a fifth-century monk named Cosmas Indicopleustes, who described the trees and the coconuts (which he dubbed "India nuts") he encountered while traveling through Sri Lanka. Part of his account details the harvesting and use of the coconuts, indicating that such processes were already well established.

Coconut palms adorn the coasts of tropical beaches worldwide, from the Caribbean to Madagascar and Hawaii, but they are not native species to these regions. Indicopleustes' accounts, along with other ancient Sanskrit texts, suggest that coconuts most likely originated in Malaysia, Polynesia and southern Asia; however, since coconut palms have been crossed, cultivated and transported for thousands of years, it has been difficult to pinpoint their origins.

New research in 2011, however, brought the coconut's origins to light. A comprehensive analysis of the DNA of 1,322 coconut palms from around the world reveals that most coconuts belong to one of two genetically distinct groups: one from the coasts of India; the other from palms in Southeast Asia. Even palms that now grow on the opposite side of the world are still members of one of these two groups.

Noting the numerous and distinct differences between the groups, the researchers concluded that the coconut palm was domesticated not once but twice: in India and on the Malay Peninsula. Following the Pacific domestication, explorers and settlers likely transported coconuts to the Polynesian islands and later to Middle America. The Indian coconut palms spread west, first to East Africa, then to West Africa and later South America via European ships.

The two lineages have notable biological differences, too: the coconuts of the Indo-Atlantic palms are elongated and angular, while the Pacific coconuts tend to be squatter and rounder. Original theories for these differences were that the palms with elongated fruits were from "wild" palms, whereas the trees with rounder fruits were domesticated in one way or another. The new genetic findings put these theories to rest.

The Complete Coconut Pantry

Virgin Coconut Oil

All of the recipes in this collection that use oil call for virgin coconut oil. It is the most healthful variety of coconut oil for two reasons: 1) the oil is harvested from fresh, young coconuts; and 2) a minimal amount of processing is used to produce it. A bonus of this minimal processing is that the oil retains a delicate coconut scent and aroma.

Virgin coconut oil is made without chemicals or high heat in one of two methods. One is the quick-dry method, which involves heating the coconut meat at a very low temperature to quick-dry it. This is followed by mechanical pressing of the meat to expel the oil. The other is wet-milling, which uses the same mechanical pressing as the quick-dry method but without first drying the meat. The result

Other Types of Coconut Oil

• **Refined (RBD) coconut oil:** Refined coconut oil is made from the dried meat (copra) of mature coconuts. It is also known as RBD coconut oil because, following extraction, the oil is refined, bleached and deodorized; it is the common method for producing coconut oil. To preserve its shelf life, the oil is also treated with sodium hydroxide, which removes any free fatty acids, and in some cases, the refined oil is also hydrogenated to remain solid in varying climates. Refined coconut oil is a popular cooking oil around the world because it is low in cost; it is also used in the production of toiletries such as lotions and soaps.

• **Expeller-pressed coconut oil:** Expeller-pressed coconut oil is the next best thing to virgin coconut oil. It is considered "refined" coconut oil, but unlike RBD coconut oil, which uses chemical solvents to extract oil, expeller-pressed coconut oil uses machines in a process known as "physical refining." Further, the oil is deodorized with steam instead of solvents and is not hydrogenated. The end result is a high-quality, almost tasteless oil that retains a high level of medium-chain fatty acids.

• **Extra virgin coconut oil:** "Extra virgin" is a legitimate marker of quality for olive oil, but for coconut oil it is merely a marketing ploy. Extra virgin coconut oil is simply virgin coconut oil, so don't be fooled into paying a premium price.

• **Liquid coconut oil:** Introduced in 2013, this product is being marketed as a coconut oil that stays liquid, even when refrigerated, for ease of measuring. This product is "fractionated" coconut oil, which means that most or all of the saturated lauric acid has been removed. It is sometimes labeled "MCT oil" or "MCT coconut oil." Since lauric acid is one of the most healthful components of virgin coconut oil, this is merely a clever marketing tactic, not a benefit to consumers.

of this pressing is coconut milk (oil plus water). The second half of wet-milling involves separating the oil from the water, most often by mechanical centrifuge or refrigeration.

Using Virgin Coconut Oil

Virgin coconut oil is 90% saturated fat. It has a low melting point (76°F/24°C), largely due to its unique composition of medium-chain fatty acids, and a smoke point of 350°F (180°C), the same as butter. A high saturated fat content also makes virgin coconut oil exceptionally stable at relatively high temperatures, which means that it does not form free radicals like polyunsaturated fats do.

Unlike other plant oils that are prone to rancidity and must be refrigerated, coconut oil can be stored at room temperature. In fact, it has the longest shelf life of any plant oil. In cool regions, during winter months, or in the refrigerator, the oil is solid, but in warm climates, such as the tropical regions in which coconuts grow, it remains a clear liquid year-round. When kept at room temperature, the oil will fluctuate from liquid to solid; this is completely normal, and unlike with other oils, it does not affect the oil's quality.

When it comes to cooking and baking, coconut oil is incredibly versatile. When solid, it can be used measure for measure in place of solid shortening or butter in baked goods or for greasing pans; when liquid, it can be used measure for measure in place of melted butter and vegetable oils for sautéing, in vinaigrettes and in other savory dishes.

It is simple to scrape out a teaspoon (5 mL) or tablespoon (15 mL) of coconut oil when it is solid, but when a larger amount is needed for a recipe, it is easier to melt the coconut oil before measuring.

As noted above, it does not harm the coconut oil to be warmed to a liquid state, so you can quickly liquefy the entire jar of coconut oil. To do this, simply hold the sealed jar under warm running water, or place it in a bowl of warm water, until there is enough liquid coconut oil to measure out.

Warming Coconut Oil in the Microwave

You can microwave coconut oil to soften or liquefy it, but use caution: it will become very hot very quickly. It will only take between 5 to 15 seconds on High to liquefy, depending on the quantity of oil in the jar. Do not microwave jars made of plastic containing BPA (bisphenol A), a toxic compound. Heating the container will increase the amount of BPA that will leach into the oil.

Topical Paradise

Coconut oil has a number of surprising and effective topical uses, too, including the following:

- **Face and body moisturizer:** Apply directly to the skin. It works wonders, even on extremely dry, chapped or cracked skin, such as on the feet and elbows. On the face, it helps to reduce the appearance of fine lines and wrinkles and aids in exfoliating the outer layer of dead skin cells.

- **Facial cleanser:** An extremely gentle way to clean off the day's dirt, makeup and grime. Massage a dollop of coconut oil onto the face and neck, then wash off with wet washcloth and pat dry.

- **Facial scrub:** Mix coconut oil with baking soda or oatmeal for a gentle exfoliating facial scrub.

- **Body scrub:** Mix equal parts coconut oil with organic cane sugar in a glass jar. Use the scrub on dry skin prior to your shower or bath.

- **Shaving lotion:** Apply a thin layer of coconut oil in place of shaving cream (on the face, legs or other areas) and shave as usual. The lauric acid in the coconut oil will also serve as an antiseptic for cuts that result from shaving.

- **Skin rashes, irritations and sores:** Apply a small amount to troubled areas. It is particularly soothing for chicken pox, shingles and cold sores.

- **Deodorant:** Applying a small amount of coconut oil directly onto your armpits can help keep odors at bay, due to the oil's antibacterial properties. Alternatively, combine 1/4 cup (60 mL) coconut oil with 1 tsp (5 mL) baking soda and 1 tbsp (15 mL) arrowroot powder for a daily "cream" deodorant.

- **Toothpaste:** Combine 1 part baking soda with 4 parts coconut oil to replace your regular toothpaste. The baking soda will gently cleanse, while the coconut oil's antibacterial properties combat harmful bacteria.

- **Mouth rinse:** Also known as "oil pulling," this is an age-old practice of swishing oil (gently warm the coconut oil until it is liquid) in the mouth for 15 minutes, then spitting it out. The antimicrobial properties of coconut oil help to fight bacteria and improve general oral health.

- **Leave-in overnight conditioner:** Rub a small amount of oil into hair (mostly at ends) and comb through; wash out in the morning.

- **Flyaway hair tamer:** Rub a tiny amount of coconut oil on hands, then rub on ends or areas with flyaways, frizzies or static.

Coconut Meat

Once the outer husk of the coconut is removed, what remains is the seed and its rich inner white lining, the coconut meat. Fresh, young coconuts have meat that is juicy, tender and almost gel-like in consistency, while the meat from mature coconuts — the brown, hairy variety most people recognize — ranges from crisp and crunchy to tough and fibrous, depending on how long the coconut has been stored.

Mature coconut can be grated or chopped to add to salads and main dishes. Raw fresh coconut is a delicious snack eaten straight up. A 2-inch (5 cm) square piece of fresh coconut meat has 4 grams of fiber and only about 7 grams of carbohydrate (far less than most fresh fruit). It is also, of course, rich in coconut fat (about 15 grams of fat for that piece).

Unsweetened Dried, Flaked Coconut

Dried, flaked coconut is the meat of a mature coconut that has been dried and cut into small pieces. Dried coconut is available in several sizes, including large flaked "chips," medium flakes and fine shreds. It is available sweetened, but the recipes in this collection call for unsweetened varieties only. Both sweetened and unsweetened varieties are readily available in supermarkets. Dried coconut is most often packaged in bags, but can occasionally be found in cans; canned varieties tend to be moister than bagged coconut. Unsweetened dried, flaked coconut will keep in an airtight container in a cool, dry place for up to 1 year.

How to Toast Flaked Coconut

- **Stovetop method:** Place the flaked coconut in a large skillet. Cook, stirring, over medium heat for 1 to 3 minutes or until the flakes are golden brown and fragrant.
- **Oven method:** Preheat oven to 325°F (160°C). Spread the flaked coconut in a thin layer on an ungreased baking sheet. Bake for 5 to 10 minutes, stirring once or twice, until golden brown and fragrant.

Coconut Butter

Coconut butter is a spread made from coconut meat, much like peanut butter is made from peanuts. It has a luscious, velvety texture and subtle natural sweetness that can be further enhanced with a hint of added sweetener (such as coconut nectar). Because it is made with whole coconut meat, it is rich in coconut oil, so it boasts all of the benefits of coconut oil with the added bonus of high fiber.

While coconut oil is used as butter and vegetable oils are used in cooking and baking, coconut butter is best categorized as a condiment. It can be used as a spread, an addition to smoothies, a dip, in no-bake natural "candy" recipes or as a measure-for-measure substitute for nut and seed butters in most baking recipes.

Coconut butter can be stored at room temperature for up to 6 months, but keep in mind that, due to its high oil content, the consistency of the butter in any given jar will vary depending on the temperature: it will be hard when it is very cold and soft when it is very warm. Depending on your intentions for use, you can warm it in the microwave on High for 5 to 10 seconds to soften it, or store it in the refrigerator to make it more firm.

Coconut butter can be purchased in jars. Occasionally it is labeled "coconut cream concentrate." It is not to be confused with coconut cream, which does not contain the fiber of the coconut and is closer in content to coconut milk. To avoid any confusion, you can make your own coconut butter at home with nothing more than a bag of unsweetened flaked coconut, a food processor or blender and roughly 5 minutes of time. See page 301 for the recipe.

Full-Fat Coconut Milk

Coconut milk is a rich, full-flavor, snow-white liquid produced from grating and pressing fresh coconut meat. It is incredibly versatile and can be used in soups, stews, curries, beverages and myriad baked goods.

Coconut milk's richness is due to its high concentration of coconut oil. All of the recipes calling for coconut milk in this collection specify full-fat, which typically has around 20 to 21 grams of fat per ½ cup (125 mL). Be careful not to use "light" coconut milk or coconut milk beverage; both have a much lower fat content and using them in place of full-fat coconut milk will lead to markedly different results, especially in baked goods recipes.

Full-fat coconut milk is available in cans and occasionally in Tetra Paks. Check the label: ideally water and coconut will be the only two ingredients. Avoid brands that have added stabilizing ingredients (such as guar gum), flavor enhancers or any kind of preservatives.

Coconut milk remains mostly liquid at room temperature. Some of the liquid and fat separate, even at room temperature; hence, it is important to stir or gently whisk the milk upon opening until it is blended smooth. Transfer any unused coconut milk to an airtight container and refrigerate for up to 5 days or freeze for up to 6 months.

Avoid bringing coconut milk to a full boil once you've added it to recipes (such as soups and stews); the fat and the water can separate, causing a curdled appearance.

Coconut Cream

Coconut cream is a rich, thick cream derived in the same manner as coconut milk, but it has a higher percentage of fat and a lower percentage of water. Do not confuse coconut cream with cream of coconut. The latter is a sweetened version of coconut cream, and is often used for desserts and mixed drinks. It is typically shelved in the beverage section of the supermarket.

Chill Coconut Milk to Get Coconut Cream

No cans of coconut cream? No problem. Simply place your can or package of full-fat coconut milk in the refrigerator for 24 hours; the fat will solidify and separate from the remaining liquid in the can. To make removing the solidified cream easier, flip the can upside down before opening it. The solidified cream, which rises to the top of the can, will now be on the bottom, making it easier to remove the top of the can and pour off the additional liquid. Scoop out the cream and store the drained liquid in an airtight container for use in smoothies or hot cereal, or to drink straight up.

Coconut Yogurt

Coconut yogurt is a dairy-free, soy-free, gluten-free, lactose-free and vegan alternative to traditional yogurt. It is produced in the same manner as dairy yogurt, but with coconut milk: the milk is combined with bacteria, heated to a low temperature and then allowed to ferment and coagulate, which thickens the milk to a rich and creamy texture while also imparting a distinctive, tangy flavor. The recipes in this collection call for plain coconut yogurt. It can be purchased in individual or tub containers, or you can make your own (see page 49).

Coconut Flour

Coconut flour, a natural byproduct of coconut milk production, is a soft, faintly sweet flour with a delicate coconut fragrance. Once the liquids are extracted from coconut meat, the remaining material is dried and then ground into a very fine flour with a consistency akin to all-purpose wheat flour. It can be used in a broad range of baked goods, as a coating or thickener in cooking or as a high-fiber addition to smoothies and shakes.

Coconut flour boasts a broad range of benefits that differentiate it from other flours. First, it is naturally gluten-free, meaning that it has none of the gluten protein molecules found in grains such as wheat, rye and barley. Gluten is highly allergenic, with symptoms ranging from mild to severe for individuals with celiac disease (a condition where gluten damages the lining of the small intestine and prevents it from absorbing nutrients in food). An increasing body of research evidence suggests that gluten — in particular, gluten from genetically modified grains — may have deleterious health effects for everyone, causing a host of modern ailments including lethargy, inability to concentrate, bloating and skin irritation.

Second, coconut flour is high in dietary fiber. According to research published in the December 2006 issue of *Innovative Food Science & Emerging Technologies*, adding coconut flour to our diets can significantly reduce our risk of developing heart disease, lower our cholesterol levels and guard us against cancer and diabetes. The researchers, all scientists at the Food and Nutrition Research Institute in the Philippines, claim that these benefits stem from coconut flour's unusually high levels of dietary fiber (a 100-gram serving contains 39 grams of fiber, almost double that of wheat bran). Because coconut flour is very rich in fiber, it is also beneficial to digestion and will help you feel full faster and stay full for longer.

Though it is free of gluten proteins, coconut flour nevertheless contains a significant amount of protein — 19.3 grams for every 100 grams of flour — more than all-purpose flour, rye flour or cornmeal. Further, since it is derived from coconut solids, coconut flour retains a large number of the fats that make coconut oil a wonder food.

Because coconut flour is high in fiber yet relatively low in digestible carbohydrates compared to processed flours, it has a gentle impact on blood sugar levels. Further, because it has an inherent sweetness, you can use less sugar when baking and cooking with it. These features make coconut flour an excellent option for people with diabetes or prediabetes, or anyone looking to avoid blood sugar spikes.

Coconut flour should be stored in an airtight container in a cool, dry place. If stored properly, coconut flour will remain fresh at room temperature for about 1 year.

Coconut Water

Coconut water is the clear liquid found inside young green coconuts. It has long been enjoyed as a refreshing beverage in tropical regions, especially in Southeast Asia, the Pacific Islands, Africa and the Caribbean. It is also known and packaged as "buko juice" (*buko* is a Filipino word meaning "young coconut").

In recent years, coconut water has become widely available — and wildly popular — in North America and Europe as an all-natural alternative to artificially flavored, colored and sweetened sports drinks. Coconut water has a mere 46 calories per cup (250 mL) and a variety of natural minerals that are beneficial to the body after a hard-core workout. When you sweat, you lose electrolytes, such as potassium and sodium; replenishing them is essential for ideal exercise recovery. Coconut water is a potassium powerhouse, with roughly 600 milligrams per cup (250 mL) — about 175 milligrams more than a banana offers and 13 times as much as is provided by most sport drinks. It also has significant levels of magnesium, which helps to enhance hydration.

But coconut water is more than a warm day refresher or a post-exercise beverage: it is used for cooking in a number of cuisines, such as Malaysian, Thai, Caribbean and Brazilian. Because coconut water is slightly sweet, it is used in place of plain water, broth or stock to balance out the salt in dishes ranging from stews to soups to rice dishes. The recipes in this collection provide inspiration and guidance for using it in a variety of cooking and baking recipes, but you can also experiment with your existing recipes, replacing all or part of the water, broth or stock with coconut water.

Coconut Water's Unique Electrolyte Balance

The balance of electrolytes in coconut water is nearly identical to human blood; in fact, coconut water is the only natural non-blood substance that can be safely injected into the human bloodstream. Coconut water has been used to replace human blood plasma in times of shortages, specifically in developing countries and during the Second World War.

Coconut Water Kefir

Coconut water kefir is a probiotic beverage made by combining coconut water and probiotic kefir grains, then allowing the mixture to ferment. Like other probiotic beverages and foods, it stimulates the growth of microorganisms, especially those with beneficial properties (such as those of the intestinal flora). An added benefit of coconut water kefir is that it is dairy-free (unlike dairy kefir and dairy yogurt), caffeine-free (unlike many varieties of kombucha, which is fermented tea) and free of added sugar.

Coconut water kefir can be purchased in a bottle, ready to drink, or you can make it for much less money and almost no effort in your own kitchen. The only ingredients are water kefir grains, which are readily available from online health food purveyors, and coconut water. Here is how to make it:

Place 1/2 cup (125 mL) kefir grains in a 4-cup (1 L) jar; add 3 cups (750 mL) coconut water. Cover loosely and let stand at room temperature for 48 hours (no longer). Using a non-metallic fine-mesh strainer, pour the culture liquid into a storage container, plastic jug or clean jar. Rinse the grains in filtered water and place in an airtight container (they can be used several more times). You can add a variety of fruits or fruit juices to the kefir — for example, a handful of berries, a few slices of apple or pear, or 1/2 cup (125 mL) of fruit juice. Store the coconut water kefir in the refrigerator for up to 1 week.

How to Open a Trimmed Young Green Coconut

Young green coconuts are increasingly available in supermarkets, and opening them to get to the coconut water and coconut meat inside is not as difficult as you might think. Here's how to do it:

1. Select a strong and heavy knife, like a butcher knife or large chef's knife.

2. Make an incision by cutting straight down into the pointed end of the coconut.

3. Make three additional incisions to form a square opening on top. Aim to make the square large enough to insert an eating spoon.

4. Use the tip of the knife to pry open the square plug.

5. The coconut water can be drunk directly from the coconut (simply insert a straw) or poured out of the opening into a container. To remove the coconut meat, insert a metal eating spoon and scrape the flesh away from the shell. The flesh of a young coconut should be very tender and will scrape away easily.

Tip: Before drinking the coconut water, check the color of the coconut meat and the clarity of the juice (you can pour out a small amount to check, if you intend to drink directly from the coconut). The meat should be a pure white and the coconut water should be clear. Do not eat the flesh or drink the water if the coconut meat has a pink hue, and do not drink the water if it is cloudy and/or the first sip is at all sour.

Coconut Sugar

Coconut sugar is an all-natural, unrefined sugar made from coconut nectar. Once the coconut nectar is collected, it is air-dried to form a crystalline sugar that looks and tastes much like brown sugar, with a very faint coconut flavor. It dissolves and melts the same as other sugars and can be used measure for measure in place of white or brown sugar. Since coconut sugar is not refined, it retains a number of key vitamins, minerals and phytonutrients, including potassium, zinc, iron and vitamins B_1, B_2, B_3 and B_6. It also contains a fiber called inulin, which may slow glucose absorption and explain why coconut sugar has a lower glycemic index than regular table sugar.

If you have shopped in Southeast Asian, Indian or Central American markets, you may have seen coconut sugar labeled as jaggery, palm sugar or Java sugar and shaped into cones or cakes.

Coconut Sugar and Sustainability

Enter the terms "sustainable" and "coconut sugar" into a web search box and you will generate almost a million hits. A quick scan of the results quickly reveals a heated debate between those who contend coconut sugar is a sustainable sweetener and those who claim the coconut sugar industry is detrimental to tropical environments and the health and livelihoods of the people who live there.

A closer look at the arguments reveals a single source for the latter camp: an online article published by a leading coconut oil manufacturer (Tropical Traditions, "The Truth About Coconut Palm Sugar: The Other Side of the Story!"). Citing research more than two decades old, the authors claim that coconut trees cannot produce both coconut sugar (derived from the nectar of the coconut blossom) and coconuts simultaneously, and that tapping a tree for its sugar is a modern phenomenon. Moreover, the article states that the increasing popularity of coconut sugar will cause the price of other coconut products (such as coconut oil, coconut flour and shredded coconut, all of which are products the company manufactures and sells) to skyrocket because low-income coconut tree farmers will choose to use their trees to produce coconut sugar instead of mature coconuts. The article advises the use of other natural sweeteners — both of which are the company's products — in place of all coconut sugar products. The article ignores copious research from reputable sources that indicates that tapping a coconut tree for its sap is a centuries-old tradition that neither harms the tree nor affects the tree's ability to produce coconuts.

The most influential research comes from the Davao Research Center, which is the research side of the Philippine Coconut Authority (a division of the Philippine Department of Agriculture). Research from one of their 2010 studies indicates that it is possible to produce both sap for making coconut sugar and coconuts from the same tree. The method involves tapping coconut sap from the first half of the coconut blossoms, then allowing the remaining half of the blossoms to develop into mature coconuts. According to the researchers, this method for tapping both sap and coconuts from the same tree yields five to seven times higher productivity than traditional methods. Moreover, once a coconut tree is tapped, sap continues to flow for the next two decades or so, which is highly sustainable and obviously supportive to the tree itself, or else it would die.

In 2011, the Food and Agriculture Organization (FAO) of the United Nations reported that coconut palm sweeteners are the single most sustainable sweetener in the world. The reason is that coconut palms are a tree crop that benefits the environment ecologically as they restore damaged soil, requiring very little water in the process. In addition, coconut palms produce more sugar per acre than sugar cane (50% to 75% more), while at the same time using less than 20% of the soil nutrients and water for that high level of production.

It is still a good idea to check the packaging or website of the coconut sugar product you choose, to make sure that the manufacturer is engaged in sustainable practices.

All of the recipes in this collection call for bagged granules of coconut sugar that can be scooped and measured.

Coconut Nectar

Coconut nectar is a dark gold syrup made from the coconut tree blossom's nectar, which naturally contains vitamins, minerals, amino acids and other nutrients, including vitamin C. In addition to its unique, full flavor — a cross between agave nectar and maple syrup — it has a lower glycemic index than many other liquid sweeteners.

Upon initial collection, the raw nectar is only 1.5% fructose. Most companies allow some of the water to evaporate, thereby thickening the syrup and intensifying the sweetness. The resulting product is typically 10% fructose, far lower than the 50% to 90% fructose found in agave products, 60% sucrose found in maple syrup or the 70% to 75% total sugar combination of glucose, fructose and sucrose found in honey.

Liquid Coconut Amino Acids

Liquid coconut amino acids look and taste like soy sauce but are made from raw coconut tree sap and sun-dried sea salt. The two ingredients are then naturally aged to produce a rich, dark, complex sauce with the familiar saltiness and umami flavor of soy sauce, as well as a hint of sweetness. It can be used measure for measure in place of soy sauce as a condiment or in recipes, or as a multipurpose seasoning in place of salt.

Coconut Vinegar

I do not call for coconut vinegar in this collection because, as of the date of publication, it is very difficult to find, due to limited production and distribution. This may change in the near future; until then, should you find it, use it. It has a mild but subtly complex flavor and can be used in any of the recipes in this book that call for vinegar.

Coconut vinegar is made from the nutrient-rich sap of the coconut palm tree's blossoms, which is allowed to ferment and age for up to a year. It is high in potassium and also quite abundant in a naturally occurring compound called fructo-oligosaccharides (FOS). FOSs are types of fructo-polysaccharides made of glucose and fructose. They are indigestible by our bodies; hence, they are transported to the large intestine, where they feed microbes and promote fermentation. As such, they have been dubbed "prebiotics," essentially serving as fertilizer for the bacteria in your colon and improving digestive health.

Completely free of soy, naturally gluten-free and vegan, free of MSG and lower in sodium than soy sauce, coconut amino acids also contain vitamins B and C, as well as various minerals. They can be found at health food stores or ordered from online health food purveyors. If liquid coconut amino acids are unavailable, regular liquid amino acids (also available at health food stores and online health food purveyors) or an equal amount of good-quality (organic, non-GMO) gluten-free soy sauce can be used as a substitute in any of the recipes in this collection.

Additional Pantry Items

Grain-Free Flours and Starches

Chickpea Flour

Chickpea flour, also known as garbanzo bean flour, besan or gram flour, is a gluten-free, light-colored, multipurpose flour made from finely ground dried chickpeas. It is also one of the keys to making a range of coconut flour baked goods without eggs.

Traditional coconut flour recipes typically call for a large quantity of eggs, sometimes as many as a half-dozen for recipes such as pancakes and tortillas and up to a dozen for a cake. The reason for the high ratio of eggs is that coconut flour lacks the protein structure (gluten) to create baked goods that do not crumble. The issue is more problematic with coconut flour than it is with gluten-free grain flours because egg replacements such as ground flaxseed gel and tofu simply do not work.

Enter chickpea flour. Thanks to its high protein content, it gives batter a comparable amount of structure and lightness as eggs. Plus, the combination of chickpea flour and coconut flour creates a taste and texture similar to all-purpose flour.

Chickpea flour provides additional benefits, too. One-half cup (125 mL) has 201 micrograms of folate, compared to 26 micrograms in whole wheat flour and 182 micrograms in enriched all-purpose flour. It is also a good source of thiamin and vitamin B_6. It offers five times the protein of an equal amount of all-purpose flour, plus it has resistant starch, an indigestible carbohydrate that does not cause a spike in blood sugar levels, as refined grain flours do.

Store chickpea flour in an airtight container in the refrigerator for up to 6 months or in the freezer for up to 1 year.

Potato Starch

Potato starch is another useful ingredient for producing great coconut flour baked goods free of grains, eggs and dairy. It is produced by pressing the starch out of potatoes; the starch is then dried to create a fine powder. The result looks and feels like cornstarch, with a neutral flavor that works beautifully in both sweet and savory preparations. Like chickpea flour, it has resistant starch, which translates to a low glycemic index that is excellent for keeping blood sugar levels in check. As a bonus, potato starch contains high amounts of vitamins B_6, potassium, thiamine, manganese, magnesium, niacin and phosphorous.

Store potato starch in an airtight container in the refrigerator for up to 6 months or in the freezer for up to 1 year.

Potato Starch versus Potato Flour

Potato starch and potato flour may sound like one and the same, but they are not. Potato flour is made from whole potatoes, either raw or cooked. The potatoes (often peel and all) are dehydrated and then ground into a heavy, cream-colored flour that has a distinct potato flavor. Whereas potato starch lends a light and fluffy texture to gluten-free baked goods, potato flour renders heavy, dry products.

Psyllium Husk

You may not have heard of psyllium as an egg replacer before now, but once you try it, you'll likely use it exclusively for all of your egg-free baking. When it comes to vegan baking with coconut flour, it is essential.

Psyllium (*Plantago ovata*) is an annual herb that is grown in India and some European countries. Its seeds contain large quantities of a type of soluble fiber known as mucilage, which absorbs water to produce a thick gel. It is this thick gel that works like magic as an egg replacement when mixed with water. It is essential in gluten-free vegan baked goods; without it, your results will literally crumble. It cannot be replaced with ground flaxseed gel or other egg replacements.

To make a psyllium "egg," mix 1 tbsp (15 mL) psyllium husk with 3 tbsp (45 mL) water or other liquid, then let stand for 5 minutes to thicken or gel.

Psyllium husk can be purchased at health food stores, pharmacies and online health food purveyors. Be sure to select whole psyllium husk (preferably organic), not psyllium husk powder. Store psyllium husk in an airtight container at room temperature for up to 6 months or in the freezer for up to 1 year.

Ground Flax Seeds (Flaxseed Meal)

Flax seeds are highly nutritious, tiny seeds from the flax plant. They have gained tremendous popularity in recent years thanks to their high levels of omega-3 fatty acids. But to reap the most benefits from the seeds, they must be ground into meal. Look for packages of ready-ground flax seeds, which may be labeled "flaxseed meal," or use a spice or coffee grinder to grind whole flax seeds to a very fine meal. The meal adds a warm, nutty flavor to a wide range of recipes. Store ground flax seeds in an airtight container in the refrigerator for up to 5 months or in the freezer for up to 8 months.

Fruits and Vegetables

Study after study indicates that diets heavy in fruits and vegetables are healthier for our hearts, help prevent cancer, keep weight in check, keep us looking and feeling younger and help us live longer. Best of all, fruits and vegetables are delicious and are far easier to add to your diet than you might think. Here are some of the terrific options to consider when you're building your fruit and vegetable reserves.

Which Fruits Ripen, Which Do Not

- **Ripen only after picking:** avocados
- **Never ripen after picking:** soft berries, cherries, citrus, grapes, pineapple, watermelon
- **Ripen in color, texture and juiciness but not in sweetness after picking:** apricots, blueberries, figs, melons (except watermelon), nectarines, passion fruit, peaches, persimmons
- **Get sweeter after picking:** apples, kiwifruit, mangos, papayas, pears
- **Ripen in every way after picking:** bananas

Fresh Fruits and Vegetables

Fresh fruits and vegetables are packed with essential vitamins and nutrients, so it's a good idea to always have some on hand. Place a bowl of fresh fruit on the counter, and keep washed and cut vegetables in the refrigerator for ready-to-eat snacks. Store hardy vegetables, such as onions, potatoes, carrots and celery, in the pantry and crisper — they're a great foundation for countless recipes.

For the freshest fruits and vegetables at the best prices, buy what is in season. In most cases, you can buy fruits a few days before their peak ripeness and let them ripen at home before use. If you choose to buy them at or past peak, use them right away — within a day or two.

Delicate fruits and vegetables, such as berries, cherries, plums, asparagus, bell peppers, corn, cucumbers, mushrooms, yellow summer squash and zucchini, should be used close to the day of purchase. The following, by contrast, keep well:

- Apples
- Bananas
- Citrus fruits (such as oranges, lemons and grapefruits)
- Cabbage
- Carrots
- Celery
- Garlic
- Onions
- Potatoes (yellow and russet)
- Sweet potatoes

Ask your grocery store's produce manager what the delivery days are, so you can purchase your favorite fruits and vegetables before their quality declines. Alternatively, buy your produce at a local farmers' market. Many communities sponsor weekly farmers' markets to provide a central, in-town site for small farms to sell their produce directly to consumers.

Fresh Dates

Fresh dates — the fruit of the date palm tree — are among the sweetest fruits in the world, with a flavor similar to brown sugar. They can be used in desserts, snacks, sauces and even soups, stews and chilis to add sweetness. The most commonly available dates in the United States and Canada are Medjool dates, which are plump and tender, and Deglet Noor dates, which are semi-soft, slender and a bit chewy; both varieties have often been left on the tree for a while after they are ripe to dry a bit (and thus last longer after harvest). When choosing fresh dates, select those that are plump-looking; it is okay if they are slightly wrinkled, but they shouldn't feel hard.

The Dirty Dozen and the Clean Fifteen

The Environmental Working Group (EWG), a non-profit organization, created the *Shopper's Guide to Pesticides in Produce*. The 2014 edition of the guide is based on the results of 28,000 tests for pesticides on produce by the U.S. Department of Agriculture and the federal Food and Drug Administration. It's important to note that the EWG states that almost all of the tests were performed on produce that had been rinsed or peeled. For more information, visit www.ewg.org.

The Dirty Dozen (Plus Two)

Here are the top 12 most pesticide-contaminated fruits and vegetables in America, along with two additional suspects, summer squash and kale. When shopping for these items, buy organic whenever possible.

1. Apples
2. Strawberries
3. Grapes
4. Celery
5. Peaches
6. Spinach
7. Bell peppers
8. Nectarines (imported)
9. Cucumbers
10. Potatoes
11. Cherry tomatoes
12. Hot peppers
13. Summer squash
14. Kale

The Clean Fifteen

These fruits and vegetables are the least contaminated by pesticides, so it's not as crucial to buy organic.

1. Sweet corn
2. Onions
3. Pineapples
4. Avocados
5. Cabbage
6. Sweet peas (frozen)
7. Papayas
8. Mangos
9. Asparagus
10. Eggplant
11. Kiwifruit
12. Grapefruit
13. Cantaloupe
14. Sweet potatoes
15. Mushrooms

Frozen Fruits and Vegetables

Keeping a selection of frozen fruits and vegetables in the freezer is a wise move for healthy cooking with coconut products, and healthy eating in general, whether for quick soups or for morning smoothies. In addition to its convenience, frozen produce can sometimes be more nutritious than fresh. When fresh fruits and vegetables are shipped long distances, they rapidly lose vitamins and minerals thanks to exposure to heat and light; by contrast, frozen fruits and vegetables are frozen immediately after being picked, ensuring that all of the vitamins and minerals are preserved.

Whenever possible, choose organic frozen fruits and vegetables. Some varieties to keep on hand include:

- Winter squash purée (typically a blend of acorn and butternut squash)
- Petite peas
- Chopped greens (spinach, Swiss chard, mustard greens)
- Chopped onions
- Broccoli florets
- Shelled edamame
- Lima beans
- Berries (blueberries, blackberries, raspberries, strawberries)
- Diced mangos
- Diced pineapples
- Sliced peaches

Interpreting Organic Labels

Understanding the various organic labels can be a challenge. Here's what the four most common labels and claims mean:

"100% Organic" USDA ORGANIC	For a food product to be 100% organic and be able to bear the USDA organic seal, it must be made with 100% organic ingredients. The food product also must have an ingredient list and list the name of the certifying agency.
"Organic" USDA ORGANIC	For a food product to be labeled as "organic" and be able to bear the USDA organic seal, it must be made with 95% organic ingredients. The food product also must list the name of the certifying agency and have an ingredient statement on the label where organic ingredients are identified as organic.
"Made with Organic Ingredients"	To make this claim, a food product must be made with at least 70% organic ingredients. The food product also must list the name of the certifying agency and have an ingredient statement on the label where organic ingredients are identified as organic.
"Some Organic Ingredients"	Food products with less than 70% organic ingredients cannot bear the USDA seal nor have information about a certifying agency, or any reference to organic content.

Shelf-Stable Tomato Products

Canned tomatoes may sound nutritionally benign (if not bereft), but nothing could be further from the truth. Unlike many canned vegetables, canned tomatoes retain almost all of their nutrients (including substantial amounts of vitamins A and C) and actually contain more lycopene than raw tomatoes.

Choose organic whenever possible, as they tend to be lower in sodium and residual chemicals. Additionally, opt for tomato products in BPA-free cans or containers.

Diced Tomatoes

Canned diced tomatoes can replace diced fresh tomatoes in most recipes, especially soups and stews. Stock up on diced fire-roasted tomatoes, too, as they add a subtle smoky flavor to dishes.

Crushed Tomatoes

Canned crushed tomatoes (sometimes called ground tomatoes) are a convenient way to add fresh tomato flavor to soups, stews and pastas without the separate step of puréeing.

Tomato Sauce

Tomato sauce can be used to make delicious sauces, stews and soups when you want to give them a distinct tomato flavor. For true tomato flavor with minimal processing, be sure to select a variety of tomato sauce that is low in sodium and has no added seasonings.

Tomato Paste

Tomato paste is made from tomatoes that have been cooked for several hours, then strained and reduced to a deep red, richly flavored concentrate. It is available in both cans and convenient squeeze tubes. Just a tablespoon or two (15 or 30 mL) can greatly enrich a wide variety of dishes, adding acidity, depth and a hint of sweetness. Select a brand that is low in sodium and has no added seasonings.

Chunky Tomato Salsa

Like marinara sauce, ready-made chunky salsa — rich with tomatoes, peppers, onions and spices but low in calories — packs tremendous flavor into recipes in an instant. For the best flavor and nutrition, select a brand that is low in sodium and has a short list of easily identifiable ingredients.

Dried Fruit

Dried fruit is essential to a well-stocked pantry. Keep a variety of dried fruits at the ready for cooking, baking or eating out of hand (especially when a craving for sweets strikes). Whenever possible, opt for organic dried fruit that is either free from added sugar or sweetened with fruit juice. The following are top picks:

- Raisins (both dark and golden)
- Dried currants (sometimes labeled "Zante currants")
- Dried cranberries
- Dried cherries
- Dried apricots
- Dried apples
- Dried pears
- Dried apples
- Dried mango
- Dried papaya
- Dried figs
- Prunes (dried plums)

Legumes

Legumes are nutritional powerhouses. One cup (250 mg) of cooked legumes has an average of 200 to 300 calories, next to no fat (with the exception of soybeans), about one-third of the protein you need in a day and lots of fiber. In addition, legumes are very low in cost and easy to prepare in a wide variety of recipes.

Canned Beans

With their high protein content, wide availability, low cost and convenience, canned beans are ideal for a wide range of quick, healthy meals and snacks. For the best flavor and versatility, select varieties that are low in sodium and have no added seasonings. The following varieties are great choices to keep on hand for everything from dips to entrées:

- Black beans
- White beans (e.g., cannellini and white navy beans)
- Pinto beans
- Red kidney beans
- Chickpeas

Dried Split Peas (Green and Yellow)

A variety of yellow and green peas are grown specifically for drying. These peas are dried and split along a natural seam (hence, "split peas"). Split peas are very inexpensive and are loaded with good nutrition, including a significant amount of protein. They are available packaged in supermarkets and in bulk in health food stores. Unlike dried beans, they do not require presoaking.

Dried Lentils

Lentils are inexpensive, require no presoaking, cook in about 30 to 45 minutes and are very high in nutrients (soybeans are the only legume with more protein). Lentils come in a variety of sizes and colors: common brown lentils and French green lentils can be found in supermarkets, and increasingly, so can red and black lentils.

Soybean Products

Be sure to select soybean products that are clearly labeled as GMO-free (free of genetically modified organisms).

Tofu
Tofu, or bean curd, is made from soybeans that have been cooked, made into milk and then coagulated. The soy milk curdles when heated, and the curds are skimmed off and pressed into blocks.

The recipes in this collection were tested with refrigerated tofu. While shelf-stable tofu is convenient, the flavor and texture are markedly inferior. Tofu can be found in extra-firm, firm and soft varieties in the refrigerated section of the supermarket. For optimal results, be sure to use the variety specified in the recipe.

Grain-Free, Gluten-Free Tempeh
Tempeh (pronounced *TEM-pay*) is a traditional Indonesian food. It is made from fully cooked soybeans that have been fermented with a mold called rhizopus and formed into cakes. Some varieties have whole grains added to the mix, so be sure to select a variety that is clearly labeled as grain- and gluten-free. Tempeh, like tofu, takes on the flavor of whatever it is marinated with, and also needs to be stored in the refrigerator.

Seeds and Seed Butters

Seeds and seed butters are very nutritious. In addition to being excellent sources of protein, seeds contain vitamins, minerals, fiber and essential fatty acids (such as omega-3 and omega-6). Seeds provide a sense of fullness and satisfaction that actually causes you to eat less of other high-calorie, high-fat foods.

Green Pumpkin Seeds (Pepitas)

Pepitas are pumpkin seeds with the white hull removed, leaving the flat, dark green inner seed. They are subtly sweet and nutty, with a slightly chewy texture when raw and a crisp, crunchy texture when toasted or roasted. They are a welcome addition to salads, soups and entrées for a pleasant, contrasting crunch, or to muffins, cookies or breads.

Shelled Sunflower Seeds

Sunflower seeds are highly nutritious and have a mild, nutty flavor and texture. The recipes in this collection call for seeds that have been removed from their shells. They can be used in place of nuts in both sweet and savory dishes.

Sesame Seeds

The delicate flavor of tiny sesame seeds increases exponentially when they are toasted. Used as a flavoring in many Asian preparations, sesame seeds are also delicious in sweet and savory baked goods.

Seed Butters

Delicious, nutritious, ultra-convenient seed butters — specifically, tahini (sesame seed butter or paste) and sunflower seed butter — are a boon for any meal of the day, as well as for a wide variety of cooking preparations. They are increasingly available at well-stocked supermarkets, co-ops and natural food stores. Tahini and sunflower seed butter may be used interchangeably in any recipe calling for seed butter unless otherwise specified. Store opened jars in the refrigerator.

Fresh Herbs

Fresh herbs add depth of flavor — as well as nutrition — to coconut recipes. Flat-leaf (Italian) parsley, cilantro and chives are readily available and inexpensive, and they store well in the produce bin of the refrigerator, so keep them on hand year-round. Basil, mint and thyme are best in the spring and summer, when they are in season in your own garden or at the farmers' market.

Flavorings

Elevating coconut dishes to exceptional levels of deliciousness can be as easy as creating a harmonious balance of simple flavorings — even if you're just adding salt and pepper. Here are my top recommendations for ingredients that will make the ordinary extraordinary.

Fine Sea Salt

Unless otherwise specified, the recipes in this collection were tested using fine-grain sea salt. Conventional salt production uses chemicals, additives and heat processing to achieve the end product commonly called table salt. By contrast, unrefined sea salt contains an abundance of naturally occurring trace minerals.

Black Pepper

Black pepper is made by grinding black peppercorns, which have been picked when the berry is not quite ripe, then dried until it shrivels and the skin turns dark brown to black. Black pepper has a strong, slightly hot flavor, with a hint of sweetness.

Spices and Dried Herbs

Spices and dried herbs can turn the simplest of coconut meals into masterpieces. They should be stored in light- and airproof containers, away from direct sunlight and heat, to preserve their flavors.

Co-ops, health food stores and mail order sources that sell herbs and spices in bulk are all excellent options for purchasing very fresh, organic spices and dried herbs, often at a low cost. With ground spices and dried herbs, freshness is everything. To determine whether a ground spice or dried herb is fresh, open the container and sniff. A strong fragrance means it is still acceptable for use.

Note that ground spices, not whole, are used throughout this collection. Here are my favorite ground spices and dried herbs:

Ground Spices
- Cinnamon
- Nutmeg
- Ginger
- Cardamom
- Coriander
- Mild curry powder
- Cumin
- Smoked paprika (both hot and sweet)
- Paprika
- Turmeric
- Black pepper (cracked and ground)
- Cayenne pepper (also labeled "ground red pepper")
- Hot pepper flakes
- Chinese five-spice powder
- Garam masala
- Chipotle chile powder
- Chili powder

Dried Herbs
- Rosemary
- Thyme
- Oregano
- Rubbed sage
- Bay leaves

Citrus Zest

Zest is the name for the colored outer layer of citrus peel. The oils in zest are intense in flavor. Use a zester, a Microplane-style grater or the small holes of a box grater to grate zest. Avoid grating the white layer (pith) just below the zest; it is very bitter.

Cocoa Powder

Select natural cocoa powder rather than Dutch process for the recipes in this collection. Natural cocoa powder has a deep, true chocolate flavor. The packaging should state whether it is Dutch process or not, but you can also tell the difference by sight: if it is dark to almost black, it is Dutch process; natural cocoa powder is much lighter and is typically brownish red in color.

Gluten-Free Vanilla Extract

Vanilla extract adds a sweet, fragrant flavor to dishes, especially baked goods. It is produced by combining an extraction from dried vanilla beans with an alcohol and water mixture. It is then aged for several months. The three most common types of vanilla beans used to make vanilla extract are Bourbon-Madagascar, Mexican and Tahitian.

Thai Curry Paste

Available in small jars, Thai curry paste is a blend of Thai chiles, garlic, lemongrass, galangal, ginger and wild lime leaves. It is a fast and delicious way to add Southeast Asian flavor to a broad spectrum of recipes in a single step. Panang and yellow curry pastes tend to be the mildest. Red curry paste is medium hot, and green curry paste is typically the hottest.

Dijon Mustard

Dijon mustard adds depth of flavor to a wide range of dishes. It is most commonly used in this collection for salad dressing because it facilitates the emulsification of oil and vinegar.

Vinegars

Vinegars are multipurpose flavor powerhouses. Delicious in vinaigrettes and dressings, they are also stealth ingredients for use at the end of cooking time to enhance and balance the natural flavors of dishes. Store vinegars in a dark place, away from heat or light.

Cider Vinegar

Cider vinegar is made from the juice of crushed apples. After the juice is collected, it is allowed to age in wooden barrels.

Red Wine Vinegar

Red wine vinegar is produced by fermenting red wine in wooden barrels. This produces acetic acid, which gives red wine vinegar its distinctive taste. Red wine vinegar has a characteristic dark red color and red wine flavor.

White Wine Vinegar

White wine vinegar is a moderately tangy vinegar made from a blend of white wines. The wine is fermented, aged and filtered to produce a vinegar with a slightly lower acidity level than red wine vinegar.

Toasted Sesame Oil

Toasted sesame oil has a dark brown color and a rich, nutty flavor. It is used sparingly, mostly in Asian recipes, to add a tremendous amount of flavor.

Ready-to-Use, Gluten-Free Vegetable Broth

Ready-made vegetable broth is useful for several recipes in this collection. Opt for certified organic broths that are all-natural, reduced-sodium and MSG-free. For convenience, look for broths in Tetra Paks, which typically come in 32-oz (1 L), 48-oz (1.5 L) and occasionally 16-oz (500 mL) sizes. Once opened, these can be stored in the refrigerator for up to 1 week.

Measuring Ingredients

Accurate measurements are important for healthy cooking — and essential for healthy baking — to achieve consistent results time and again. So take both time and care as you measure.

Measuring Dry Ingredients

When measuring a dry ingredient, such as flour, cocoa powder, sugar, spices or salt, spoon it into the appropriate-size dry measuring cup or measuring spoon, heaping it up over the top. Slide a straight-edged utensil, such as a knife, across the top to level off the extra. Be careful not to shake or tap the cup or spoon to settle the ingredient, or you will have more than you need.

Measuring Moist Ingredients

Moist ingredients, such as flaked or shredded coconut and dried fruit, must be firmly packed in a measuring cup or spoon to be measured accurately. Use a dry measuring cup for these ingredients. Fill the measuring cup to slightly overflowing, then pack down the ingredient firmly with the back of a spoon. Add more of the ingredient and pack down again until the cup is full and even with the top of the measure.

Measuring Liquid Ingredients

Use a clear plastic or glass measuring cup or container with lines up the sides to measure liquid ingredients. Set the container on the counter and pour the liquid to the appropriate mark. Lower your head to read the measurement at eye level.

Common Nutrition Terms

Amino acids: Amino acids are the chemical compounds that make up plant and animal proteins. They are classified into two categories: essential and nonessential. The eight essential amino acids are those that must be obtained from food sources because the body cannot synthesize them on its own. Nonessential amino acids are those that the body can manufacture on its own.

Antioxidants: Antioxidants protect the body from damage caused by harmful molecules called free radicals. Many experts believe this damage is a factor in the development of blood vessel disease (atherosclerosis), cancer and other conditions. Exposure to free radicals most often comes about through byproducts of normal processes that take place in the body, such as the breakdown of nutrients, but it can also be through pollutants in the environment. Antioxidants include some vitamins (such as vitamins C and E), some minerals (such as selenium) and flavonoids, which are found in plants. The best sources of antioxidants are fruits and vegetables.

Calories: A calorie is a measurement of the amount of energy released when the body breaks down food. Calories are provided by carbohydrates, proteins and fats. The more calories a food has, the more energy it can provide the body. When more calories are eaten than are needed for energy, the body stores the extra calories as fat.

Carbohydrates: Carbohydrates provide fuel for the body in the form of glucose, a sugar that is the primary source of energy for all of the body's cells. Adults should get about 45% to 65% of their calories from carbohydrates. Carbohydrate sources include many foods that are nutrient-rich, such as whole grains, fruits, vegetables and legumes, as well as foods such as candy, pastries, cookies and flavored beverages (soft drinks and fruit drinks), which provide insignificant amounts of vitamins, minerals and other essential nutrients.

Carotenoids: Carotenoids, a type of phytonutrient (see page 42), are the red, orange and yellow pigments in fruits and vegetables. Some of the most familiar carotenoids are alpha carotene, beta carotene, lycopene and lutein. Fruits and vegetables that are high in carotenoids appear to protect against certain cancers, heart disease and age-related macular degeneration.

Cholesterol: Cholesterol is a waxy, fat-like substance made in the liver and other cells and found in certain foods, such as dairy products, eggs and meat. The body needs some cholesterol to function properly. Its cell walls, or membranes, need cholesterol to produce hormones, vitamin D and the bile acids that help digest fat. But the body needs only a limited amount of cholesterol to meet its needs. When too much is present, health problems such as heart disease may develop.

Cholesterol moves through the bloodstream by attaching to a protein; in combination, these are called lipoproteins. Low-density lipoproteins (LDL), also known as "bad" cholesterol, can cause buildup of plaque on artery walls, which can lead to heart disease and other ailments. High-density lipoproteins (HDL), also known as "good" cholesterol, help the body rid itself of LDL. Hence, the higher the body's HDL cholesterol, the better; the lower the HDL, the greater the chance of heart disease.

Fat: Fat is made up of compounds called fatty acids, or lipids. Depending on their chemical structure, these fatty acids can be monounsaturated, polyunsaturated, saturated or trans fats. Trans fats and saturated fats are the unhealthiest fats.

Trans fats are formed when manufacturers turn liquid oils into solid fats (hydrogenation), such as with shortening and hard margarine. Trans fats can also be found in many processed foods, including crackers (even healthy-sounding ones), cereals, baked goods, snack foods, salad dressings and fried foods.

Saturated fats are found in meats and whole dairy products such as milk, cheese, cream and ice cream. They are also present in some plant foods, such as coconut oil. When margarine or vegetable shortening is made from soybean oil, corn oil or other vegetable oils, hydrogen atoms are added, making some of the fat molecules "saturated." This also makes the fat solid at room temperature.

Unsaturated fat is liquid at room temperature. It is found mostly in plant oils. Eating unsaturated fat instead of saturated fat may improve your cholesterol levels. Try to eat mostly unsaturated fats. Monounsaturated fat and polyunsaturated fat are both types of unsaturated fat. Monounsaturated fat is found in vegetable oils such as canola, olive and peanut oil. Eating foods high in monounsaturated fats may help lower your "bad" LDL cholesterol. Monounsaturated fats may also keep "good" HDL cholesterol levels high. Polyunsaturated fat is found mainly in vegetable oils such as safflower, sunflower, sesame, soybean and corn oil. Polyunsaturated fat is also the main fat in seafood. Eating polyunsaturated fat in place of saturated fat may lower LDL cholesterol. Omega-3 fatty acids are a type of polyunsaturated fat that may reduce the risk of heart disease. To get the health benefits of omega-3s, eat a 3-ounce (90 g) serving of fatty fish, such as salmon or mackerel, twice a week. Ground flax seeds, flaxseed oil, nuts and seeds also provide omega-3 fatty acids.

Coconut Meat

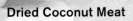

Dried Coconut Meat

Unsweetened Dried, Flaked Coconut

Virgin Coconut Oil

Shredded Coconut

Coconut Flour

Coconut Sugar

Full-Fat Coconut Milk

Baked Blueberry Banana Porridge (page 48)

Essential Coconut Pancakes (page 51)

Strawberry Beet Smoothie (page 76)
and Papaya Dream Smoothie (page 78)

Sesame and Green Onion Bread (page 92)

Fiber: Dietary fiber is found naturally in edible plants. It does not break down in the gastrointestinal system and instead passes through the body undigested. Dietary fiber is either soluble or insoluble, and both forms are needed for optimal health.

Soluble fiber attracts water and forms a gel, which slows down digestion. Soluble fiber delays the emptying of your stomach and makes you feel full, which helps control weight. Slower stomach emptying may also affect blood sugar levels and have a beneficial effect on insulin sensitivity, which may help control diabetes. In addition, soluble fiber can help lower LDL ("bad") blood cholesterol by interfering with the absorption of dietary cholesterol. Sources of soluble fiber include oats, oat bran, psyllium, nuts, flax seeds, lentils, beans, dried peas, apples, oranges, pears, strawberries, blueberries, cucumbers, celery and carrots.

Insoluble fiber has a laxative effect and adds bulk to the diet, helping prevent constipation. It does not dissolve in water, so it passes through the gastrointestinal tract relatively intact. Insoluble fiber is found mainly in whole grains and vegetables. Sources of insoluble fiber include whole wheat, wheat bran, corn bran, bulgur, barley, couscous, brown rice, seeds, nuts, raisins, grapes, zucchini, celery, broccoli, cabbage, onions, tomatoes, carrots, cucumbers, green beans, dark leafy vegetables and root vegetable skins.

Flavonoids: Flavonoids are polyphenols, natural components in thousands of plants that give them their beautiful colors. Most flavonoids function in the human body as antioxidants, helping to neutralize and prevent overly reactive oxygen-containing molecules from damaging cells. Foods rich in flavonoids include onions, apples, red grapes, strawberries, raspberries, blueberries, cranberries, grape juice, tea, red wine and certain nuts.

Micronutrients: Vitamins and minerals are called micronutrients because the body needs them in small amounts. Micronutrients are vital to the body's ability to process macronutrients — fats, proteins and carbohydrates.

Minerals: Minerals, like vitamins, must come from diet; the body does not make them. Many minerals, such as calcium, potassium and iron, are vital to the body's proper function and must be consumed in relatively large amounts. Others, including the trace minerals zinc, selenium and copper, are needed only in small amounts to maintain good health.

Phytonutrients: The prefix "phyto-" comes from a Greek word meaning "plant." Phytonutrients — such as beta carotene, lycopene and resveratrol — are organic components of plants and are thought to promote human health. Fruits, vegetables, grains, legumes, nuts and teas are rich sources of phytonutrients. Unlike the traditional nutrients (protein, fat, carbohydrates, vitamins and minerals), phytonutrients are not "essential" for life, so some people prefer the term "phytochemicals."

Protein: Proteins are nutrients that are essential to the building, maintenance and repair of body tissue, such as the skin, internal organs and muscles. They are also the major components of the immune system and hormones. Proteins are made up of substances called amino acids, 22 of which are considered vital for health. Of these, the adult body can make 14; the other eight (the essential amino acids) can only be obtained from diet.

Recommended Dietary Allowance (RDA): A subset of assessment values for the Dietary Reference Intakes (DRI), a new means of assessing dietary needs for healthy individuals, the RDA is the amount of nutrients most people need daily to prevent the development of disease, as outlined by the U.S. Department of Agriculture (USDA). As an example, the RDA for vitamin C is 70 milligrams; if you consume less than that each day, you run the risk of developing scurvy.

Vitamins: Vitamins help with chemical reactions in the body. In general, vitamins must come from the diet; the body doesn't make them. Thirteen vitamins are essential to the body. They are divided into two categories: water-soluble (vitamin C and all the B vitamins) and fat-soluble (vitamins A, D, E and K). The fat-soluble vitamins are more easily stored by the body. Because the water-soluble vitamins aren't stored for long in the body, they must be consumed daily.

Breakfast

Sunflower, Pepita and Chia Granola

A serving of this superpower granola — free of grains, dairy and nuts, but loaded with fiber, healthy minerals and protein — will help you breeze through the morning with nary a thought of lunchtime.

Makes 4 servings

Tips

You can flavor this granola in countless ways by adding a small amount of ground spice (such as cinnamon, cardamom or ginger), extracts (such as vanilla or lemon) or finely grated citrus zest (such as lemon, lime or orange).

Either small- or large-flaked coconut will work, but for a texture and appearance similar to oats, use large-flaked. Coarsely break the coconut into smaller pieces with your fingers.

Because of their high fat content, seeds can become rancid quickly. To keep them as fresh as possible, store them in an airtight container in the freezer for up to 6 months.

Be sure not to add the dried fruit until after the granola is baked; if baked with the seeds and coconut, it will become very hard and may burn.

- Preheat oven to 300°F (150°C)
- Large rimmed baking sheet, lined with parchment paper

1 1/2 cups	unsweetened flaked coconut	375 mL
1 1/4 cups	sunflower seeds	300 mL
3/4 cup	green pumpkin seeds (pepitas)	175 mL
1/3 cup	chia seeds, sesame seeds or hemp hearts	75 mL
1/3 cup	coconut nectar or coconut sugar	75 mL
1/3 cup	warmed virgin coconut oil	75 mL
2/3 cup	chopped dried fruit (apricots, dates, raisins, cherries)	150 mL

1. In a large bowl, whisk together coconut, sunflower seeds, pumpkin seeds and chia seeds.

2. In a medium bowl, whisk together coconut nectar and coconut oil until well blended.

3. Add the oil mixture to the coconut mixture and stir until well coated. Spread mixture in a single layer on prepared baking sheet.

4. Bake in preheated oven for 20 to 25 minutes or until coconut and sunflower seeds are golden brown. Let cool completely on pan.

5. Transfer granola to an airtight container and stir in dried fruit. Store at room temperature for up to 2 weeks or freeze for up to 3 months.

Coconut Chia Breakfast Bowl

This simple breakfast bowl is a great way to start enjoying the benefits of chia seeds. The seeds plump up overnight, creating a pudding-like texture akin to tapioca pudding. It's filling, delicious and a snap to prepare the night before.

Makes 4 servings

Tips

If you do not like the tapioca consistency of chia seeds, in step 1 process the ingredients in a blender until smooth. Refrigerate and serve as directed.

Feel free to leave off the fresh berries, if desired.

You can vary the flavor of this breakfast bowl in countless ways by adding a small amount of ground spices (such as cinnamon, cardamom or ginger), by subbing finely grated citrus zest (such as lemon, lime or orange) for the vanilla, or by using unsweetened fruit juice in place of the coconut water.

1½ cups	well-stirred coconut milk (full-fat)	375 mL
½ cup	coconut water or water	125 mL
6 tbsp	chia seeds	90 mL
2 tbsp	coconut sugar	30 mL
⅛ tsp	fine sea salt	0.5 mL
½ tsp	gluten-free vanilla extract	2 mL
1 cup	fresh berries or chopped fruit (blueberries, raspberries, mango, apple)	250 mL

Suggested Accompaniments

Plain or toasted flaked or shredded coconut

Raw or toasted seeds (hemp, sunflower, green pumpkin, sesame)

Ground flax seeds (flaxseed meal)

Dried fruit (raisins, cherries, cranberries)

1. In a small bowl, whisk together coconut milk, coconut water, chia seeds, coconut sugar, salt and vanilla until blended. Cover and refrigerate for at least 4 hours, until thickened, or overnight.

2. Divide chia mixture among bowls and top with berries and any of the suggested accompaniments, as desired.

✳ Power Ingredient

Chia Seeds
Chia seeds are an excellent source of omega-3 fatty acids and fiber — about 10 grams of fiber per 2 tbsp (30 mL). They are also a good source of protein and a variety of minerals, including iron, calcium, magnesium and zinc. Emerging research suggests that including chia seeds as part of a healthy diet may help improve cardiovascular risk factors by lowering cholesterol, triglycerides and blood pressure.

Instant Coconut Flax Hot Cereal

Raise your hand if packets of instant oatmeal or other hot cereals have made an appearance in your breakfasts past. The convenience is hard to beat, but if you are looking for a grain-free version, you won't find it at the grocery store. The search ends here. This three-ingredient mix take seconds to throw together, and preparing the porridge in the morning is as easy as adding boiling water and your favorite toppings.

Makes about 4 cups (1 L)

Tips

This recipe works best with finely flaked coconut, but if you have large-flaked coconut, you can still use it: simply crumble it into fine pieces (with your fingers) or chop before using.

You can use an equal amount of whole psyllium husks in place of the ground flax seeds.

If desired, replace half of the chia seeds with hemp hearts.

For the Porridge Mix

2 cups	unsweetened finely flaked or shredded coconut	500 mL
1 cup	ground flax seeds (flaxseed meal)	250 mL
1 cup	chia seeds	250 mL

For 1 Serving Porridge

½ cup	porridge mix	125 mL
¾ cup	boiling water	175 mL
2 tbsp	well-stirred coconut milk (full-fat)	30 mL
Pinch	fine sea salt (optional)	Pinch

Suggested Accompaniments

Coconut sugar or coconut nectar

Dried fruit

Chopped fresh fruit or berries

Toasted seeds (green pumpkin, sunflower, sesame)

1. *Mix:* In a large airtight container or sealable plastic bag, whisk together coconut, flax seeds and chia seeds. Store at room temperature for up to 1 month or in the refrigerator or freezer for up to 6 months.

2. *Porridge:* In a serving bowl or mug, stir porridge mix and boiling water until blended. Let stand for 3 to 4 minutes to thicken. Stir in coconut milk and salt (if using). Top with any of the suggested accompaniments, as desired.

Apple Cinnamon Hemp Porridge

You don't need to wait for a chilly morning to savor this cozy apple breakfast. A hint of ground cinnamon adds complementary zing to each spoonful.

Tips

For the apple, try Braeburn, Gala or Golden Delicious.

One large apple will yield the amount needed for this recipe.

An equal amount of raw sunflower seeds can be used in place of the hemp hearts.

For a different flavor, try ground ginger, cardamom or allspice in place of the cinnamon.

Use an equal amount of chopped pear, mango, peaches or apricots in place of the apple.

- Food processor

½ cup	hemp hearts (hulled hemp seeds)	125 mL
⅔ cup	coconut water	150 mL
1⅓ cups	coarsely chopped peeled tart-sweet apple	325 mL
2 tbsp	ground flax seeds (flaxseed meal)	30 mL
1 tbsp	golden or dark raisins	15 mL
¾ tsp	ground cinnamon	3 mL
Pinch	fine sea salt	Pinch
¼ cup	well-stirred coconut milk (full-fat)	60 mL
1 tbsp	coconut sugar (optional)	15 mL

1. In a small bowl, combine hemp hearts and coconut water. Cover and refrigerate for at least 4 hours or overnight.

2. Drain hemp hearts, reserving coconut water. In food processor, combine hemp hearts, apple, flax seeds, raisins, cinnamon and salt; pulse until finely chopped.

3. In a small saucepan, combine reserved coconut water and coconut milk. Bring to a simmer over medium-low heat. Add hemp heart mixture and cook, stirring, for 4 to 5 minutes or until warmed through.

4. Divide porridge between two bowls and sprinkle with coconut sugar, if desired.

Baked Blueberry Banana Porridge

Despite the newfangled, grain-free combination of ingredients, this baked porridge has plenty of old-fashioned comfort-food appeal.

Makes 9 servings

Tips

Let leftovers cool and cut into individual squares or bars. Store in an airtight container in the refrigerator and enjoy cold (much like an energy bar) or at room temperature, or reheat each portion in the microwave on High for 10 to 15 seconds.

You can substitute ¼ cup (60 mL) whole psyllium husk for the ground flax seeds.

For variety, an equal amount of other fruits (raspberries, blackberries, diced pears, apples, strawberries, mangos, peaches, apricots, firm-ripe bananas) can be used in place of the blueberries.

- Preheat oven to 375°F (190°C)
- 9-inch (23 cm) square metal baking pan, greased with coconut oil

½ cup	coconut flour	125 mL
6 tbsp	ground flax seeds (flaxseed meal)	90 mL
⅓ cup	coconut sugar	75 mL
¼ tsp	fine sea salt	1 mL
2 cups	coconut water or water	500 mL
1 cup	mashed very ripe bananas	250 mL
½ cup	well-stirred coconut milk (full-fat)	125 mL
2 tsp	gluten-free vanilla extract	10 mL
2 tsp	gluten-free baking powder	10 mL
1½ cups	blueberries	375 mL
⅓ cup	green pumpkin seeds (pepitas) (optional)	75 mL

1. In a large bowl, whisk together coconut flour, flax seeds, coconut sugar, salt, coconut water, bananas, coconut milk and vanilla until blended. Let stand for 10 minutes to thicken. Stir in baking powder until well blended. Gently fold in blueberries.

2. Spread mixture evenly in prepared pan. Sprinkle with pepitas (if using).

3. Bake in preheated oven for 50 to 55 minutes or until set at the center and golden. Let cool on a wire rack for 10 minutes. Cut into servings and serve warm.

Coconut Yogurt

You do not need to eat dairy to reap the benefits of yogurt's probiotics: just make coconut yogurt!

**Makes 2 cups
(500 mL)**

Tips

Probiotic capsules for yogurt-making are available at health and natural food stores, as well as in the health food sections of well-stocked supermarkets.

If coconut cream is not available, you can make coconut cream from full-fat, high-quality coconut milk. Place the coconut milk in the refrigerator until cold. Avoid shaking when opening the can. Scoop out the solid coconut cream that settles on the top (reserve the remaining, thin coconut milk portion for smoothies or for any recipe calling for coconut water). You'll need about four 14-oz (398 mL) cans of coconut milk to get 2 cups (500 mL) cream.

You can use 2 tbsp (30 mL) purchased probiotic coconut yogurt or kefir in place of the probiotic capsules. Once you have made a batch of coconut yogurt, you can use 2 tbsp (30 mL) of that in place of the probiotic capsules.

- Electric yogurt maker

2 cups	coconut cream	500 mL
2	probiotic capsules	2

1. Place the coconut cream in a medium bowl. Empty the contents of the capsules over the cream, discarding the casings, then whisk until smooth.

2. Transfer coconut cream mixture into yogurt maker jars; place jars in yogurt maker. Follow the manufacturer's directions for processing the yogurt.

❖ About Probiotics

Probiotics are live microorganisms (in most cases, bacteria) that are similar to the beneficial microorganisms naturally found in the human gut. These "good bacteria" can prevent and alleviate a variety of conditions, facilitate digestion and provide nutrients (B vitamins, vitamin K, folate and some short-chain fatty acids) by combining with other "good" bacteria in the gut. Probiotics also provide multiple benefits for your immune system. When probiotics are abundant in your body, it's harder for bacteria that cause illness to get a foothold. Some probiotics also keep you healthy by making bacteriocins, which suppress the growth of harmful bacteria.

Variations

Coconut Yogurt Kefir: Use an equal amount of well-stirred coconut milk (full-fat) in place of the coconut cream. (Note that this is akin to dairy-style kefir; it is not like coconut kefir made from fermented coconut water).

Greek-Style Coconut Yogurt: After step 2, strain the yogurt through doubled layers of cheesecloth, or a coffee filter, overnight in the refrigerator. Reserve the drained liquid for use in smoothies or any recipe calling for coconut water.

Seasonal Fruit Parfaits

Sweet but not cloying, filling but not heavy, fresh with a bit of crunch and distinctive tropical vibe, these ever-so-simple parfaits can be assembled the night before.

Makes 2 servings

Tips
....

An equal amount of well-stirred coconut milk (full-fat) can be used in place of the coconut yogurt. If desired, whisk 1 tbsp (15 mL) freshly squeezed lemon or lime juice into the coconut milk first, to give it some tang.

You can also assemble these parfaits in small mason jars, for a portable breakfast extraordinaire.

- 2 parfait glasses

½ cup	assorted raw seeds (green pumpkin, sunflower seeds, hemp hearts, sesame seeds), toasted	125 mL
½ cup	unsweetened flaked or shredded coconut, toasted	125 mL
1 cup	plain regular or Greek-style coconut yogurt (store-bought or see recipe, page 49)	250 mL
3 tbsp	coconut nectar or coconut sugar	45 mL
1½ cups	assorted diced seasonal fruit and/or berries	375 mL

1. In a small bowl, combine seeds and coconut.
2. Spoon half the coconut yogurt into each parfait glass. Drizzle 1 tbsp (15 mL) coconut nectar into each glass. Top each with half the seed mixture and half the fruit. Drizzle with the remaining nectar.

✳ Power Ingredient

Seeds
Seeds are truly nutrition superstars. Packed with niacin and folate, seeds also offer high levels of iron and zinc. Moreover, they are good sources of protein and provide more fiber per ounce (28 g) than nuts.

Essential Coconut Pancakes

Few things top homemade pancakes and this coconut variation is a winner with kids and adults alike. You'll stay satisfied for hours, too, thanks to the high protein content of the chickpea flour (10 grams in 1 cup/250 mL, compared to 8 grams in wheat flour) and the high fiber content of the coconut flour.

Makes 14 pancakes

Tip

Serve the pancakes with any or all of your favorite toppings, such as maple syrup, coconut nectar, fresh fruit or a dab of coconut oil.

Storage Tip

Refrigerate pancakes between sheets of waxed paper, tightly covered in plastic wrap, for up to 2 days or freeze, enclosed in a sealable plastic bag, for up to 1 month. Let thaw at room temperature or defrost in the microwave.

⅔ cup	chickpea flour	150 mL
6 tbsp	coconut flour	90 mL
1½ tbsp	potato starch	22 mL
2½ tsp	gluten-free baking powder	12 mL
½ tsp	fine sea salt	2 mL
1 cup	well-stirred coconut milk (full-fat)	250 mL
⅔ cup	coconut water or water	150 mL
1 tbsp	psyllium husk	15 mL
2 tbsp	coconut sugar	30 mL
2 tbsp	melted virgin coconut oil	30 mL
1 tsp	gluten-free vanilla extract	5 mL
	Additional melted virgin coconut oil	

1. In a large bowl, whisk together chickpea flour, coconut flour, potato starch, baking powder and salt.

2. In a medium bowl, whisk together coconut milk, coconut water and psyllium. Let stand for 10 minutes to thicken. Whisk in coconut sugar, 2 tbsp (30 mL) coconut oil and vanilla until blended.

3. Add the coconut milk mixture to the flour mixture and stir until just blended.

4. Heat a griddle or skillet over medium heat. Brush with coconut oil. For each pancake, pour about ¼ cup (60 mL) batter onto griddle. Cook until bubbles appear on top. Turn pancake over and cook for about 1 minute or until golden brown. Repeat with the remaining batter, brushing griddle and adjusting heat as necessary between batches.

Variations

Blueberry Coconut Pancakes: After pouring the batter onto the griddle, sprinkle each pancake with 4 to 5 blueberries.

Apple Cinnamon Pancakes: Add 1½ tsp (7 mL) ground cinnamon in step 1. Stir in 1 cup (250 mL) shredded tart-sweet apple at the end of step 2.

Banana Flapjacks

These pancakes are guaranteed to leave you smiling, both from the great taste and because the bananas contain a high level of tryptophan, which is converted into serotonin, the good-mood neurotransmitter.

Tip

You can peel and freeze very ripe bananas in a sealed plastic bag or airtight container and thaw when ready to use.

Storage Tip

Refrigerate pancakes between sheets of waxed paper, tightly covered in plastic wrap, for up to 2 days or freeze, enclosed in a sealable plastic bag, for up to 1 month. Let thaw at room temperature or defrost in the microwave.

½ cup	chickpea flour	125 mL
¼ cup	coconut flour	60 mL
1 tbsp	potato starch	15 mL
2¼ tsp	gluten-free baking powder	11 mL
½ tsp	ground cinnamon	2 mL
¼ tsp	fine sea salt	1 mL
1 tbsp	coconut sugar	15 mL
⅔ cup	mashed very ripe bananas	150 mL
½ cup	well-stirred coconut milk (full-fat)	125 mL
½ cup	coconut water or water	125 mL
2 tbsp	melted virgin coconut oil	30 mL
2 tsp	cider vinegar	10 mL
	Additional melted virgin coconut oil	

1. In a large bowl, whisk together chickpea flour, coconut flour, potato starch, baking powder, cinnamon and salt.

2. In a medium bowl, whisk together coconut sugar, bananas, coconut milk, coconut water, 2 tbsp (30 mL) coconut oil and vinegar until blended.

3. Add the banana mixture to the flour mixture and stir until just blended.

4. Heat a griddle or skillet over medium heat. Brush with coconut oil. For each pancake, pour about ¼ cup (60 mL) batter onto griddle. Cook until bubbles appear on top. Turn pancake over and cook for about 1 minute or until golden brown. Repeat with the remaining batter, brushing griddle and adjusting heat as necessary between batches.

Variations

Pumpkin Spice Flapjacks: Replace the bananas with an equal amount of pumpkin purée (not pie filling). Replace the cinnamon with 1¼ tsp (6 mL) pumpkin pie spice and increase the coconut sugar to 2 tbsp (30 mL).

Applesauce Flapjacks: Replace the bananas with an equal amount of unsweetened applesauce. Increase the coconut sugar to 2 tbsp (30 mL).

Make-Ahead Coconut Crêpes

The French sure know how to do pancakes. This super-satisfying, high-fiber variation of classic crêpes can be made in advance, then reheated with just about any filling — sweet or savory — that suits your fancy.

Makes 12 crêpes

Storage Tip

Refrigerate crêpes between sheets of waxed paper, tightly covered in plastic wrap, for up to 2 days or freeze, enclosed in a sealable plastic bag, for up to 1 month.

Crêpe Filling Ideas

Lemon juice and a drizzle of coconut nectar or sprinkle of coconut sugar.

A thin spread of coconut butter or seed butter and fruit-sweetened jam.

Coconut yogurt (store-bought or see recipe, page 49) and fresh fruit or fruit-sweetened jam.

Grated bittersweet chocolate.

Sautéed greens (spinach, kale, chard) and a sprinkle of nutritional yeast.

Thinly sliced pears sprinkled with coconut sugar.

Tofu Scramble with Mushrooms and Peppers (page 57).

½ cup	chickpea flour	125 mL
⅓ cup	coconut flour	75 mL
1 tbsp	potato starch	15 mL
½ tsp	fine sea salt	2 mL
1 cup	coconut water or water	250 mL
⅔ cup	well-stirred coconut milk (full-fat)	150 mL
	Melted virgin coconut oil	

1. In a large bowl, whisk together chickpea flour, coconut flour, potato starch and salt. Whisk in coconut water and coconut milk until smooth. Cover and refrigerate for 1 hour.

2. Heat a large skillet over medium–high heat. Remove from heat and lightly grease pan with coconut oil. Whisk the crêpe batter slightly. For each crêpe, pour about ¼ cup (60 mL) batter into pan, quickly tilting in all directions to cover bottom of pan. Cook for about 45 seconds or until just golden at the edges. With a spatula, carefully lift edge of crêpe to test for doneness. The crêpe is ready to turn when it is golden brown on the bottom and can be shaken loose from the pan. Turn crêpe over and cook for about 15 to 30 seconds or until golden brown.

3. Transfer crêpe to an unfolded kitchen towel to cool completely. Repeat with the remaining batter, greasing skillet and adjusting heat as necessary between crêpes, stacking cooled crêpes between sheets of waxed paper to prevent sticking.

Variation

Coconut Flour Tortillas: Use a medium skillet. For each tortilla, pour about ⅓ cup (75 mL) batter into a hot skillet that has been lightly greased with melted virgin coconut oil. Cook for about 60 to 75 seconds on the first side and 30 to 45 seconds on the second side. Store in the same manner as the crêpes and use as you would wheat or corn tortillas.

Good Morning Grain-Free Waffles

I won't say these grain-free waffles are as good as the original . . . because they are better! The texture is right in line with classic grain flour waffles, but these are far lower in sugar and higher in protein. The result? You'll feel satisfied and energized for far longer.

Storage Tip

Refrigerate waffles between sheets of waxed paper, tightly covered in plastic wrap, for up to 2 days or freeze, enclosed in a sealable plastic bag, for up to 1 month. Toast in a toaster for 1 to 2 minutes before serving.

- Preheat waffle maker to medium-high

2 tbsp	psyllium husk	30 mL
1 tbsp	coconut sugar	15 mL
1 cup	well-stirred coconut milk (full-fat)	250 mL
½ cup	water	125 mL
2 tbsp	melted virgin coconut oil	30 mL
1 tbsp	gluten-free vanilla extract	15 mL
1½ tsp	cider vinegar	7 mL
½ cup	chickpea flour	125 mL
¼ cup	coconut flour	60 mL
1 tbsp	potato starch	15 mL
1½ tsp	gluten-free baking powder	7 mL
½ tsp	baking soda	2 mL
⅛ tsp	fine sea salt	0.5 mL
	Additional melted virgin coconut oil	

1. In a medium bowl, whisk together psyllium, coconut sugar, coconut milk, water, 2 tbsp (30 mL) coconut oil, vanilla and vinegar. Let stand for 5 minutes.

2. In a large bowl, whisk together chickpea flour, coconut flour, potato starch, baking powder, baking soda and salt. Add psyllium mixture and stir until just blended.

3. Lightly brush preheated waffle maker with coconut oil. For each waffle, pour about ⅓ cup (75 mL) batter into waffle maker. Cook according to manufacturer's instructions until golden brown.

Variation

Chocolate Chip Waffles: Stir ⅓ cup (75 mL) miniature semisweet chocolate chips (vegan, gluten-free) into the batter at the end of step 2.

Pumpkin Latte Waffles

Pumpkin, spice and everything nice is rejigged into a supercharged, super-easy breakfast reminiscent of your favorite autumn latte — you may never go back to the coffeehouse again.

Makes 10 waffles

Storage Tip

Refrigerate waffles between sheets of waxed paper, tightly covered in plastic wrap, for up to 2 days or freeze, enclosed in a sealable plastic bag, for up to 1 month. Toast in a toaster for 1 to 2 minutes before serving.

- Preheat waffle maker to medium-high

3 tbsp	coconut sugar	45 mL
2 tbsp	psyllium husk	30 mL
1 cup	pumpkin purée (not pie filling)	250 mL
1 cup	well-stirred coconut milk (full-fat)	250 mL
1/2 cup	strong-brewed coffee, cooled	125 mL
2 tbsp	melted virgin coconut oil	30 mL
2/3 cup	chickpea flour	150 mL
1/3 cup	coconut flour	75 mL
4 tsp	potato starch	20 mL
2 1/2 tsp	gluten-free baking powder	12 mL
2 tsp	pumpkin pie spice	10 mL
1/2 tsp	fine sea salt	2 mL
	Additional melted virgin coconut oil	

1. In a medium bowl, whisk together coconut sugar, psyllium, pumpkin, coconut milk, coffee and 2 tbsp (30 mL) coconut oil. Let stand for 5 minutes.

2. In a large bowl, whisk together chickpea flour, coconut flour, potato starch, baking powder, pumpkin pie spice and salt.

3. Add the pumpkin mixture to the flour mixture and stir until just blended.

4. Lightly brush preheated waffle maker with coconut oil. For each waffle, pour about 1/3 cup (75 mL) batter into waffle maker. Cook according to manufacturer's instructions until golden brown.

Variations

Pumpkin Spice Waffles: Replace the coffee with an equal amount of coconut water or water.

Banana Waffles: Decrease the coconut sugar to 2 tbsp (30 mL), replace the pumpkin with an equal amount of mashed very ripe bananas, and replace the coffee with an equal amount of coconut water or water.

Garlicky Kale Frittata

I've turned the frittata — a baked or broiled Italian omelet — on its head by omitting the primary ingredient: eggs. Tofu stands in with great success, and the addition of kale and garlic make this a brunch-worthy bake.

Tips

An equal amount of packed baby spinach leaves (no need to chop) can be used in place of the kale. Reduce the cooking time for the greens to 1 to 2 minutes.

Leftovers can be wrapped in individual portions and stored in an airtight container for up to 3 days. Enjoy cold or at room temperature, or reheat each portion in the microwave on High for 20 to 30 seconds.

- Preheat oven to 400°F (200°C)
- 8-inch (20 cm) square glass baking pan or pie plate, greased with coconut oil

2 tbsp	virgin coconut oil	30 mL
6	cloves garlic, thinly sliced	6
4 cups	packed chopped kale leaves	1 L
	Fine sea salt and freshly ground black pepper	
1	package (16 oz/500 g) extra-firm or firm tofu, drained	1
¼ cup	nutritional yeast	60 mL
¼ tsp	ground turmeric	1 mL
2 tbsp	coconut cream or well-stirred coconut milk (full-fat)	30 mL
1 tsp	Dijon mustard	5 mL

1. In a medium skillet, melt coconut oil over medium heat. Add garlic and cook, stirring, for 3 to 4 minutes or until golden. Add kale, increase heat to medium–high and cook, stirring, for 4 to 5 minutes or until kale is wilted. Season to taste with salt and pepper.

2. Meanwhile, in a medium bowl, mash tofu with a fork until it resembles ricotta cheese. Add nutritional yeast, ¾ tsp (3 mL) salt, turmeric, coconut cream and mustard, mixing until well blended. Add kale mixture, stirring until combined. Season to taste with pepper.

3. Transfer tofu mixture to prepared baking pan, pressing down firmly and smoothing top.

4. Bake in preheated oven for 20 to 25 minutes or until frittata is firm and golden brown. Let cool in pan for 3 minutes, then invert onto a plate. Serve warm.

Tofu Scramble with Mushrooms and Peppers

Bronzed in a hot skillet with mushrooms and peppers, crumbled tofu absorbs a delectable blend of flavors. It's an excellent source of protein, which means you'll feel satisfied for hours, and iron, providing 33.8% of the daily value per 4-oz (125 g) serving.

Makes 4 servings

Tips

An equal amount of gluten-free soy sauce can be used in place of the liquid coconut amino acids.

Other colors of bell pepper can be used in place of the red pepper.

2 tbsp	virgin coconut oil	30 mL
1	large red bell pepper, chopped	1
12 oz	mushrooms, chopped	375 g
1	package (16 oz/500 g) extra-firm or firm tofu, drained and coarsely mashed with a fork	1
¼ cup	chopped green onions	60 mL
2 tbsp	well-stirred coconut milk (full-fat)	30 mL
1 tbsp	gluten-free liquid coconut amino acids	15 mL
Pinch	freshly ground black pepper	Pinch

1. In a large skillet, melt coconut oil over medium heat. Add red pepper and mushrooms; increase heat to medium–high and cook, stirring, for 4 to 5 minutes or until softened.

2. Add tofu, green onions, coconut milk and liquid amino acids; cook, stirring, for 5 to 6 minutes or until flavors are blended and tofu is golden brown. Season with pepper.

✳ Power Ingredient

Bell Peppers
Bell peppers are excellent sources of vitamins C and A, both of which are antioxidants that neutralize free radicals, thus helping to reduce the risk of heart disease, some cancers and cataracts, and to alleviate symptoms of arthritis and asthma. Bell peppers also contain vitamin B_6, folate and fiber, all of which may help reduce the risk of heart attack and stroke.

Smoky Sweet Potato Hash

I've swapped in sweet potatoes in place of traditional white potatoes in this smoky, hearty dish. And though this recipe is in the breakfast chapter, it makes a terrific dinner, too.

Tips
....

To vary the flavor, you can replace the smoked paprika with an equal amount of ground cumin, sweet paprika or chili powder.

An equal amount of pinto or kidney beans can be used in place of the black beans.

2 tbsp	virgin coconut oil	30 mL
1½ cups	chopped onions	375 mL
1	red bell pepper, chopped	1
2	cloves garlic, minced	2
2 tsp	smoked paprika	10 mL
2 cups	diced peeled sweet potatoes	500 mL
1¼ cups	coconut water or water	300 mL
¼ tsp	fine sea salt	1 mL
1 cup	rinsed drained canned black beans	250 mL
	Fine sea salt and cracked black pepper	

Suggested Accompaniments

Chopped fresh cilantro or flat-leaf (Italian) parsley

Chopped fresh chives or green onions

Plain coconut yogurt (store-bought or see recipe, page 49)

Salsa

Hot sauce

1. In a large skillet, melt coconut oil over medium heat. Add onions and red pepper; increase heat to medium–high and cook, stirring, for 6 to 8 minutes or until softened. Add garlic and paprika; cook, stirring, for 1 minute.

2. Stir in sweet potatoes, coconut water and salt; bring to a boil. Reduce heat, cover and simmer, without stirring, for 12 minutes. Uncover and stir with a spatula. Add black beans and cook, stirring, for 4 to 5 minutes or until liquid is absorbed and sweet potatoes are tender and slightly browned. Cover and let stand for 5 minutes.

3. Serve warm with any of the suggested accompaniments, as desired.

You can increase the health benefits you receive from garlic by letting it stand for about 15 minutes after mincing it. Researchers at the American Institute for Cancer Research found that when chopped, minced or crushed garlic was allowed to stand before it was cooked or combined with acidic ingredients (such as vinegar or lemon juice in a salad dressing), more of its cancer-fighting compounds were preserved.

Variation

Chickpea Masala Hash: Replace the black beans with rinsed drained canned chickpeas, and replace the smoked paprika with an equal amount of garam masala or curry powder.

✳ Power Ingredient

Garlic
Valued as a contributor to good health for thousands of years, garlic is a useful antibiotic and inhibits fungal infections such as athlete's foot. Its powerful sulfur compounds are the cause of its strong odor but are also the main source of its health benefits. Eating garlic appears to boost our natural supply of hydrogen sulfide, which acts as an antioxidant and transmits cellular signals that relax blood vessels and increase blood flow. The human body already produces hydrogen sulfide, but boosted production could help explain why a garlic-rich diet may protect against various cancers, including breast, prostate and colon cancer. Additional research suggests that higher hydrogen sulfide might also protect the heart, preventing formation of blood clots and arterial plaque. Garlic also appears to minimize stomach ulcers. Eaten in reasonable quantity, it is a good source of vitamin C, selenium, potassium and calcium.

Raspberry Breakfast Clafouti

This amazingly delicious and healthy baked breakfast is satisfying without being heavy. The possibilities for variation are endless, so pick and choose the fruits and flavorings of your choice. Coconut milk adds mellow flavor and creaminess (to replace the traditional eggs and milk in clafouti) while simultaneously contributing to your daily iron and potassium requirements.

Makes 8 servings

Tips

Although the clafouti is delicious plain, consider topping servings with small dollops of coconut cream or coconut yogurt (see page 49).

If using fruits larger than raspberries, such as apples, peaches or pears (see the variation, page 61), be sure to cut or chop them into small pieces (about ½ inch/1 cm) to ensure even baking.

Consider making the clafouti in individual-size portions. Grease a 6-cup muffin pan with coconut oil. Prepare batter as directed, then spoon and spread into prepared cups. Sprinkle with raspberries and remaining coconut sugar. Bake for 14 to 19 minutes or until set at the center and golden. Let cool as directed.

- Preheat oven to 350°F (180°C)
- 9-inch (23 cm) glass pie plate, greased with coconut oil

⅓ cup	potato starch	75 mL
⅓ cup	coconut flour	75 mL
7 tbsp	coconut sugar, divided	105 mL
2 tsp	gluten-free baking powder	10 mL
½ tsp	fine sea salt	2 mL
2¼ cups	well-stirred coconut milk (full-fat)	550 mL
2 tsp	gluten-free vanilla extract	10 mL
1 cup	raspberries	250 mL

1. In a large bowl, whisk together potato starch, coconut flour, 6 tbsp (90 mL) coconut sugar, baking powder, salt, coconut milk and vanilla until smooth.

2. Spoon and spread coconut mixture into prepared pan. Sprinkle with raspberries and remaining coconut sugar.

3. Bake in preheated oven for 25 to 35 minutes or until set at the center and golden. Let cool on a wire rack for 20 minutes. Cut or spoon into servings and serve warm.

Storage Tip

Let clafouti cool completely, then wrap individual portions in plastic wrap and store in an airtight container in the refrigerator for up to 3 days or in the freezer for up to 1 month. Thaw in the refrigerator or microwave. Serve cold or at room temperature, or reheat each portion in the microwave on High for 15 to 30 seconds.

Variation

An equal amount of other fresh fruits, such as diced apples, bananas, pears, peaches or blueberries, may be used in place of the raspberries. Alternatively, use ½ cup (125 mL) dried fruit (raisins, dried cherries, chopped dried apricots).

✳ Power Ingredient

Raspberries
Packed with vitamin C, high in fiber and loaded with antioxidants to protect the heart, raspberries are one of the most nutritious fruits. They are best eaten raw, because cooking or processing destroys some of these antioxidants, especially anthocyanins — red and purple pigments that have been shown to help prevent heart disease and cancer and may help prevent varicose veins. Raspberries also contain high levels of ellagic acid, a compound with anticancer properties, and good amounts of iron, which the body absorbs well thanks to the high levels of vitamin C.

Chocolate Chip Breakfast Bars

If you are weary of grain-laden, preservative-packed energy bars and granola bars, give these chocolate chip breakfast bars a try. Recent research indicates that the medium-chain triglycerides (MCTs) in coconut oil can increase energy expenditure compared to the same amount of calories from longer-chain fats. One study in the *European Journal of Clinical Nutrition* found that 15 to 30 grams of MCTs per day increased 24-hour energy expenditure by 5% — so grab a breakfast bar and get busy!

Makes 16 bars

Tips

Lining a pan with foil is easy. Begin by turning the pan upside down. Tear off a piece of foil longer than the pan, and then mold the foil over the pan. Remove the foil and set it aside. Flip the pan over and gently fit the shaped foil into the pan, allowing the foil to hang over the sides (the overhang ends will work as "handles" when the contents of the pan are removed).

An equal amount of chopped dried fruit (such as prunes, apricots or figs) can be used in place of the chocolate chips.

An equal amount of hemp hearts can be used in place of the sunflower seeds, or you can use half of each.

- Food processor
- 9-inch (23 cm) square metal baking pan, lined with foil (see tip, at left)

⅔ cup	virgin coconut oil	150 mL
2 cups	sunflower seeds (raw, toasted or roasted)	500 mL
1 cup	unsweetened flaked or shredded coconut	250 mL
½ cup	sunflower seed butter or tahini	125 mL
3 tbsp	coconut flour	45 mL
½ tsp	fine sea salt	2 mL
1½ tbsp	coconut sugar	22 mL
1 tbsp	gluten-free vanilla extract	15 mL
½ cup	miniature semisweet chocolate chips (vegan, gluten-free)	125 mL

1. In a small saucepan, melt coconut oil over medium-low heat.

2. In food processor, pulse sunflower seeds and coconut until chopped (not too fine). Add sunflower seed butter, coconut flour, salt, coconut sugar and vanilla; pulse until mixture begins to hold together as dough.

3. Transfer mixture to prepared pan and press flat with a square of waxed paper.

Wrap bars individually and refrigerate for up to 2 weeks.

4. Melt chocolate chips in the microwave according to package directions (or in a heatproof bowl set over a saucepan of hot water). Drizzle or spread over bar mixture. Freeze for 30 minutes. Using foil liner, lift mixture from pan. Peel off foil and place bar mixture on a cutting board. Cut into 16 bars.

✳ Power Ingredient

Sunflower Seeds
Besides the filling nutrients protein and fiber, sunflower seeds are rich in polyunsaturated fats, plant sterols (which have a cholesterol-lowering effect), iron and selenium. They contain B vitamins, magnesium, manganese and copper, all of which help with energy production, connective tissue formation and nerve function. Notably, 1 ounce (28 g) of sesame seeds provides nearly 50% of the recommended daily value of vitamin E, an important fat-soluble vitamin that boosts immune function and benefits the health of your hair, nails and complexion. Vitamin E also neutralizes the free radicals that, in excess, can damage the body's cells and speed up the aging process, helps protect against inflammatory conditions such as asthma and rheumatoid arthritis, and is linked with a lower risk of cardiovascular disease and with protection from colon cancer.

Apricot Breakfast Bites

Packed with coconut, assorted seeds, tart-sweet apricots and aromatic cardamom, these portable breakfast bites are far more exciting — and nutritious — than what you'll find on the breakfast bar shelf.

Tips

Ground cardamom is my favorite spice to use in this recipe, but ground cinnamon or ginger are delicious too.

An equal amount of other moist dried fruits (such as prunes, raisins or cherries) or fresh dates can be used in place of the apricots.

Storage Tip

Store balls in an airtight container at room temperature for up to 3 days or in the refrigerator for up to 3 weeks. Or wrap them in plastic wrap, then foil, completely enclosing them, and freeze for up to 6 months. Let thaw at room temperature for 1 hour before serving.

- Food processor

1 cup	moist, soft dried apricots	250 mL
¾ cup	unsweetened flaked coconut	175 mL
1 tbsp	virgin coconut oil	15 mL
¼ tsp	ground cardamom (optional)	1 mL
¾ cup	assorted raw seeds (sunflower, hemp, chia, sesame, green pumpkin)	175 mL

1. In food processor, combine apricots, coconut, coconut oil and cardamom (if using); pulse until mixture resembles a thick paste. Transfer to a medium bowl.

2. In the same food processor bowl (no need to clean it), pulse seeds until finely chopped. Add seeds to apricot paste and, using your fingers or a wooden spoon, combine well.

3. Roll mixture into twenty 1-inch (2.5 cm) balls. Cover and refrigerate for at least 30 minutes before eating.

✳ Power Ingredient

Apricots

Apricots are an excellent source of vitamins A, C and E, potassium and iron, and a great source of beta carotene. Two to 3 dried apricots provide nearly 50% of the daily value of vitamin A. Apricots are also rich in powerful antioxidants, such as lycopene, which helps to strengthen the immune system. Moreover, the golden fruits are a good source of fiber, which benefits digestive health.

Beverages

Cucumber and Mint Coconut Water

This is a spa-style drink, if ever there was one. Coconut water contains a wealth of nutrients, including vitamins, minerals, amino acids and antioxidants. It is also considered the second most pure liquid after water, so it's an excellent choice for hydration in general and skin hydration in particular.

Tips

Give the lemon and cucumber a vigorous scrub before use to remove any wax or dirt.

Whenever possible, use organic fruits and vegetables to avoid pesticide residue.

8 cups	coconut water	2 L
1	small lemon, quartered	1
½	English cucumber, sliced	½
½ cup	packed fresh mint leaves	125 mL

1. In a pitcher, combine coconut water, lemon, cucumber and mint. Refrigerate for at least 12 hours to blend the flavors. Strain, discarding solids.
2. Store in the refrigerator for up to 2 days.

Variation

Orange and Basil Coconut Water: Replace the lemon with ½ navel orange, cut into 4 pieces, and replace the mint with an equal amount of fresh basil leaves.

Apple Ginger Juice

"An apple a day" is great health advice, and this blender juice gives the adage a fresh, bold spin.

Makes 2 servings

Tip

For the apples, try Braeburn, Gala or Golden Delicious.

- Blender

2	tart-sweet apples, peeled and chopped	2
2 tsp	grated gingerroot	10 mL
1⅓ cups	coconut water, chilled	325 mL
1 tbsp	coconut nectar or coconut sugar	15 mL

1. In blender, purée apples, ginger, coconut water and coconut nectar until smooth. Pour into two glasses and serve immediately.

Variation

Apple Cinnamon Juice: Replace the ginger with ½ tsp (2 mL) ground cinnamon.

✳ Power Ingredient

Apples

Apples are packed full of antioxidants, especially vitamin C for healthy skin and gums, and contain a form of soluble fiber called pectin that can help lower blood cholesterol levels and keep the digestive system healthy. In fact, research published in the December 2013 *British Medical Journal* found that eating an apple every day could be just as effective as statins in preventing vascular deaths among people over 50.

Honeydew Detox Drink

A symphony in green, this beautiful beverage will refresh and revive you with each sip.

Makes 2 servings

Tips

Try cantaloupe, casaba or Crenshaw melon in place of the honeydew.

An equal amount of fresh mint can be used in place of the basil.

- Blender

3 cups	chopped peeled honeydew melon, chilled	750 mL
1 cup	coconut water, chilled	250 mL
1/4 cup	fresh basil leaves	60 mL
2 tbsp	freshly squeezed lime juice	30 mL

1. In blender, purée melon, coconut water, basil and lime juice until smooth. Pour into two glasses and serve immediately.

Variation

Honeydew Detox Shake: Replace the coconut water with well-stirred coconut milk (full-fat).

✳ Power Ingredient

Honeydew Melon
Honeydew melon possesses one of the highest vitamin C contents of all melons. Vitamin C aids in tissue repair, iron absorption and building a strong immune system, and can even guard against the cancer-causing effects of free radicals. The most unique (and tongue-twisting) component of honeydew has to be zeaxanthin, from which it gets its green hue and vision-protecting superpowers. Its potassium content aids in muscle repair, and its soluble and insoluble fiber not only aid digestion, but also help regulate blood sugar levels.

Kiwi Coconut Freeze

Kiwifruit is the belle of the ball in this summertime slush.

Tips

Use this basic recipe as a template to make a host of slushy variations. Simply replace the kiwifruit with 1¼ cups (300 mL) chopped fresh fruit, such as blueberries, pineapple, peaches or plums.

You can leave out the coconut nectar if the kiwifruit are especially sweet.

- Blender

6	small ripe kiwifruit, peeled and halved	6
1 cup	ice cubes	250 mL
¾ cup	coconut water	175 mL
1 tbsp	coconut nectar or coconut sugar	15 mL

1. In blender, purée kiwis, ice cubes, coconut water and coconut nectar until smooth. Pour into two glasses and serve immediately.

✳ Power Ingredient

Kiwifruit
Kiwifruit is as nutritious as it is delicious. In addition to being high in folate, vitamin C (which helps heal wounds, increases iron absorption and boosts the immune system) and vitamin E (which decreases the risk of heart disease), kiwis are also rich in phytonutrients, which repair DNA, act as the body's protection against some cancers and function as antioxidants.

Coconut Vanilla Shake

Reaping the benefits of coconut milk has never been more delectable than in this rich, thick, vanilla-enhanced shake. And talk about great benefits: with every sip, you're drinking vitamins C, E, B_1, B_3, B_5 and B_6 and trace amounts of several minerals, including iron, selenium, sodium, calcium, magnesium and phosphorous.

Tip

For a lighter shake, replace the coconut milk with an equal amount of coconut water.

- Blender

2 cups	well-stirred coconut milk (full-fat)	500 mL
1 cup	ice cubes	250 mL
3 tbsp	coconut sugar or coconut nectar	45 mL
2 tsp	gluten-free vanilla extract	10 mL

1. In blender, purée coconut milk, ice cubes, coconut sugar and vanilla until smooth. Pour into two glasses and serve immediately.

Variations

Vanilla Mint Shake: Add 1/3 cup (75 mL) fresh mint leaves.

Coconut Latte Shake: Add 2 to 3 tsp (10 to 15 mL) instant espresso powder.

Banana Shake: Replace the ice cubes with an equal amount of sliced frozen bananas, and decrease the coconut sugar to 1 tbsp (15 mL).

Deep Chocolate Coconut Shake

Potassium-rich, high-fiber banana is the only sweetener you need in this decadent chocolate shake.

Makes 2 servings

Tip

For a lighter shake, replace the coconut milk with an equal amount of coconut water.

- Blender

1 cup	well-stirred coconut milk (full-fat)	250 mL
½ cup	ice cubes	125 mL
1 cup	sliced frozen very ripe bananas	250 mL
3 tbsp	unsweetened natural cocoa powder	45 mL
1 tbsp	coconut sugar or coconut nectar	15 mL

1. In blender, purée coconut milk and ice cubes until smooth. Add banana, cocoa and coconut sugar; purée until smooth. Pour into two glasses and serve immediately.

Variations

Chocolate Mint Shake: Add 3 tbsp (45 mL) fresh mint leaves with the banana.

Mocha Shake: Add 1 to 2 tsp (5 to 10 mL) instant espresso powder with the banana.

✳ Power Ingredient

Bananas
One medium banana has over 400 milligrams of potassium, an electrolyte necessary for good nerve and muscle function, as well as for maintaining a healthy balance of fluids in the body. Bananas also have a small amount of vitamin A, a fat-soluble vitamin that is vital for protecting your eyes and normal vision.

Pumpkin Pie Shake

Brimming with antioxidants, fiber and vitamin A, pumpkin delivers great health and great taste in equal measure. Here, it stars in a sweet, creamy smoothie, offering delicious proof that it deserves a place in your pantry year-round.

Tip

For a lighter shake, replace the coconut milk with an equal amount of coconut water.

- Blender

¾ cup	well-stirred coconut milk (full-fat)	175 mL
⅔ cup	sliced frozen ripe banana	150 mL
½ cup	pumpkin purée (not pie filling)	125 mL
½ cup	ice cubes	125 mL
1 tbsp	coconut nectar or coconut sugar	15 mL
¼ tsp	pumpkin pie spice or ground cinnamon	1 mL
1 tsp	gluten-free vanilla extract	5 mL

1. In blender, purée coconut milk, banana, pumpkin, ice cubes, coconut nectar, pumpkin pie spice and vanilla until smooth. Pour into two glasses and serve immediately.

Brain Power Shake

Every ingredient in this mindful shake is bursting with brain-power nutrients, but avocado is the superstar.

Tips

You can replace the strawberries and bananas with an equal amount (1¼ cups/ 300 mL total) of other frozen fruits, such as peaches, mangos, pineapple and/or blueberries.

For a richer shake, replace ¾ cup (175 mL) of the coconut water with well-stirred coconut milk (full-fat).

- Blender

1	small ripe Hass avocado, peeled, pitted and diced	1
¾ cup	frozen strawberries	175 mL
½ cup	sliced frozen ripe banana	125 mL
1¼ cups	coconut water, chilled	300 mL
1 tbsp	coconut nectar or coconut sugar (optional)	15 mL

1. In blender, purée avocado, strawberries, banana, coconut water and coconut nectar (if using) until smooth. Pour into two glasses and serve immediately.

❋ Power Ingredient

Avocados
Avocados are rich in nutrients, including vitamins C, E and B$_6$, folate, iron, magnesium and potassium, and the antioxidant plant chemicals beta sitosterol (which can help lower blood cholesterol) and glutathione (which protects against cancer). Avocado is also very high in both insoluble and soluble fiber while still being very gentle on the gut mucosa, making it ideal for gently cleansing the colon and carrying toxins out of the body. Its high fiber content also helps lower HDL cholesterol levels and manage diabetes.

Avocados are very high in fat, but it is mostly heart-healthy monounsaturated fat, which helps your body to better absorb vitamin A, a potent antioxidant that is involved in the natural detox process. Avocados are particularly rich in a fatty acid called oleic acid, which can lower the risk of breast cancer and help reduce "bad" blood cholesterol levels. Further, oleic acid helps build the coating of insulation, known as myelin, found in the brain's white matter. Myelin helps information travel at speeds of up to 200 miles (320 km) per hour. Neurons without myelin (gray matter) process information at slower speeds. Oleic acid makes up over a third of the fat in myelin. Thus, avocados are helpful for speedy messaging within your brain. We can make some oleic acid on our own if we have other good fats in our diet, but avocados are a tasty way to enjoy it.

Purple Power Shake

Each sip of this deep purple smoothie delivers antioxidants, protein, vitamins and so much more. Be sure to choose a dark purple grape juice, rather than a white grape juice, to reap the most benefits.

Makes 2 servings

Tips

For the berries, try strawberries, blueberries, blackberries and/or raspberries.

You can replace the bananas with an equal amount of other frozen fruits, such as peaches, mangos or pineapple.

An equal amount of well-stirred coconut milk (full-fat) or coconut water can be used in place of the coconut yogurt.

- Blender

1½ cups	mixed frozen berries	375 mL
½ cup	sliced frozen ripe banana	125 mL
¾ cup	plain coconut yogurt (store-bought or see recipe, page 49)	175 mL
¾ cup	unsweetened grape juice	175 mL

1. In blender, purée berries, banana, yogurt and grape juice until smooth. Pour into two glasses and serve immediately.

✳ Power Ingredient

Fresh Fruits
Fresh fruits contain a bounty of antioxidants and healthful nutrients, and their cellular structure, made of fiber, makes us feel full and provides other metabolic benefits. When you crunch into an apple, for example, the fruit's fiber helps slow your absorption of fructose, the main sugar in most fruits. When eaten at breakfast, fiber will help keep you from overeating before lunchtime by making you feel fuller. Unlike processed foods, which are usually digested in the first few feet of our intestines, fiber-rich fruit breaks down more slowly, so it travels more slowly in the digestive tract, making you feel satisfied for a long time.

Banana Date Coconut Smoothie

Naturally sweetened with dates and banana, this creamy concoction may fool you into thinking you're sipping a thick ice cream shake. Go ahead and savor the folly: the combination of high-fiber ingredients makes this a fantastic detox smoothie for your digestive system.

Makes 2 servings

Tips

You can still make this smoothie if you only have fresh (as opposed to frozen) bananas. It will be less thick, but the flavor will be the same.

If your dates are hard or tough, let them soak in hot water for 10 to 15 minutes. Drain, then use as directed.

In place of the dates, you can use 2 to 3 tbsp (30 to 45 mL) coconut sugar or coconut nectar. Increase the coconut water to 1 cup (250 mL).

- Blender

1 cup	sliced frozen ripe banana	250 mL
1/3 cup	pitted Medjool or other soft dates, roughly chopped	75 mL
3/4 cup	well-stirred coconut milk (full-fat), chilled	175 mL
3/4 cup	coconut water or water, chilled	175 mL

1. In blender, purée banana, dates, coconut milk and coconut water until smooth. Pour into two glasses and serve immediately.

✳ Power Ingredient

Dates

In addition to high levels of fiber, copper and potassium, dates contain notable amounts of several other essential nutrients. One $3\frac{1}{2}$-oz (100 g) serving provides 15%, 13.5% and 12% of the daily values for manganese, magnesium and vitamin B_6, respectively. The same serving delivers 8% each of the daily values for niacin and pantothenic acid, 6% each of the daily values for calcium and phosphorus, and 5% of the daily value for iron. Dates also provide lesser amounts of folate, zinc, thiamine, riboflavin and vitamin K. A 2009 study published in the *Journal of Agricultural and Food Chemistry* found dates to be high in antioxidant phenols, which may help reduce high blood triglyceride levels.

Strawberry Beet Smoothie

Breakfast, lunch, snack — this gorgeous glassful is the all-in-one answer for a fast, fresh energy boost.

Tips

Consider wearing rubber gloves while shredding the beets, to avoid stained hands.

An equal amount of coconut milk plus 1 tbsp (15 mL) lemon juice can be used in place of the yogurt.

- Blender

1 cup	frozen strawberries	250 mL
1/3 cup	finely shredded beets	75 mL
2/3 cup	plain coconut yogurt (store-bought or see recipe, page 49)	150 mL
2/3 cup	unsweetened apple juice	150 mL

1. In blender, purée strawberries, beets, coconut yogurt and apple juice until smooth. Pour into two glasses and serve immediately.

Variation

Triple Red Elixir: Replace the apple juice with cranberry juice and the coconut yogurt with coconut water.

❋ Power Ingredient

Strawberries

Strawberries contain good amounts of fiber, folate and potassium, as well as anthocyanin, a powerful antioxidant that offers protection from the damaging effects of the environment, especially the sun. Strawberries can also help you "chill out" in the summertime and year-round: just 1 cup (250 mL) contains more than 100% of the daily recommended allowance of vitamin C. Recent research suggests that, when vitamin C is consumed during times of stress, it has the ability to decrease blood pressure to a normal level, preventing the development of hypertension. Vitamin C also boosts the immune system and helps to heal wounds, prevent arterial damage, promote iron absorption and strengthen blood vessel walls.

Mango Carrot Coconut Smoothie

Begin the day by drinking your vegetables. This sunshiny blend of mango and carrots has more than enough zing to launch you into your day.

Makes 2 servings

Tips

An equal amount of coconut yogurt (store-bought or see recipe, page 49) can be used in place of the coconut milk.

For a lighter smoothie, replace the coconut milk with an equal amount of coconut water.

- Blender

1 cup	frozen mango chunks	250 mL
¾ cup	finely shredded carrots	175 mL
⅔ cup	orange juice	150 mL
½ cup	well-stirred coconut milk (full-fat)	125 mL

1. In blender, purée mango, carrots, orange juice and coconut milk until smooth. Pour into two glasses and serve immediately.

✵ Power Ingredient

Carrots

Carrots are an excellent source of antioxidant compounds and the richest vegetable source of carotenes, which give them their bright orange color and may reduce the incidence of heart disease by about 45%. High intake of carotenes has been linked with a 20% decrease in postmenopausal breast cancer and up to a 50% decrease in cancers of the cervix, bladder, colon, prostate, larynx and esophagus. Extensive studies have shown that a diet that includes at least one carrot per day could cut the rate of lung cancer in half. Another chemical found in carrots, falcarinol, has been shown to suppress tumors in animals by a third.

Carrots also offer an excellent source of fiber, vitamin K and biotin, the latter of which is beneficial for strong nails and hair. They are a good source of vitamins B_6, C and E, potassium, calcium and thiamine.

Furthermore, the old adage is true: munching on carrots is great for your eyes. Research continues to indicate that carrots are very effective at promoting good vision, especially night vision. Their high levels of beta carotene provide protection against macular degeneration and the development of senile cataracts, the leading cause of blindness in the elderly.

Papaya Dream Smoothie

This beautiful tropical smoothie is a good choice for keeping colds at bay. Both pineapple juice and papaya are excellent sources of vitamin C, which is vital for increasing the body's natural resistance to colds and disease.

Makes 2 servings

Tips

An equal amount of coconut water, unsweetened apple juice or orange juice can be used in place of the pineapple juice.

An equal amount of plain coconut yogurt (store-bought or see recipe, page 49) can be used in place of the coconut milk.

For a lighter smoothie, replace the coconut milk with an equal amount of coconut water.

- Blender

1 cup	frozen papaya chunks	250 mL
1 cup	unsweetened pineapple juice	250 mL
¾ cup	well-stirred coconut milk (full-fat)	175 mL
1 tbsp	freshly squeezed lemon or lime juice	15 mL

1. In blender, purée papaya, pineapple juice, coconut milk and lemon juice until smooth. Pour into two glasses and serve immediately.

Variation

Mango Ginger Smoothie: Replace the papaya with an equal amount of frozen mango chunks and add 1 tbsp (15 mL) roughly chopped gingerroot.

Green Coconut Smoothie

Eschew the drive-through once and for all: this is what real fast food is all about. Ready in minutes, this refreshing, nutrient-dense elixir will satisfy and energize you all morning long.

Tips

You can replace the grapes with an equal amount of chopped fresh honeydew melon, cantaloupe, pineapple or mango.

For a richer smoothie, replace the coconut water with an equal amount of well-stirred coconut milk (full fat) or coconut yogurt (store-bought or see recipe, page 49).

- Blender

2 cups	loosely packed spinach leaves or trimmed kale leaves	500 mL
1 cup	green grapes	250 mL
¾ cup	sliced frozen ripe banana	175 mL
½ cup	chopped kiwifruit	125 mL
1 cup	coconut water, chilled	250 mL

1. In blender, purée spinach, grapes, banana, kiwi and coconut water until smooth. Pour into two glasses and serve immediately.

Variation

Green Tea Energy Smoothie: Add 1 tsp (5 mL) green tea powder (matcha).

✻ Power Ingredient

Grapes
An excellent source of antioxidants, vitamins A, C and B_6 and folate, grapes are superfoods by any measure. Purple grapes also contain the phytonutrient resveratrol, known for its helpful effects on circulation. While resveratrol is concentrated in red wine, you can still get plenty by drinking dark purple grape juice. Grapes help prevent circulatory problems by keeping blood vessels healthy, raising HDL ("good") cholesterol and lowering LDL ("bad") cholesterol.

Super C Elixir

This refreshing, tart-sweet smoothie is a drinkable wake-up call. The berries are loaded with antioxidants, and the oranges boost the dietary fiber and are an excellent source of vitamin C and flavonoids.

Makes 2 servings

Tips

Leave some of the pith (the white part beneath the peel) on the orange — it contains high levels of fiber, phytochemicals and antioxidants.

For the berries, try strawberries, blueberries, blackberries and/or raspberries.

For a richer smoothie, replace the coconut water with an equal amount of well-stirred coconut milk (full-fat) or coconut yogurt (store-bought or see recipe, page 49).

- Blender

2	oranges, peel and pith removed, flesh cut into chunks	2
1 cup	frozen mixed berries	250 mL
1 cup	coconut water, chilled	250 mL

1. In blender, purée oranges, berries and coconut water until smooth. Pour into two glasses and serve immediately.

Variation

Green C Monster: Add 1½ cups (375 mL) loosely packed spinach leaves or trimmed kale leaves.

Coconut Nog

This nog needs neither eggs nor sugar to make it seductively rich, sweet and creamy — just coconut milk, coconut water, dates and some spices. Cinnamon is important, but ground nutmeg is the quintessential nog spice.

Makes 4 servings

Tips

If you want to give your nog a pale yellow hue to resemble traditional eggnog, add about ½ tsp (2 mL) ground turmeric. It will not contribute any flavor, just color.

If your dates are hard or tough, let them soak in hot water for 10 to 15 minutes. Drain, then use as directed.

- Blender

1 cup	pitted Medjool or other soft dates, roughly chopped	250 mL
2 cups	well-stirred coconut milk (full-fat)	500 mL
1½ cups	coconut water or water	375 mL
1½ tsp	ground cinnamon	7 mL
¾ tsp	ground nutmeg	3 mL
1 tsp	natural rum extract, brandy extract or gluten-free vanilla extract (optional)	5 mL

1. In blender, purée dates, coconut milk, coconut water, cinnamon, nutmeg and rum extract (if using) until smooth.

2. Store in an airtight container in the refrigerator for up to 5 days. Shake or stir before serving.

✳ Power Ingredient

Nutmeg
Nutmeg is the fruit of an evergreen native to Indonesia and now grown in several countries. The spice is made from the seed of this fruit. Like many other spices, nutmeg has antibacterial action and can help protect us from food poisoning bacteria, such as *E. coli*. The spice has been used to treat Crohn's disease, an inflammatory condition of the bowel, and it is said that the essential oil of the fruit can help painful gums.

Coconut Hot Chocolate

Looking for the perfect warm drink to help you jumpstart a chilly morning? You found it. Cocoa powder contains a mild hit of caffeine — just enough to rev your engine — and increases blood flow to the brain, improving cognitive function.

Tip

To get the most health benefits from cocoa powder, opt for natural rather than Dutch process. With the latter, the cocoa beans are washed in an alkali bath that reduces their acidity but also significantly reduces the health-boosting compounds (notably, a class of antioxidants called flavonoids). Natural cocoa powder is readily available in the baking section of supermarkets; so long as the container does not specifically say "Dutch Process," you can safely assume it is natural.

¼ cup	unsweetened natural cocoa powder	60 mL
3 tbsp	coconut sugar	45 mL
⅛ tsp	fine sea salt	0.5 mL
1¼ cups	coconut milk, divided	300 mL
¾ cup	coconut water or water	175 mL
½ tsp	gluten-free vanilla extract	2 mL

1. In a small saucepan, whisk together cocoa powder, coconut sugar, salt and ¾ cup (175 mL) of the coconut milk until well blended. Whisk in the remaining coconut milk until smooth, then whisk in coconut water until blended.

2. Bring mixture to a simmer over medium-low heat, whisking occasionally. Whisk in vanilla. Divide between two mugs or cups and serve immediately.

Variations

Mexican Hot Chocolate: Add ¼ tsp (1 mL) ground cinnamon and ⅛ tsp (0.5 mL) cayenne pepper with the cocoa powder.

Chai Spice Hot Chocolate: Add ¼ tsp (1 mL) pumpkin pie spice and ⅛ tsp (0.5 mL) ground cardamom with the cocoa powder.

Breads and Muffins

Coconut Soda Bread

Irish soda bread is one of the easiest breads you can bake, and now you can make it 100% grain-free. Coconut milk and water are mixed with vinegar to make a mock "buttermilk" (a traditional ingredient in soda bread). The acid in the vinegar reacts with the base of the baking soda to provide the bread's leavening. This one is basic, but you can add more frills (see the variations, below) if you like.

Makes 2 loaves, 6 slices per loaf

Tip

Consider making soda breads in muffin-size portions. Grease a 12-cup muffin pan with coconut oil. Prepare batter as directed, then spoon and spread into prepared cups. Bake for 28 to 32 minutes or until tops are golden brown and a toothpick inserted in the center of a muffin comes out clean. Let cool as directed.

- Preheat oven to 350°F (180°C)
- Two 5- by 3-inch (12.5 by 7.5 cm) metal loaf pans, greased with coconut oil

¾ cup	well-stirred coconut milk (full-fat)	175 mL
¾ cup	water	175 mL
1 tbsp	cider or white vinegar	15 mL
3 tbsp	psyllium husk	45 mL
¾ cup	chickpea flour	175 mL
⅓ cup	coconut flour	75 mL
2 tbsp	potato starch	30 mL
1½ tsp	baking soda	7 mL
½ tsp	fine sea salt	2 mL

1. In a small bowl, whisk together coconut milk, water and vinegar. Let stand for 10 minutes or until mixture appears curdled. Whisk in psyllium; let stand for 5 minutes to thicken.

2. In a large bowl, whisk together chickpea flour, coconut flour, potato starch, baking soda and salt.

3. Add the coconut milk mixture to the flour mixture and stir until just blended.

4. Divide batter evenly between prepared pans.

5. Bake in preheated oven for 40 to 45 minutes or until tops are golden brown and a toothpick inserted in the center of a loaf comes out clean. Let cool in pans on a wire rack for 10 minutes, then transfer to the rack to cool completely.

Store the cooled
bread, wrapped in foil
or plastic wrap, in the
refrigerator for up to
1 week. Alternatively,
wrap it in plastic wrap,
then foil, completely
enclosing bread,
and freeze for up to
3 months. Let thaw
at room temperature
for 4 to 6 hours
before serving.

Variations

Caraway Currant Soda Bread: Gently fold in $3/4$ cup (175 mL) dried currants and 2 tsp (10 mL) caraway seeds at the end of step 3.

Sesame Soda Bread: Gently fold in 2 tbsp (30 mL) toasted sesame seeds at the end of step 3.

Golden Raisin Soda Bread: Gently fold in $1/2$ cup (125 mL) golden raisins and 2 tsp (10 mL) finely grated orange zest at the end of step 3.

Fresh Herb Soda Bread: Gently fold in 3 tbsp (45 mL) chopped fresh basil, parsley or dill, or 1 tbsp (15 mL) chopped fresh rosemary, at the end of step 3.

✴ Power Ingredient

Vinegar
More than 2,000 years ago, Hippocrates, the father of modern medicine, recommended using vinegar for treating sores and ulcerations. Some modern research indicates that he was right: vinegar does indeed work as an antimicrobial for wounds. In 2009, Japanese researchers found that vinegar consumption increases calcium absorption, and researchers in Spain found that adding a small amount of vinegar to foods produced bactericidal activity and was effective in destroying strains of salmonella. Additionally, a growing and significant body of cell and animal research indicates that vinegar has anti-tumor properties. Although the anti-tumor factors have not been identified, acetic acid appears to be a major player, as it forms acetate ions in the stomach, which may have direct anti-tumor effects.

Date Bread

Move over, candy — dates, with their honey-like sweetness, are in town.

Makes 12 slices

Tip

A glass pan of the same dimensions may also be used. Add 4 to 8 minutes to the baking time.

Storage Tip

Store the cooled bread, wrapped in foil or plastic wrap, in the refrigerator for up to 5 days. Alternatively, wrap it in plastic wrap, then foil, completely enclosing bread, and freeze for up to 3 months. Let thaw at room temperature for 4 to 6 hours before serving.

- 9- by 5-inch (23 by 12.5 cm) metal loaf pan, greased with coconut oil

¾ cup	well-stirred coconut milk (full-fat)	175 mL
⅔ cup	coconut water or water	150 mL
1½ tsp	ground cinnamon	7 mL
1 cup	chopped pitted dates	250 mL
¾ cup	chickpea flour	175 mL
6 tbsp	coconut flour	90 mL
1½ tbsp	potato starch	22 mL
1½ tsp	baking soda	7 mL
½ tsp	fine sea salt	2 mL
½ cup	coconut sugar	125 mL
2 tbsp	psyllium husk	30 mL
2 tbsp	melted virgin coconut oil	30 mL

1. In a small saucepan, combine coconut milk, coconut water and cinnamon. Bring to a simmer over medium–high heat. Stir in dates, remove from heat, cover and let stand for 20 minutes.

2. Preheat oven to 350°F (180°C).

3. In a large bowl, whisk together chickpea flour, coconut flour, potato starch, baking soda and salt.

4. Stir coconut sugar, psyllium and coconut oil into date mixture until well blended. Let stand for 5 minutes to thicken.

5. Add the date mixture to the flour mixture and stir until just blended.

6. Spread batter evenly in prepared pan.

7. Bake for 50 to 55 minutes or until a toothpick inserted in the center comes out clean. Let cool in pan on a wire rack for 10 minutes, then transfer to the rack to cool completely.

Banana Bread

Everybody needs a great banana bread recipe in their repertoire, and this one fits the bill, with fantastic flavor and a tender, moist texture. As a bonus, you'll reap the potassium and vitamin A from the bananas, high fiber from the coconut flour and protein from the chickpea flour.

Makes 16 slices

Tip

A glass pan of the same dimensions may also be used. Add 4 to 8 minutes to the baking time.

Storage Tip

Store the cooled bread, wrapped in foil or plastic wrap, in the refrigerator for up to 5 days. Alternatively, wrap it in plastic wrap, then foil, completely enclosing bread, and freeze for up to 3 months. Let thaw at room temperature for 4 to 6 hours before serving.

- Preheat oven to 350°F (180°C)
- 9- by 5-inch (23 by 12.5 cm) metal loaf pan, greased with coconut oil

¾ cup	chickpea flour	175 mL
6 tbsp	coconut flour	90 mL
1½ tbsp	potato starch	22 mL
1 tsp	baking soda	5 mL
½ tsp	gluten-free baking powder	2 mL
¼ tsp	fine sea salt	1 mL
¼ tsp	ground nutmeg	1 mL
⅓ cup	coconut sugar	75 mL
2 tbsp	psyllium husk	30 mL
1 cup	mashed very ripe bananas	250 mL
½ cup	well-stirred coconut milk (full-fat)	125 mL

1. In a large bowl, whisk together chickpea flour, coconut flour, potato starch, baking soda, baking powder, salt and nutmeg.

2. In a medium bowl, combine coconut sugar, psyllium, bananas and coconut milk until well blended. Let stand for 5 minutes to thicken.

3. Add the banana mixture to the flour mixture and stir until just blended.

4. Spread batter evenly in prepared pan.

5. Bake in preheated oven for 45 to 50 minutes or until top is golden brown and a toothpick inserted in the center comes out clean. Let cool in pan on a wire rack for 10 minutes, then transfer to the rack to cool completely.

Spiced Pear Bread

Loaded with fall pears, this sophisticated loaf will please your palate and body in equal measure.

Tips

A glass pan of the same dimensions may also be used. Add 4 to 8 minutes to the baking time.

Do not chop the pears too finely; too much juice will release, altering the dry-to-liquid ingredient ratio of the bread.

- Preheat oven to 350°F (180°C)
- 9- by 5-inch (23 by 12.5 cm) metal loaf pan, greased with coconut oil

³⁄₄ cup	chickpea flour	175 mL
6 tbsp	coconut flour	90 mL
1½ tbsp	potato starch	22 mL
½ tsp	ground nutmeg	2 mL
2 tsp	gluten-free baking powder	10 mL
¼ tsp	baking soda	1 mL
¼ tsp	fine sea salt	1 mL
½ cup	coconut sugar	125 mL
3 tbsp	psyllium husk	45 mL
½ cup	well-stirred coconut milk (full-fat)	125 mL
²⁄₃ cup	coconut water or water	150 mL
1½ tsp	gluten-free vanilla extract	7 mL
1½ cups	chopped pears (unpeeled)	375 mL

1. In a large bowl, whisk together chickpea flour, coconut flour, potato starch, nutmeg, baking powder, baking soda and salt.

2. In a medium bowl, whisk together coconut sugar, psyllium, coconut milk, coconut water and vanilla until well blended. Let stand for 5 minutes to thicken.

3. Add the coconut milk mixture to the flour mixture and stir until just blended. Gently fold in pears.

4. Spread batter evenly in prepared pan.

5. Bake in preheated oven for 55 to 60 minutes or until top is golden brown and a toothpick inserted in the center comes out clean. Let cool in pan on a wire rack for 10 minutes, then transfer to the rack to cool completely.

Storage Tip

Store the cooled bread, wrapped in foil or plastic wrap, in the refrigerator for up to 3 days. Alternatively, wrap it in plastic wrap, then foil, completely enclosing bread, and freeze for up to 3 months. Let thaw at room temperature for 4 to 6 hours before serving.

Variation

Spiced Apple Bread: Substitute chopped apples (unpeeled) for the pears.

✳ Power Ingredient

Pears

Pears may have a delicate flavor, but they pack a nutritional punch: one medium-sized pear supplies 212 milligrams of potassium (a mineral that helps your heart beat normally and keeps your muscles working the way they are supposed to), 7.5 milligrams of vitamin C (about 10% of your daily needs), which helps prevent infection and keeps your immune system strong, and 5.5 grams of fiber. Pears also supply a good dose of vitamin K to help clot your blood, as well as vitamin A for your eyes.

Cardamom Carrot Bread

Cardamom is a beloved spice for sweets in Scandinavia, India and the Middle East. Here, it complements carrots in a quick, easy and deliciously moist bread.

Tips

A glass pan of the same dimensions may also be used. Add 4 to 8 minutes to the baking time.

This bread is also incredibly delicious when made with shredded parsnips in place of the carrots.

The raisins can be swapped out for an equal amount of almost any other dried fruit (currants, cherries, chopped figs), or omit them altogether, if you prefer.

Ground cinnamon or ginger can be used in place of the cardamom.

- Preheat oven to 350°F (180°C)
- 9- by 5-inch (23 by 12.5 cm) metal loaf pan, greased with coconut oil

2 tbsp	psyllium husk	30 mL
1 cup	well-stirred coconut milk (full-fat)	250 mL
1/3 cup	coconut water or water	75 mL
2/3 cup	chickpea flour	150 mL
1/3 cup	coconut flour	75 mL
2 tbsp	potato starch	30 mL
2 1/2 tsp	gluten-free baking powder	12 mL
1 tsp	ground cardamom	5 mL
1/4 tsp	fine sea salt	1 mL
1/2 cup	coconut sugar	125 mL
1 tsp	gluten-free vanilla extract	5 mL
1 1/2 cups	shredded carrots	375 mL
1/3 cup	raisins	75 mL

1. In a medium bowl, whisk together psyllium, coconut milk and coconut water. Let stand for 5 minutes to thicken.

2. In a large bowl, whisk together chickpea flour, coconut flour, potato starch, baking powder, cardamom and salt.

3. Whisk coconut sugar and vanilla into coconut milk mixture. Add to the flour mixture and stir until just blended. Gently fold in carrots and raisins.

4. Spread batter evenly in prepared pan.

Store the cooled bread, wrapped in foil or plastic wrap, in the refrigerator for up to 3 days. Alternatively, wrap it in plastic wrap, then foil, completely enclosing bread, and freeze for up to 3 months. Let thaw at room temperature for 4 to 6 hours before serving.

5. Bake in preheated oven for 50 to 55 minutes or until top is golden brown and a toothpick inserted in the center comes out clean. Let cool in pan on a wire rack for 10 minutes, then transfer to the rack to cool completely.

✳ Power Ingredient

Cardamom

Cardamom, a citrusy, exotic spice native to the evergreen forests of India, has long been prized in Ayurvedic medicine for its health-promoting properties, and now it's garnering attention in Western medicine as well. Recent studies indicate that cardamom contains cancer-fighting compounds with the potential to kill cancer cells as well as stunt new cancer cell growth. A study in the September 2012 issue of the *British Journal of Nutrition*, for example, found that cardamom regulates gene activity in skin cancer cells and reduces the activity of genes linked to cancer growth.

Sesame and Green Onion Bread

Green onions lend moisture and a delicate onion flavor to this bread, along with high levels of vitamins A and C.

Makes 12 slices

Tips

A glass pan of the same dimensions may also be used. Add 4 to 8 minutes to the baking time.

An equal amount of chopped fresh chives can be used in place of the green onions.

- Preheat oven to 350°F (180°C)
- 9- by 5-inch (23 by 12.5 cm) metal loaf pan, greased with coconut oil

2 tbsp	psyllium husk	30 mL
2/3 cup	well-stirred coconut milk (full-fat)	150 mL
2/3 cup	coconut water or water	150 mL
3 tbsp	melted virgin coconut oil	45 mL
1 tbsp	toasted sesame oil	15 mL
3/4 cup	chickpea flour	175 mL
6 tbsp	coconut flour	90 mL
2 tbsp	potato starch	30 mL
2 1/4 tsp	gluten-free baking powder	11 mL
1/4 tsp	fine sea salt	1 mL
3/4 cup	chopped green onions	175 mL
1 tbsp	sesame seeds	15 mL

1. In a small bowl, whisk together psyllium, coconut milk, coconut water, coconut oil and sesame oil. Let stand for 5 minutes to thicken.

2. In a large bowl, whisk together chickpea flour, coconut flour, potato starch, baking powder and salt.

3. Add the coconut milk mixture to the flour mixture and stir until just blended. Gently fold in green onions.

4. Spread batter evenly in prepared pan. Sprinkle with sesame seeds.

5. Bake in preheated oven for 50 to 55 minutes or until top is golden brown and a toothpick inserted in the center comes out clean. Let cool in pan on a wire rack for 10 minutes, then transfer to the rack to cool completely.

Storage Tip

Store the cooled bread, wrapped in foil or plastic wrap, in the refrigerator for up to 3 days. Alternatively, wrap it in plastic wrap, then foil, completely enclosing bread, and freeze for up to 3 months. Let thaw at room temperature for 4 to 6 hours before serving.

Variation

French Green Onion Bread: Omit the sesame oil and sesame seeds, and increase the melted virgin coconut oil to $\frac{1}{4}$ cup (60 mL). Add 2 tsp (10 mL) Dijon mustard in step 1 and add 2 tsp (10 mL) dried thyme in step 2.

✳ Power Ingredient

Sesame Seeds
Sesame seeds contain two special types of fiber, sesamin and sesamolin, which are members of the lignans group and can lower "bad" cholesterol and help prevent high blood pressure. Sesamin is a powerful antioxidant in its own right and has been shown to protect the liver from damage. Plant sterols contained in sesame seeds also have a cholesterol-lowering action. The seeds are particularly rich in copper, which may be of use to arthritis sufferers because it is thought to have an anti-inflammatory action, reducing pain and swelling. Finally, sesame seeds provide iron, zinc, calcium and potassium in varying quantities.

Coconut "Corn" Bread

It may sound odd — "corn" bread without any corn — but take a bite of this home-style bread and you'll swear you're eating the real thing.

Makes 9 pieces

Tip

A glass pan of the same dimensions may also be used. Add 3 to 6 minutes to the baking time.

Storage Tip

Store the cooled bread, wrapped in foil or plastic wrap, in the refrigerator for up to 3 days. Alternatively, wrap it in plastic wrap, then foil, completely enclosing bread, and freeze for up to 3 months. Let thaw at room temperature for 4 to 6 hours before serving.

- Preheat oven to 350°F (180°C)
- 9-inch (23 cm) square metal baking pan, greased with coconut oil

¾ cup	well-stirred coconut milk (full-fat)	175 mL
½ cup	water	125 mL
3 tbsp	pumpkin purée (not pie filling)	45 mL
2 tsp	cider or white vinegar	10 mL
2 tbsp	psyllium husk	30 mL
1 tbsp	coconut sugar (optional)	15 mL
¾ cup	chickpea flour	175 mL
6 tbsp	coconut flour	90 mL
1½ tbsp	potato starch	22 mL
2 tsp	gluten-free baking powder	10 mL
¼ tsp	baking soda	1 mL
½ tsp	ground cumin	2 mL
½ tsp	fine sea salt	2 mL

1. In a small bowl, whisk together coconut milk, water, pumpkin and vinegar. Let stand for 10 minutes or until mixture appears curdled. Whisk in psyllium and coconut sugar (if using); let stand for 5 minutes to thicken.

2. In a large bowl, whisk together chickpea flour, coconut flour, potato starch, baking powder, baking soda, cumin and salt.

3. Add the coconut milk mixture to the flour mixture and stir until just blended.

4. Spread batter evenly in prepared pan.

5. Bake in preheated oven for 40 to 45 minutes or until top is golden brown and a toothpick inserted in the center comes out clean. Let cool in pan on a wire rack for 10 minutes, then transfer to the rack to cool completely.

Variation

Calico "Corn" Bread: Gently fold in ⅓ cup (75 mL) chopped green onions and ¼ cup (60 mL) chopped drained jarred roasted red bell peppers at the end of step 3.

Pumpkin Bread

This is a perfect pumpkin bread: moist, flavorful and subtly sweet, it's grand for breakfast, a snack or dessert. Pumpkin is one of the most nutritionally valuable foods around, packing an abundance of disease-fighting nutrients. Moreover, it is inexpensive and available year-round, so you can make this delectable bread anytime.

Tips

A glass pan of the same dimensions may also be used. Add 4 to 8 minutes to the baking time.

An equal amount of winter squash or butternut squash purée (canned or thawed frozen) can be used in place of the pumpkin purée.

For a bit of crunch, add ¾ cup (175 mL) lightly toasted green pumpkin seeds (pepitas), coarsely chopped, in step 3.

Storage Tip

Store the cooled bread, wrapped in foil or plastic wrap, in the refrigerator for up to 3 days. Alternatively, wrap it in plastic wrap, then foil, completely enclosing bread, and freeze for up to 3 months. Let thaw at room temperature for 4 to 6 hours before serving.

- Preheat oven to 350°F (180°C)
- 8- by 4-inch (20 by 10 cm) metal loaf pan, greased with coconut oil

¾ cup	chickpea flour	175 mL
⅓ cup	coconut flour	75 mL
1½ tbsp	potato starch	22 mL
2 tsp	gluten-free baking powder	10 mL
1½ tsp	pumpkin pie spice	7 mL
½ tsp	fine sea salt	2 mL
¼ tsp	baking soda	1 mL
⅔ cup	coconut sugar	150 mL
2 tbsp	psyllium husk	30 mL
1¼ cups	pumpkin purée (not pie filling)	300 mL
½ cup	melted virgin coconut oil	125 mL
½ cup	coconut water or water	125 mL

1. In a large bowl, whisk together chickpea flour, coconut flour, potato starch, baking powder, pumpkin pie spice, salt and baking soda.

2. In a medium bowl, whisk together coconut sugar, psyllium, pumpkin, coconut oil and coconut water until well blended. Let stand for 5 minutes to thicken.

3. Add the pumpkin mixture to the flour mixture and stir until just blended.

4. Spread batter evenly in prepared pan.

5. Bake in preheated oven for 55 to 65 minutes or until top is golden and a toothpick inserted in the center comes out clean. Let cool in pan on a wire rack for 10 minutes, then transfer to the rack to cool completely.

Zucchini Bread

Add a hint of color to your baking routine with zucchini bread, glinting with green. Moist and fragrant, it's perfect for breakfast, teatime or even dessert.

<table>
<tr><td colspan="2">**Makes 12 slices**</td></tr>
</table>

Tip

A glass pan of the same dimensions may also be used. Add 4 to 8 minutes to the baking time.

- Preheat oven to 350°F (180°C)
- 9- by 5-inch (23 by 12.5 cm) metal loaf pan, greased with coconut oil

¾ cup	chickpea flour	175 mL
6 tbsp	coconut flour	90 mL
1½ tbsp	potato starch	22 mL
2 tsp	gluten-free baking powder	10 mL
1 tsp	ground cinnamon	5 mL
½ tsp	fine sea salt	2 mL
⅔ cup	coconut sugar	150 mL
2 tbsp	psyllium husk	30 mL
¾ cup	well-stirred coconut milk (full-fat)	175 mL
¼ cup	melted virgin coconut oil	60 mL
2 tsp	gluten-free vanilla extract	10 mL
1 cup	shredded zucchini	250 mL

1. In a large bowl, whisk together chickpea flour, coconut flour, potato starch, baking powder, cinnamon and salt.

2. In a medium bowl, whisk together coconut sugar, psyllium, coconut milk, coconut oil and vanilla until well blended. Let stand for 5 minutes to thicken.

3. Add the coconut milk mixture to the flour mixture and stir until well blended. Gently fold in zucchini.

4. Spread batter evenly in prepared pan.

5. Bake in preheated oven for 40 to 45 minutes or until top is golden and a toothpick inserted in the center comes out clean. Let cool in pan on a wire rack for 10 minutes, then transfer to the rack to cool completely.

✻ Power Ingredient

Zucchini

High in fiber and vitamins A and C, zucchini is also a good source of the B-complex vitamins, including thiamin, pyridoxine and riboflavin, and minerals such as iron, phosphorus, zinc and potassium. In addition, it is an excellent source of manganese, which helps the body metabolize protein and carbohydrates, participates in the production of sex hormones and catalyzes the synthesis of fatty acids and cholesterol. Manganese has two additional functions: it increases the levels of superoxide dismutase, the enzyme responsible for protecting mitochondria (the power plants of the cell) against oxidative stress; and it is essential for the production of proline, an amino acid that allows collagen to form, allowing for healthy skin and proper wound healing.

Coconut Flour Focaccia

The taste and texture of this grain-free, rosemary-scented focaccia make it a winner, and the trio of superpower coconut ingredients — coconut flour, coconut oil and coconut milk — elevates it to star status.

Makes 16 servings

Tips

If you don't have fresh rosemary on hand, you can use 1½ tsp (7 mL) dried rosemary in its place.

For a more traditional Italian flavor, use an equal amount of olive oil in place of the coconut oil.

- Preheat oven to 400°F (200°C)
- Large baking sheet, lined with parchment paper

2 tbsp	psyllium husk	30 mL
1 cup	well-stirred coconut milk (full-fat)	250 mL
½ cup	coconut water or water	125 mL
2 tbsp	melted virgin coconut oil	30 mL
¾ cup	chickpea flour	175 mL
⅓ cup	coconut flour	75 mL
1½ tbsp	potato starch	22 mL
1 tbsp	gluten-free baking powder	15 mL
1 tsp	fine sea salt	5 mL
	Melted virgin coconut oil	
1 tbsp	chopped fresh rosemary	15 mL

1. In a small bowl, whisk together psyllium, coconut milk, coconut water and coconut oil. Let stand for 5 minutes to thicken.

2. In a large bowl, whisk together chickpea flour, coconut flour, potato starch, baking powder and salt.

3. Using a wooden spoon, stir coconut milk mixture into flour mixture until blended and sticky.

4. Turn dough out onto prepared baking sheet. With moist fingers, pat into a 12- by 10-inch (30 by 25 cm) rectangle. Poke indentations all over top of dough with your fingertips. Gently brush dough with coconut oil and sprinkle with rosemary.

5. Bake in preheated oven for 14 to 18 minutes or until golden brown at edges and firm to the touch at center. Using parchment paper, transfer to a wire rack. Let cool completely before slicing.

Storage Tip

Store the cooled focaccia, wrapped in foil or plastic wrap, at room temperature for up to 2 days. Alternatively, wrap it in plastic wrap, then foil, completely enclosing focaccia, and freeze for up to 3 months. Let thaw at room temperature for 4 to 6 hours before serving.

Variations

Tomato Focaccia: In step 4, arrange 3 thinly sliced plum (Roma) tomatoes on top of the dough before brushing with coconut oil. Replace the rosemary with 2 tsp (10 mL) chopped fresh oregano or 1 tsp (5 mL) dried oregano.

Onion Sage Focaccia: In step 4, arrange 1 cup (250 mL) thinly sliced red onion on top of the dough before brushing with coconut oil. Replace the rosemary with an equal amount of chopped fresh sage or 1½ tsp (5 mL) dried rubbed sage.

Focaccia Dolce: Soak ¾ cup dried fruit (such as raisins, tart cherries or chopped apricots) in hot water for 15 minutes; drain and pat dry with paper towels. Add 1 tbsp (15 mL) coconut sugar and 1 tsp (5 mL) ground cinnamon, cardamom or ginger with the salt in step 2. In step 4, arrange fruit and, if desired, ¼ cup (60 mL) seeds (such as green pumpkin seeds or sesame seeds) on top of the dough before brushing with coconut oil. Omit the rosemary and sprinkle dough with an additional 1 tbsp (15 mL) coconut sugar.

* Power Ingredient

Rosemary

Rosemary, a member of the mint family, has been used for centuries in both savory and sweet dishes, as well as medicinally to help alleviate muscle pain, improve memory, boost the immune and circulatory systems, and promote hair growth. Modern scientific research has found that many of its ancient health claims have some validity. In addition to being a good source of iron, calcium and vitamin B_6, rosemary is a rich source of antioxidants and anti-inflammatory compounds, both of which are thought to help boost the immune system and improve blood circulation. Antioxidants also play an important role in neutralizing harmful particles called free radicals. Some research shows that rosemary can indeed improve memory and cognitive function, thanks to carnosic acid, a compound that fights off free radical damage in the brain and may help prevent brain aging. Carnosic acid may also be useful in promoting eye health, by providing protection against macular degeneration.

Coconut Flax Tortillas

With a rustic texture reminiscent of corn tortillas, these flax and coconut tortillas are the perfect accompaniment to all of your favorite Mexican and Latin American–inspired dishes and make a great bread alternative for quick and easy sandwich roll-ups. They make adding flaxseed to your diet a breeze.

Makes eight 6-inch (15 cm) tortillas

Storage Tip

Stack the cooled tortillas between sheets of waxed paper and store, wrapped in foil or plastic wrap, in the refrigerator for up to 3 days. Alternatively, wrap them in plastic wrap, then foil, completely enclosing them, and freeze for up to 3 months. Let thaw at room temperature for 4 to 6 hours before serving.

- Parchment paper or waxed paper

1¼ cups	ground flax seeds (flaxseed meal), divided	300 mL
6 tbsp	coconut water or water	90 mL
2 tbsp	coconut flour	30 mL
1 tsp	fine sea salt	5 mL
	Melted virgin coconut oil	

1. In a small bowl, combine ¼ cup (60 mL) flax seeds and coconut water until blended. Let stand for 5 minutes or until thickened.

2. In a large bowl, whisk together the remaining flax seeds, coconut flour and salt. Add the coconut water mixture, stirring until blended (mixture will be very thick). Turn out onto a flat surface and knead until dough is no longer sticky.

3. Divide dough into 8 equal pieces and roll each piece into a ball. Roll each ball out between two sheets of parchment paper into a 6-inch (15 cm) round.

4. Heat a medium skillet (preferably cast iron) over medium-high heat until hot, then lightly brush with coconut oil. Place one round in skillet and cook for 30 to 40 seconds or until edges begin to brown. Flip over and cook for 30 to 40 seconds or until tortilla appears dry. Transfer to a wire rack. Repeat with the remaining rounds, lightly brushing the pan with oil each time and adjusting heat as necessary to prevent burning.

Variations

Spiced Coconut Flax Tortillas: Add 1 tsp (5 mL) ground cumin, curry powder, chili powder, smoked paprika, garlic powder or onion powder with the coconut flour.

Herbed Coconut Flax Tortillas: Add 1 tsp (5 mL) dried herbs (crumbled rosemary, rubbed sage, basil, Italian seasoning, oregano) or 1 to 2 tbsp (15 to 30 mL) chopped fresh herbs (flat-leaf parsley, cilantro, basil) with the coconut flour.

Coconut Flour Flatbread

This ultra-easy bread is destined to become one of your go-to recipes for its great taste and versatility.

Storage Tip

Refrigerate flatbread between sheets of waxed paper, tightly covered in plastic wrap, for up to 2 days or freeze, enclosed in a sealable plastic bag, for up to 1 month.

²⁄₃ cup	coconut flour	150 mL
2 tbsp	psyllium husk	30 mL
1 tsp	gluten-free baking powder	5 mL
½ tsp	fine sea salt	2 mL
1⅓ cups	boiling water	325 mL
2½ tbsp	melted virgin coconut oil	37 mL
	Additional melted virgin coconut oil	

1. In a medium bowl, whisk together coconut flour, psyllium, baking powder and salt. Stir in boiling water and oil until oil is melted and mixture comes together as a cohesive dough. Let stand for 5 minutes to thicken.

2. Divide dough into 8 equal pieces and roll each piece into a ball. Press each ball into a 4-inch (10 cm) round.

3. Heat a large skillet (preferably cast iron) over medium-high heat until hot, then lightly grease with coconut oil. Place two rounds in skillet and cook for 30 to 60 seconds per side or until golden brown in spots. Transfer flatbreads to a wire rack. Repeat with the remaining rounds, lightly greasing the pan each time and adjusting heat as necessary to prevent burning. Serve warm or at room temperature.

Farinata

Farinata is a savory flatbread whose origins lie in Liguria, Italy. In other regions and countries, it goes by other names, such as faina, cecina or socca (French). Farinata is made with a loose batter of chickpea flour, water and salt. Olive oil is the traditional fat used, but coconut oil makes an irresistible alternative. It is baked in a hot cast-iron skillet, which renders a golden crispiness to the outside while keeping the center soft and tender. You can eat it plain or add toppings, much like a pizza crust.

Makes 8 servings

Storage Tip

Farinata is also delicious cold or at room temperature. You can make it ahead and refrigerate it, tightly covered in plastic wrap, for up to 5 days, or freeze it, enclosed in an airtight plastic container, for up to 1 month.

- 10-inch (25 cm) cast-iron skillet

1 cup	chickpea flour	250 mL
1 tsp	fine sea salt	5 mL
½ tsp	freshly ground black pepper	2 mL
1¾ cups	lukewarm water	425 mL
5 tbsp	melted virgin coconut oil, divided	75 mL

1. In a large bowl, whisk together chickpea flour, salt and pepper. Slowly whisk in water until blended and smooth. Cover and let stand at room temperature for at least 1 hour or up to 12 hours.

2. Preheat oven to 450°F (230°C). Place skillet in oven for 15 minutes.

3. Add 3 tbsp (45 mL) coconut oil to skillet, tilting to coat bottom. Rewhisk batter and slowly pour into skillet. Bake for 10 to 15 minutes or until flatbread feels firm to the touch.

4. Remove skillet from oven and position rack 6 to 8 inches (15 to 20 cm) from broiler. Preheat broiler and brush top of flatbread with the remaining coconut oil. Broil for 30 to 60 seconds or until golden brown in spots. Cut into wedges and serve hot or warm.

Multi-Seed Crackers

With their crispy crunch and toasty flavor, these little numbers are especially delectable. Spread them with seed butter or jam in the morning, top them with hummus at lunch or serve them alongside soup at supper. They make a great between-meal snack, too.

Makes 2 dozen medium crackers

Tip

Do not bother trying to separate the cracker dough before baking; it is tricky and the dough is prone to tearing. Once baked, it is easy to separate the crackers along the score lines.

Storage Tip

Store the cooled crackers in a tin at room temperature for up to 3 days.

- Preheat oven to 325°F (160°C)
- Parchment paper
- Food processor
- Large baking sheet

¾ cup	sunflower seeds	175 mL
3 tbsp	psyllium husk	45 mL
¼ tsp	fine sea salt	1 mL
¼ tsp	baking soda	1 mL
¼ tsp	garlic powder	1 mL
½ cup	sesame seeds	125 mL
2 tbsp	melted virgin coconut oil	30 mL
2 to 3 tbsp	coconut water or water	30 to 45 mL

1. Cut two pieces of parchment paper, each large enough to line baking sheet.

2. In food processor, pulse sunflower seeds until finely ground. Add psyllium, salt, baking soda and garlic powder; pulse two or three times to combine. Add sesame seeds and coconut oil; pulse two or three times, until just blended. Add coconut water, 1 tbsp (15 mL) at a time, until the mixture begins to come together as a cohesive dough.

3. Place one piece of parchment paper on a flat surface. Transfer dough to parchment and cover with second piece of parchment. Using a rolling pin, roll dough into a ⅛-inch (3 mm) thick rectangle. Remove top piece of parchment and use your fingers to patch any small tears in the dough.

4. Using a knife or a pizza cutter, score dough into 2 dozen squares or rectangles (do not separate crackers). Slide the piece of parchment paper, with the dough, onto baking sheet.

5. Bake in preheated oven for 18 to 22 minutes or until golden brown. Using the parchment paper, slide the crackers (on the paper) onto a wire rack; let cool completely. Once cool, carefully snap crackers apart along score lines.

Coconut Biscuits

Who knew that grain-free, vegan, nut-fee biscuits were not only possible, but also fabulous? They've got great substance, too, with a satisfyingly golden exterior and a pillowy interior that begs for a drizzle of coconut nectar, a schmear of fruit-sweetened jam or a dollop of coconut butter.

- Preheat oven to 425°F (220°C)
- Large baking sheet, lined with parchment paper

2 tbsp	psyllium husk	30 mL
2/3 cup	well-stirred coconut milk (full-fat)	150 mL
1/3 cup	coconut water or water	75 mL
3/4 cup	chickpea flour	175 mL
6 tbsp	coconut flour	90 mL
1 tbsp	potato starch	15 mL
1 tbsp	gluten-free baking powder	15 mL
1/2 tsp	fine sea salt	2 mL
3 tbsp	cold virgin coconut oil, cut into small pieces	45 mL
	Additional potato starch	

1. In a small bowl, combine psyllium, coconut milk and coconut water. Let stand for 5 minutes to thicken.

2. In a large bowl, whisk together chickpea flour, coconut flour, potato starch, baking powder and salt. Using a pastry blender or two knives, cut in coconut oil until crumbly.

3. Add the coconut milk mixture to the flour mixture and stir until just blended.

4. Turn dough out onto a surface very lightly dusted with potato starch and knead briefly until dough comes together. Gently pat into a 7- by 5-inch (18 by 12.5 cm) rectangle, about 1/2 inch (1 cm) thick. Cut into 8 squares and place 2 inches (5 cm) apart on prepared baking sheet.

5. Bake in preheated oven for 15 to 20 minutes or until golden brown. Transfer biscuits to a wire rack and let cool slightly. Serve warm.

Pumpkin Biscuits

Pumpkin adds lovely color, subtle sweetness and moisture to these biscuits, with few calories and zero fat.

Storage Tip

Store the cooled biscuits in an airtight container at room temperature for up to 2 days or in the freezer for up to 3 months. Let thaw at room temperature for 1 to 2 hours before serving.

- Preheat oven to 400°F (200°C)
- Large baking sheet, lined with parchment paper

¾ cup	chickpea flour	175 mL
6 tbsp	coconut flour	90 mL
1 tbsp	potato starch	15 mL
1 tbsp	gluten-free baking powder	15 mL
¾ tsp	ground cinnamon	3 mL
½ tsp	fine sea salt	2 mL
3 tbsp	cold virgin coconut oil, cut into small pieces	45 mL
2 tbsp	psyllium husk	30 mL
1 tbsp	coconut sugar	15 mL
¾ cup	pumpkin purée (not pie filling)	175 mL
½ cup	well-stirred coconut milk (full-fat)	125 mL
	Additional potato starch	

1. In a large bowl, whisk together chickpea flour, coconut flour, potato starch, baking powder, cinnamon and salt. Using a pastry blender or two knives, cut in coconut oil until crumbly.

2. In a small bowl, whisk together psyllium, coconut sugar, pumpkin and coconut milk until well blended. Let stand for 5 minutes to thicken.

3. Add the pumpkin mixture to the flour mixture and stir until just blended.

4. Turn dough out onto a surface very lightly dusted with potato starch and knead briefly until dough comes together. Gently pat into a 7- by 5-inch (18 by 12.5 cm) rectangle, about ½ inch (1 cm) thick. Cut into 8 squares and place 2 inches (5 cm) apart on prepared baking sheet.

5. Bake in preheated oven for 15 to 20 minutes or until golden brown. Transfer biscuits to a wire rack and let cool slightly. Serve warm.

Coconut Scones

Tender, fragrant and subtly sweet, these are everything good scones should be.

Makes 8 scones

Tips

If you have cool hands, you can use your fingertips to cut in the coconut oil in step 1.

For a light and tender texture, it's very important to chill the coconut oil before adding it to the flour mixture, and then to refrigerate the flour-oil mixture for 10 minutes. If your coconut oil is not chilled, measure what you need and place it in the freezer; it will be firm in about 20 minutes.

The scones can be prepared through step 4 up to 24 hours in advance. Cover and refrigerate until ready to bake, then proceed with step 5.

- Preheat oven to 400°F (200°C)
- Large baking sheet, lined with parchment paper

⅔ cup	chickpea flour	150 mL
⅓ cup	coconut flour	75 mL
¼ cup	coconut sugar	60 mL
1½ tbsp	potato starch	22 mL
2 tsp	gluten-free baking powder	10 mL
¼ tsp	fine sea salt	1 mL
¼ cup	cold virgin coconut oil, cut into small pieces	60 mL
2 tbsp	psyllium husk	30 mL
¾ cup	well-stirred coconut milk (full-fat)	175 mL
2 tbsp	coconut water or water	30 mL
1 tsp	gluten-free vanilla extract	5 mL
	Additional potato starch	

1. In a large bowl, whisk together chickpea flour, coconut flour, coconut sugar, potato starch, baking powder and salt. Using a pastry blender or two knives, cut in coconut oil until crumbly. Refrigerate for 10 minutes.

2. Meanwhile, in a medium bowl, whisk together psyllium, coconut milk, coconut water and vanilla until well blended. Let stand for 5 minutes to thicken.

3. Add the coconut milk mixture to the flour mixture and stir until just blended.

4. Turn dough out onto a surface lightly dusted with potato starch and knead briefly until dough comes together. Gently pat into a 9-inch (23 cm) circle, about ¾ inch (2 cm) thick. Cut into 8 wedges and place 2 inches (5 cm) apart on prepared baking sheet.

Store the cooled scones
in an airtight container
at room temperature
for up to 2 days or in
the freezer for up to
3 months. Let thaw
at room temperature
for 1 to 2 hours
before serving.

5. Bake in preheated oven for 17 to 22 minutes or until golden brown and firm to the touch. Transfer scones to a wire rack and let cool for 5 minutes. Serve warm or let cool completely.

Variations

Citrus Scones: Replace the vanilla with 1 tbsp (15 mL) finely grated citrus zest (lemon, orange, tangerine, lime).

Dried Fruit Scones: In step 4, knead in ½ cup (125 mL) raisins, dried cranberries, chopped dates or dried cherries.

Chocolate Chip Scones: In step 4, knead in ½ cup (125 mL) semisweet chocolate chips (vegan, gluten-free).

❖ Make Your Own Baking Powder

You may want to consider making your own baking powder if: a) you have run out; b) you are unsure if what you have is gluten-free and/or grain-free (many commercial brands have added cornstarch); or c) you have concerns about the aluminum used in many commercial brands. Baking powder is easy to make. You can either make it as you need it or prepare a larger quantity in advance and store it in an airtight container for up to 3 months.

The formula is simple: one part baking soda to one part potato starch (arrowroot or tapioca starch can also be used) and two parts cream of tartar. For example: ¼ tsp (1 mL) baking soda + ¼ tsp (1 mL) potato starch + ½ tsp (2 mL) cream of tartar = 1 tsp (5 mL) homemade baking powder.

Mocha Chip Drop Scones

Nutritionists have long said that eating dark chocolate in moderation can be good for our health (yippee!), so feel free to up the quantity of chocolate chips.

<table>
<tr><td>**Makes 8 scones**</td></tr>
</table>

Tip

The instant espresso powder can be replaced with 2 tbsp (30 mL) instant coffee powder.

- Preheat oven to 400°F (200°C)
- Large baking sheet, lined with parchment paper

2 tbsp	psyllium husk	30 mL
1 tbsp	instant espresso powder	15 mL
1 cup	well-stirred coconut milk (full-fat)	250 mL
1/3 cup	coconut water or water	75 mL
3/4 cup	chickpea flour	175 mL
6 tbsp	coconut flour	90 mL
1 tbsp	potato starch	15 mL
2 tsp	gluten-free baking powder	10 mL
1/4 tsp	fine sea salt	1 mL
1/3 cup	coconut sugar	75 mL
1/4 cup	melted virgin coconut oil	60 mL
1 1/2 tsp	gluten-free vanilla extract	7 mL
1/2 cup	miniature semisweet chocolate chips (vegan, gluten-free)	125 mL

1. In a medium bowl, whisk together psyllium, espresso, coconut milk and coconut water. Let stand for 5 minutes to thicken.

2. In a large bowl, whisk together chickpea flour, coconut flour, potato starch, baking powder and salt.

3. Whisk coconut sugar, coconut oil and vanilla into coconut milk mixture until well blended. Add to the flour mixture and stir until just blended. Gently stir in chocolate chips.

4. Drop dough by 1/4-cup (60 mL) measures 2 inches (5 cm) apart on prepared baking sheet.

Store the cooled
scones in an airtight
container at room
temperature for up to
2 days or in the freezer
for up to 3 months.
Let thaw at room
temperature for 1 to
2 hours before serving.

5. Bake in preheated oven for 18 to 23 minutes or until tops are golden brown and a toothpick inserted in the center comes out clean. Let cool on pan on a wire rack for 5 minutes, then transfer to the rack to cool for 5 minutes. Serve warm or let cool completely.

Variations

Chocolate Chip Drop Scones: Omit the espresso powder and add ¾ tsp (3 mL) ground cinnamon in step 2.

Fruity Drop Scones: Omit the espresso powder and replace the chocolate chips with an equal amount of raisins, chopped dates or dried cherries.

✻ Power Ingredient

Dark Chocolate
Nutritionists have long said that eating dark chocolate in moderation can be good for our health. A 2014 report indicates that it may reduce the risk of atherosclerosis — the thickening and hardening of the arteries — by restoring flexibility to the arteries and preventing white blood cells from sticking to the blood vessel walls. Research links moderate consumption of dark chocolate to a wide-ranging list of health perks, including boosting immune function and helping muscles recover after a tough workout. In addition to being chock full of heart-healthy antioxidants, dark chocolate also stimulates endorphin production and contains serotonin, which acts as an antidepressant.

Vanilla Coconut Baked Doughnuts

Few things beat a warm, fresh doughnut, and these are no exception.

Makes 12 doughnuts

Tip

If you don't own a doughnut pan, you can prepare the batter in a regular or mini muffin pan. For a regular muffin pan, grease 6 cups with coconut oil, fill with batter and bake for 11 to 14 minutes or until a toothpick inserted in the center comes out clean. For a mini muffin pan, grease 12 cups with coconut oil, fill with batter and bake for 7 to 10 minutes or until a toothpick inserted in the center comes out clean.

- Preheat oven to 375°F (190°C)
- 6-count doughnut pan, greased with coconut oil

Doughnuts

½ cup	chickpea flour	125 mL
¼ cup	coconut flour	60 mL
1 tbsp	potato starch	15 mL
2 tsp	gluten-free baking powder	10 mL
¼ tsp	fine sea salt	1 mL
½ cup	coconut sugar	125 mL
2 tbsp	psyllium husk	30 mL
⅔ cup	well-stirred coconut milk (full-fat)	150 mL
¼ cup	coconut water or water	60 mL
2 tbsp	melted virgin coconut oil	30 mL
2 tsp	gluten-free vanilla extract	10 mL

Icing

⅓ cup	coconut butter (store-bought or see recipe, page 301)	75 mL
1 tbsp	coconut nectar	15 mL
½ tsp	gluten-free vanilla extract	2 mL

1. *Doughnuts:* In a medium bowl, whisk together chickpea flour, coconut flour, potato starch, baking powder and salt.

2. In a small bowl, whisk together coconut sugar, psyllium, coconut milk, coconut water, coconut oil and vanilla until well blended. Let stand for 5 minutes to thicken.

3. Add the coconut milk mixture to the flour mixture and stir until well blended.

Tip

The doughnuts may also be prepared in two batches in a 12-count mini doughnut pan. Prepare as directed, baking mini doughnuts for 5 to 9 minutes.

4. Divide half the batter equally among prepared doughnut forms (they should be about half full).

5. Bake in preheated oven for 12 to 17 minutes or until doughnuts are golden and spring back when lightly touched. Let cool in pan on a wire rack for 2 minutes, then transfer to the rack.

6. Regrease the pan and repeat steps 4 and 5 with the remaining batter.

7. *Icing:* In a small saucepan set over low heat, melt coconut butter with coconut nectar. Remove from heat and stir in vanilla. Drizzle or spread over doughnuts. Let cool completely.

✳ Power Ingredient

Chickpea Flour

Chickpea flour (ground dried chickpeas) delivers a boost of magnesium — 76 milligrams per ½ cup (125 mL) — which helps maintain vascular health and regulates blood pressure. Like whole chickpeas, chickpea flour is rich in fiber and protein. It also contains vitamins and minerals, such as folate (chickpeas tend to be higher in folate than other beans) and zinc.

Cinnamon Sugar Muffins

Ground cinnamon gives these muffins their signature zing. Cinnamon's nutritional benefits are a zinger, too: it contains calcium, iron and vitamin C, vitamin K and manganese.

Makes 12 muffins

Tip

Other spices work beautifully in place of the cinnamon in this recipe. For example, use an equal amount of pumpkin pie spice or ground ginger in the topping and in the batter; or use 2 tsp (10 mL) ground cardamom or ground allspice in the topping and 1 tsp (5 mL) in the batter; or use 1½ tsp (7 mL) ground nutmeg in the topping and ¾ tsp (3 mL) in the batter.

- Preheat oven to 350°F (180°C)
- 12-cup muffin pan, greased with coconut oil

Topping

2 tbsp	coconut sugar	30 mL
1 tbsp	ground cinnamon	15 mL

Muffins

½ cup	chickpea flour	125 mL
⅓ cup	coconut flour	75 mL
1 tbsp	potato starch	15 mL
2½ tsp	gluten-free baking powder	12 mL
2 tsp	ground cinnamon	10 mL
½ tsp	fine sea salt	2 mL
⅓ cup	coconut sugar	75 mL
2 tbsp	psyllium husk	30 mL
1 cup	well-stirred coconut milk (full-fat)	250 mL
¼ cup	water	60 mL
2 tsp	gluten-free vanilla extract	10 mL

1. *Topping:* In a small cup, stir together coconut sugar and cinnamon.

2. *Muffins:* In a large bowl, whisk together chickpea flour, coconut flour, potato starch, baking powder, cinnamon and salt.

3. In a medium bowl, whisk together coconut sugar, psyllium, coconut milk, water and vanilla until well blended. Let stand for 5 minutes to thicken.

4. Add the coconut milk mixture to the flour mixture and stir until just blended.

5. Divide batter equally among prepared muffin cups and sprinkle with topping.

6. Bake in preheated oven for 28 to 33 minutes or until tops are golden brown and a toothpick inserted in the center comes out clean. Let cool in pan on a wire rack for 3 minutes, then transfer to the rack to cool completely.

Storage Tip

Store the cooled muffins, wrapped in foil or plastic wrap, in the refrigerator for up to 3 days. Alternatively, wrap them in plastic wrap, then foil, completely enclosing them, and freeze for up to 3 months. Let thaw at room temperature for 1 to 2 hours before serving.

Variations

Dried Fruit Muffins: Gently fold in ½ cup (125 mL) dried fruit (raisins, cranberries, chopped apricots, blueberries) at the end of step 3.

Toasted Seed Muffins: Gently fold in ¾ cup (175 mL) chopped toasted seeds (green pumpkin seeds, sunflower seeds, chia seeds, hemp hearts) at the end of step 3.

✳ Power Ingredient

Cinnamon

Chinese medicine and Ayurveda have long used cinnamon to treat illnesses such as colds, indigestion and cramps, and also believed it to improve energy, vitality and circulation. Now, researchers in the Western medical tradition are singing cinnamon's praises too. Among its myriad benefits, studies indicate cinnamon may be effective at boosting cognitive function, fighting *E. coli* bacteria, treating type 2 diabetes and reducing the proliferation of leukemia and lymphoma cancer cells.

Cinnamon contains several volatile oils and compounds, including cinnamaldehyde, cinnamyl acetate and cinnamyl alcohol, that have a variety of benefits. Cinnamaldehyde acts as an anticoagulant, meaning it can help protect against strokes, and is anti-inflammatory, relieving the symptoms of arthritis and asthma.

Dark Chocolate Muffins

It's not a dream: dark chocolate really is good for you. In addition to being chock full of heart-healthy antioxidants, it also stimulates endorphin production and contains serotonin, which acts as an antidepressant (i.e., chocolate = happiness).

Makes 12 muffins

Tip

Select natural cocoa powder rather than Dutch process. Natural cocoa powder has a deep, true chocolate flavor. The packaging should state whether it is Dutch process or not, but you can also tell by sight: if it is dark to almost black, it is Dutch process; natural cocoa powder is much lighter and is typically reddish brown in color.

- Preheat oven to 350°F (180°C)
- 12-cup muffin pan, greased with coconut oil

2 tbsp	psyllium husk	30 mL
1 cup	well-stirred coconut milk (full-fat)	250 mL
1/4 cup	coconut water or water	60 mL
1 tsp	cider vinegar	5 mL
1/3 cup	chickpea flour	75 mL
1/4 cup	unsweetened natural cocoa powder (see tip, at left)	60 mL
1/4 cup	coconut flour	60 mL
1 1/2 tsp	gluten-free baking powder	7 mL
1/2 tsp	baking soda	2 mL
1/4 tsp	fine sea salt	1 mL
1/2 cup	coconut sugar	125 mL
1/4 cup	melted virgin coconut oil	60 mL
1 tsp	gluten-free vanilla extract	5 mL

1. In a medium bowl, whisk together psyllium, coconut milk, coconut water and vinegar. Let stand for 5 minutes to thicken.

2. In a large bowl, whisk together chickpea flour, cocoa powder, coconut flour, baking powder, baking soda and salt.

3. Whisk coconut sugar, coconut oil and vanilla into coconut milk mixture until well blended. Add to the flour mixture and stir until just blended.

4. Divide batter equally among prepared muffin cups.

5. Bake in preheated oven for 28 to 33 minutes or until a toothpick inserted in the center comes out clean. Let cool in pan on a wire rack for 3 minutes, then transfer to the rack to cool completely.

Store the cooled muffins, wrapped in foil or plastic wrap, in the refrigerator for up to 3 days. Alternatively, wrap them in plastic wrap, then foil, completely enclosing them, and freeze for up to 3 months. Let thaw at room temperature for 1 to 2 hours before serving.

Variations

Double Chocolate Muffins: Gently fold in ½ cup (125 mL) miniature semisweet chocolate chips (vegan, gluten-free) at the end of step 3.

Carob Muffins: Use unsweetened carob powder in place of the cocoa powder. If desired, gently fold in ½ cup (125 mL) carob chips, chopped, at the end of step 3.

✳ Power Ingredient

Cocoa Powder

Cocoa powder is made from cocoa beans, which are rich in antioxidant flavonoids, fiber and minerals. Cocoa powder is also low in sodium and high in potassium, and it contains several chemical compounds that have a positive effect on mood and cognitive health, including phenethylamine (PEA), the chemical your brain creates when you're falling in love. PEA encourages your brain to release endorphins, which reduce stress and promote positive feelings.

But its antioxidants have garnered the most attention from researchers in recent years, because they can have an anticoagulant action, protecting against the oxidation of cholesterol in the body. It's important to note, however, that most of the research conducted on the health benefits of cocoa powder was performed on natural, or non-alkalized, cocoa powder (not Dutch process cocoa powder). Alkalization mellows the flavor of cocoa, but it also destroys the polyphenolic compounds.

Not-Bran Muffins

Who needs wheat bran when you can create delectable grain-free muffins with flax seeds? Despite their tiny size, they are loaded with nutrition.

Storage Tip

Store the cooled muffins, wrapped in foil or plastic wrap, in the refrigerator for up to 3 days. Alternatively, wrap them in plastic wrap, then foil, completely enclosing them, and freeze for up to 3 months. Let thaw at room temperature for 1 to 2 hours before serving.

- Preheat oven to 350°F (180°C)
- 12-cup muffin pan, cups greased with coconut oil

½ cup	chickpea flour	125 mL
⅓ cup	ground flax seeds (flaxseed meal)	75 mL
¼ cup	coconut flour	60 mL
1 tbsp	potato starch	15 mL
2 tsp	gluten-free baking powder	10 mL
1 tsp	ground cinnamon	5 mL
¼ tsp	fine sea salt	1 mL
⅓ cup	coconut sugar	75 mL
1 tbsp	psyllium husk	15 mL
1¼ cups	unsweetened applesauce	300 mL
½ cup	well-stirred coconut milk (full-fat)	125 mL

1. In a large bowl, whisk together chickpea flour, flax seeds, coconut flour, potato starch, baking powder, cinnamon and salt.

2. In a medium bowl, whisk together coconut sugar, psyllium, applesauce and coconut milk until well blended. Let stand for 5 minutes to thicken.

3. Add the applesauce mixture to the flour mixture and stir until just blended.

4. Divide batter evenly among prepared cups.

5. Bake in preheated oven for 28 to 32 minutes or until tops are golden and a toothpick inserted in the center comes out clean. Let cool in pan on a wire rack for 10 minutes, then transfer to the rack to cool completely.

✳ Power Ingredient

Applesauce
Applesauce contains quercetin, an antioxidant bioflavonoid that research indicates may reduce the risk of several cancers. Further, some research suggests that quercetin benefits neurological health by reducing cellular death caused by oxidation and inflammation of neurons.

Super-Seed Muffins

No arguments will occur over whether these are seriously delicious muffins — because they are, plain and simple. The array of seeds adds terrific crunch and flavor, not to mention healthy fats, fiber and a kick of protein, too.

Makes 12 muffins

Tip

If you're in a hurry, you can skip resting the batter in step 3. The results are superior with the resting time, but even without it, the muffins are extremely good.

Storage Tip

Store the cooled muffins, wrapped in foil or plastic wrap, in the refrigerator for up to 3 days. Alternatively, wrap them in plastic wrap, then foil, completely enclosing them, and freeze for up to 3 months. Let thaw at room temperature for 1 to 2 hours before serving.

- Food processor
- 12-cup muffin pan, greased with coconut oil

3 tbsp	psyllium husk	45 mL
1½ cups	coconut water or water	375 mL
1¾ cups	green pumpkin seeds (pepitas)	425 mL
1 cup	sunflower seeds	250 mL
⅔ cup	flaked unsweetened coconut	150 mL
½ cup	sesame seeds	125 mL
⅓ cup	ground flax seeds (flaxseed meal)	75 mL
1 tsp	fine sea salt	5 mL
3 tbsp	virgin coconut oil, melted	45 mL

1. In a small bowl, whisk together psyllium and water. Let stand for 5 minutes to thicken.

2. Meanwhile, in food processor, combine pumpkin seeds, sunflower seeds, coconut and sesame seeds. Pulse five or six times, until coarsely chopped.

3. Add seed mixture to psyllium mixture, along with flax seeds, salt and coconut oil. Stir until blended. Let stand for 1 hour.

4. Meanwhile, preheat oven to 350°F (180°C).

5. Divide batter equally among prepared muffins cups.

6. Bake for 28 to 33 minutes or until a toothpick inserted in the center comes out clean. Let cool in pan on a wire rack for 10 minutes, then transfer to the rack to cool completely.

Variations

Chocolate Seed Muffins: Add ½ cup (125 mL) miniature semisweet chocolate chips or chopped semisweet chocolate (vegan, gluten-free) with the flax seeds.

Super-Seed and Fruit Muffins: Add ⅔ cup (150 mL) chopped dried fruit (prunes, dates, apricots) with the flax seeds.

Seeded Power Muffins: Add 1 cup (250 mL) coarsely shredded beets, apples, pears, zucchini or carrots with the flax seeds.

Applesauce Raisin Muffins

Whether you use store-bought applesauce or make your own, you'll love the not-too-sweet comfort of these old-fashioned muffins.

Tip

An equal amount of any other dried fruit (such as cranberries, chopped apricots or chopped prunes) can be used in place of the raisins.

Storage Tip

Store the cooled muffins, wrapped in foil or plastic wrap, in the refrigerator for up to 3 days. Alternatively, wrap them in plastic wrap, then foil, completely enclosing them, and freeze for up to 3 months. Let thaw at room temperature for 1 to 2 hours before serving.

- Preheat oven to 350°F (180°C)
- 12-cup muffins tin, greased with coconut oil

¾ cup	chickpea flour	175 mL
6 tbsp	coconut flour	90 mL
1½ tbsp	potato starch	22 mL
2 tsp	ground cinnamon	10 mL
2 tsp	gluten-free baking powder	10 mL
½ tsp	baking soda	2 mL
¼ tsp	fine sea salt	1 mL
⅓ cup	coconut sugar	75 mL
2 tbsp	psyllium husk	30 mL
1½ cups	unsweetened applesauce	375 mL
¼ cup	melted virgin coconut oil	60 mL
1 tsp	gluten-free vanilla extract	5 mL
½ cup	raisins	125 mL

1. In a large bowl, whisk together chickpea flour, coconut flour, potato starch, cinnamon, baking powder, baking soda and salt.

2. In a medium bowl, whisk together coconut sugar, psyllium, applesauce, coconut oil and vanilla until well blended. Let stand for 5 minutes to thicken.

3. Add the applesauce mixture to the flour mixture and stir until just blended. Gently fold in raisins.

4. Divide batter evenly among prepared cups.

5. Bake in preheated oven for 28 to 33 minutes or until tops are golden brown and a toothpick inserted in the center comes out clean. Let cool in pan on a wire rack for 10 minutes, then transfer to the rack to cool completely.

Variation

Apple Cinnamon Power Muffins: Replace the raisins with an equal amount of hemp hearts or chopped sunflower seeds.

Blueberry Muffins

A perennial summer favorite, plump, juicy blueberries add sweet flavor to these tender, lemon-scented muffins.

Makes 12 muffins

Tip

The lemon zest can be replaced with 1 tsp (5 mL) lemon extract.

Storage Tip

Store the cooled muffins, wrapped in foil or plastic wrap, in the refrigerator for up to 3 days. Alternatively, wrap them in plastic wrap, then foil, completely enclosing them, and freeze for up to 3 months. Let thaw at room temperature for 1 to 2 hours before serving.

- Preheat oven to 350°F (180°C)
- 12-cup muffin pan, cups greased with coconut oil

¾ cup	chickpea flour	175 mL
⅓ cup	coconut flour	75 mL
1½ tbsp	potato starch	22 mL
2½ tsp	gluten-free baking powder	12 mL
¼ tsp	fine sea salt	1 mL
½ cup	coconut sugar	125 mL
2 tbsp	psyllium husk	30 mL
2 tsp	finely grated lemon zest	10 mL
¾ cup	well-stirred coconut milk (full-fat)	175 mL
⅔ cup	coconut water or water	150 mL
1⅓ cups	blueberries	325 mL

1. In a large bowl, whisk together chickpea flour, coconut flour, potato starch, baking powder and salt.

2. In a medium bowl, whisk together coconut sugar, psyllium, lemon zest, coconut milk and coconut water until well blended. Let stand for 5 minutes to thicken.

3. Add the coconut milk mixture to the flour mixture and stir until just blended. Gently fold in blueberries.

4. Divide batter equally among prepared muffin cups.

5. Bake in preheated oven for 28 to 33 minutes or until tops are golden brown and a toothpick inserted in the center comes out clean. Let cool in pan on a wire rack for 3 minutes, then transfer to the rack to cool completely.

Variation

Raspberry Lime Muffins: Replace the blueberries with raspberries and the lemon zest with lime zest.

Cranberry Orange Muffins

The cranberry is praised for its sauce capabilities at the Thanksgiving table, but the ruby fruit is underappreciated as a healthy food. Cranberries are teamed with whole-grain flour and antioxidant-rich orange zest and juice to create these muffins, destined to be a favorite.

Makes 12 muffins

Tip

......

Cranberries freeze very well, so when they are in season, stock the freezer with multiple bags for baking throughout the year.

- Preheat oven to 350°F (180°C)
- 12-cup muffin pan, greased with coconut oil

½ cup	chickpea flour	125 mL
⅓ cup	coconut flour	75 mL
2 tbsp	potato starch	30 mL
2½ tsp	gluten-free baking powder	12 mL
¼ tsp	fine sea salt	1 mL
⅓ cup	coconut sugar	75 mL
2 tbsp	psyllium husk	30 mL
2 tsp	finely grated orange zest	10 mL
½ cup	freshly squeezed orange juice	125 mL
½ cup	well-stirred coconut milk (full-fat)	125 mL
¾ cup	fresh or thawed frozen cranberries, coarsely chopped	175 mL

1. In a large bowl, whisk together chickpea flour, coconut flour, potato starch, baking powder and salt.

2. In a medium bowl, whisk together coconut sugar, psyllium, orange zest, orange juice and coconut milk until well blended. Let stand for 5 minutes to thicken.

3. Add the orange juice mixture to the flour mixture and stir until just blended. Gently fold in cranberries.

4. Divide batter evenly among prepared cups.

Store the cooled muffins, wrapped in foil or plastic wrap, in the refrigerator for up to 3 days. Alternatively, wrap them in plastic wrap, then foil, completely enclosing them, and freeze for up to 3 months. Let thaw at room temperature for 1 to 2 hours before serving.

5. Bake in preheated oven for 25 to 30 minutes or until tops are golden and a toothpick inserted in the center comes out clean. Let cool in pan on a wire rack for 10 minutes, then transfer to the rack to cool completely.

✳ Power Ingredient

Cranberries

Cranberries are loaded with disease-fighting antioxidants and are a good source of vitamin C, fiber, manganese and potassium. Cranberries are perhaps best known for their role in preventing urinary tract infections, especially for people with recurrent infections. The high level of proanthocyanidins in cranberries helps reduce the adhesion of certain bacteria to the urinary tract walls, fighting off infections. Some preliminary evidence also suggests that the polyphenols in cranberries may reduce the risk of cardiovascular disease by preventing platelet buildup and reducing blood pressure via anti-inflammatory mechanisms.

Spinach and Basil Muffins

Here, I've pepped up a basic savory muffin with a combination of spinach, garlic and basil. The delectable result is great paired with soup, but one muffin is practically a meal unto itself.

Storage Tip

Store the cooled muffins, wrapped in foil or plastic wrap, in the refrigerator for up to 3 days. Alternatively, wrap them in plastic wrap, then foil, completely enclosing them, and freeze for up to 3 months. Let thaw at room temperature for 1 to 2 hours before serving.

- Preheat oven to 350°F (180°C)
- 12-cup muffin pan, greased with coconut oil

2 tbsp	psyllium husk	30 mL
2/3 cup	well-stirred coconut milk (full-fat)	150 mL
1/2 cup	coconut water or water	125 mL
1	package (10 oz/300 g) frozen chopped spinach, thawed and squeezed dry	1
1/2 cup	chickpea flour	125 mL
1/4 cup	coconut flour	60 mL
1 tbsp	potato starch	15 mL
2 1/2 tsp	gluten-free baking powder	12 mL
2 tsp	dried basil	10 mL
3/4 tsp	garlic powder	3 mL
1/2 tsp	fine sea salt	2 mL

1. In a medium bowl, whisk together psyllium, coconut milk and coconut water. Let stand for 5 minutes to thicken. Stir in spinach.

2. In a large bowl, whisk together chickpea flour, coconut flour, potato starch, baking powder, basil, garlic powder and salt.

3. Add the spinach mixture to the flour mixture and stir until just blended.

4. Divide batter equally among prepared muffin cups.

5. Bake in preheated oven for 28 to 32 minutes or until tops are golden brown and a toothpick inserted in the center comes out clean. Let cool in pan on a wire rack for 5 minutes, then transfer to the rack to cool completely.

Variation

Roasted Pepper and Oregano Muffins: Substitute an 8-oz (230 mL) jar of roasted red bell peppers, drained, patted dry and chopped, for the spinach. Replace the basil with 1 1/4 tsp (6 mL) dried oregano.

Salads

Coconut Waldorf Salad

The rich tropical flavor of coconut milk brings out the sweet-tart flavors of the apples and red grapes. The bittersweet edge of Belgian endive further enhances this reinvention of a New York City original.

Tip

If desired, you can sprinkle the salad with 1/4 cup (60 mL) roasted sunflower seeds, green pumpkin seeds (pepitas) or hemp hearts after stirring in the endive.

2 tsp	coconut sugar	10 mL
1/2 cup	well-stirred coconut milk (full-fat)	125 mL
2 tbsp	freshly squeezed lemon juice	30 mL
4	Granny Smith or other tart apples, peeled and diced	4
1 1/2 cups	thinly sliced celery	375 mL
1 1/2 cups	red seedless grapes, halved	375 mL
1/4 cup	golden or dark raisins	60 mL
1	small head Belgian endive, coarsely chopped	1

1. In a small bowl, whisk together coconut sugar, coconut milk and lemon juice.

2. In a large bowl, combine apples, celery, grapes and raisins. Add dressing and gently toss to coat. Cover and refrigerate for at least 30 minutes, until chilled, or for up to 2 hours.

3. Just before serving, stir in endive.

Variation

Coconut Radicchio Waldorf Salad: Replace the celery with chopped fennel bulb (about 1 large bulb) and replace the endive with 2 cups (500 mL) coarsely chopped radicchio. Add 3 tbsp (45 mL) chopped fennel fronds.

✳ Power Ingredient

Belgian Endive
Belgian endive's bitter flavor comes from coumarin and lactucin, anti-inflammatory chemicals that can relieve gout and arthritis. In addition, endive contains a type of fiber called inulin, which acts as a prebiotic in the digestive system, stimulating the bacteria essential for gut health. Inulin also helps regulate blood sugar levels, boosts the immune system and can increase HDL ("good") cholesterol and reduce LDL ("bad") cholesterol.

Fennel, Apple and Coconut Salad

Unmistakable for its delicate crunch and licorice undertones, fresh fennel — which happens to be rich in fiber, vitamin C, potassium and manganese — becomes even more enticing when paired with tart-crisp apples and tossed with a lemon-coconut dressing.

Makes 6 side-dish servings

Tip

To prepare the fennel bulb, trim off the tough stalks from the top and the bottom root end before cutting the bulb in half lengthwise. If the outer layers of the bulb are tough and stringy, you can discard them or peel off the outer layer with a sharp vegetable peeler.

2 tbsp	melted virgin coconut oil	30 mL
1 tsp	finely grated lemon zest	5 mL
2 tsp	freshly squeezed lemon juice	10 mL
1/8 tsp	fine sea salt	0.5 mL
1/8 tsp	cracked black pepper	0.5 mL
1	large bulb fennel, halved lengthwise (see tip, at left), cored and very thinly sliced crosswise, fronds reserved	1
1	large Granny Smith apple, peeled, cored and thinly sliced	1
3 tbsp	unsweetened shredded or flaked coconut, toasted	45 mL

1. In a small bowl, whisk together coconut oil, lemon zest, lemon juice, salt and pepper.

2. Chop enough of the reserved fennel fronds to measure 2 tbsp (30 mL).

3. In a large bowl, combine fennel fronds, fennel bulb and apple. Add dressing and gently toss to coat. Let stand for 10 minutes to blend the flavors. Sprinkle with coconut.

✳ Power Ingredient

Fennel

Fennel is one of the best antioxidant and anti-inflammatory foods you can eat, packed with vitamin C, folate, potassium and dietary fiber. Moreover, a recent study from the University of Texas MD Anderson Cancer Center found that anethole, a phytonutrient that is plentiful in fennel, blocks both inflammation and carcinogenesis, the transformation of regular cells into cancerous ones.

Mango and Avocado Salad

With sunshiny mangos, velvety avocados and crunchy jicama, this salad will send your palate on a delectable trip to Central America.

Makes 6 side-dish servings

Tip

Avocados come in several varieties, but Hass are the most widely available. A Hass avocado — notable for its dark, bumpy skin and rich, buttery flesh — is ideal in this simple salad, but any other variety may be used in its place.

1/2 tsp	ground coriander	2 mL
1/2 tsp	fine sea salt	2 mL
3 tbsp	melted virgin coconut oil	45 mL
2 tbsp	freshly squeezed lime juice	30 mL
1 tbsp	coconut nectar or coconut sugar	15 mL
2	large firm-ripe mangos, diced	2
1	small firm-ripe Hass avocado, diced	1
6 oz	baby spinach (about 6 cups/ 1.5 L packed)	175 g
1 cup	matchstick-size strips peeled jicama	250 mL
2 tbsp	chopped fresh mint or cilantro	30 mL

1. In a small bowl, whisk together coriander, salt, coconut oil, lime juice and coconut nectar.

2. In a large bowl, combine mangos, avocado, spinach, jicama and mint. Add dressing and gently toss to coat.

✴ Power Ingredient

Mangos

Mangos are rich in antioxidants, are a premier source of vitamins C and A, and contain more than 20 different vitamins and minerals. They have particularly high levels of vitamin A (beta carotene), vitamin E and selenium, all of which offer protection against heart disease and several types of cancer. Mangos are also a great source of potassium, which helps to regulate blood pressure and muscle contraction and keep your bodily processes working correctly. In addition, mangos contain vitamin E, which can help the hormonal system perform more efficiently.

Watermelon Salad with Creamy Coconut Dressing

Fresh and creamy all at once, this salad is summer on a plate. You would be hard-pressed to a find a more refreshing side dish!

Makes 6 side-dish servings

Tips

It's best not to cut the watermelon into small pieces until a few hours before serving; the cut pieces will release their juices over time, making it less crisp.

Cantaloupe or another musk melon can be used in place of the watermelon.

Consider replacing the cardamom with an equal amount of freshly cracked black pepper.

²/₃ cup	well-stirred coconut milk (full-fat)	150 mL
2 tbsp	coconut nectar or coconut sugar	30 mL
2 tbsp	freshly squeezed lime juice	30 mL
¼ tsp	ground cardamom (optional)	1 mL
⅛ tsp	fine sea salt	0.5 mL
5 cups	cubed seedless watermelon (¾-inch/2 cm cubes)	1.25 L
⅓ cup	unsweetened flaked or shredded coconut, toasted	75 mL

1. In a small bowl, whisk together coconut milk, coconut nectar, lime juice, cardamom (if using) and salt. Refrigerate for 20 to 30 minutes or until chilled.

2. Arrange watermelon on a platter or in individual serving dishes. Whisk dressing, then drizzle over watermelon. Sprinkle with coconut.

✳ Power Ingredient

Watermelon
Watermelon is one of the most refreshing, thirst-quenching fruits available year-round, and it is also very nutritious. Deep red varieties have displaced the tomato as one of the best sources of lycopene. A mounting body of clinical evidence indicates that lycopene may benefit heart health by boosting the body's natural antioxidant defenses and protecting against DNA damage.

Roasted Golden Beet Salad

Golden beets are every bit as gorgeous as their crimson cousins, but with a far more mellow flavor. Here, they find sophisticated complements from Middle Eastern flavors: ground coriander, cumin, dill and tangy yogurt.

Makes 6 side-dish servings

Tip

......

Other types of beets (such as red or red-and-white-striped Chioggia) would be great in this salad. To avoid stained hands, wear plastic gloves when peeling dark-colored beets.

- Preheat oven to 400°F (200°C)
- Large rimmed baking sheet

6	golden beets, with greens attached (about 2 lbs/1 kg)	6
4	cloves garlic, minced, divided	4
1½ tsp	ground cumin, divided	7 mL
1¼ tsp	ground coriander, divided	6 mL
¾ tsp	fine sea salt, divided	3 mL
3 tbsp	melted virgin coconut oil	45 mL
1½ tbsp	cider vinegar	22 mL
1 cup	plain coconut yogurt (store-bought or see recipe, page 49)	250 mL
1 tbsp	chopped fresh dill	15 mL
⅛ tsp	cayenne pepper	0.5 mL

1. Trim greens from beets. Cut off and discard stems, then coarsely chop leaves. Set beet leaves aside.

2. Tightly wrap each beet in foil and place on baking sheet. Roast in preheated oven for about 90 minutes or until fork-tender. Let cool completely in foil on baking sheet.

3. Meanwhile, in a large saucepan of boiling water, cook beet leaves for 2 to 3 minutes or until tender. Drain and let cool completely.

4. Peel beets and cut each into 8 wedges. Place beets in a medium bowl.

5. Squeeze beet leaves to remove any excess water and add to beets.

6. In a small bowl, whisk together half the garlic, 1 tsp (5 mL) cumin, ¾ tsp (3 mL) coriander, ½ tsp (2 mL) salt, coconut oil and vinegar. Add to beets, tossing to coat.

If you don't have fresh dill on hand, you can use 1½ tsp (7 mL) dried dillweed in its place.

An equal amount of other fresh herbs, such as basil, mint, cilantro or flat-leaf (Italian) parsley, can be used in place of the dill.

7. In a small bowl, whisk together coconut yogurt, dill, cayenne and the remaining garlic, cumin, coriander and salt.

8. Transfer salad to a serving platter and spoon some of the yogurt sauce over top. Serve the remaining sauce on the side.

✳ Power Ingredient

Dill

Dill has a long history that dates back to the ancient Egyptians. It was also favored by the ancient Romans and Greeks and was used for medicinal purposes and culinary applications, and as a symbol of wealth. Bowls of dill seeds often appeared on the table after big meals and banquets, a practice that is still common in Italy, Greece and the Middle East. A concoction of dill seeds and hot water sweetened with sugar or honey, known as "gripe water," was given to babies who suffered from colic and abdominal pains. This is, in fact, most likely where the name for the herb originated, as the Old Norse word *dilla* means "to lull" or "to soothe." Dill is still highly regarded as a source of fresh and vibrant flavor in a variety of dishes, and is now known to be a good source of vitamin C, vitamin A, calcium, manganese, iron and magnesium.

Shredded Beet, Coconut and Sesame Salad

Crisp fresh beets, fragrant coconut and earthy sesame team up in a sophisticated salad that makes a terrific side dish for any number of meals.

Makes 4 side-dish servings

Tips

Use the coarse side of a box cheese grater to shred the beets and carrots. Or, to make quick work of the task, use the shredding disk on a food processor. To prevent the carrots from turning purple, shred them first, then measure them, then shred the beets.

To toast sesame seeds, place up to 3 tbsp (45 mL) seeds in a medium skillet set over medium heat. Cook, shaking the skillet, for 3 to 5 minutes or until seeds are fragrant. Let cool completely before use.

3 tbsp	melted virgin coconut oil	45 mL
1 tbsp	cider vinegar	15 mL
2 tsp	coconut nectar or coconut sugar	10 mL
¼ tsp	fine sea salt	1 mL
3 cups	coarsely shredded peeled beets (about 3 large)	750 mL
1 cup	coarsely shredded carrots	250 mL
⅓ cup	packed fresh mint leaves, chopped	75 mL
½ cup	unsweetened flaked or shredded coconut, toasted	125 mL
1½ tbsp	toasted sesame seeds (see tip, at left)	22 mL

1. In a small bowl, whisk together coconut oil, vinegar, coconut nectar and salt.

2. In a large bowl, combine beets and carrots. Add dressing and gently toss to coat. Cover and refrigerate for at least 30 minutes, until chilled, or for up to 4 hours.

3. Just before serving, stir in mint, coconut and sesame seeds.

✳ Power Ingredient

Mint

Mint has been revered as a digestive aid and natural stimulant for centuries, but a new body of research has examined the effects mint has on alertness, retention and general cognitive function. Early research indicates that consumption of mint (fresh, dried or in oil form) may enhance memory retention and mental alertness. Mint may also be effective at fighting a variety of allergies. Mint contains high levels of rosmarinic acid, an antioxidant that destroys free radicals and reduces allergy symptoms.

Bok Choy Salad with Ginger Dressing

So simple to prepare, this Asian-inspired salad showcases the versatility of coconut oil and coconut sugar.

Makes 4 side-dish servings

2 tsp	minced gingerroot	10 mL
1½ tbsp	cider vinegar	22 mL
1½ tbsp	melted virgin coconut oil	22 mL
1½ tsp	coconut nectar or coconut sugar	7 mL
6 cups	sliced bok choy (about 1 large)	1.5 L
1 tbsp	toasted black or regular sesame seeds (see tip, at left)	15 mL

1. In a small bowl, whisk together ginger, vinegar, coconut oil and coconut nectar.

2. Place bok choy in a large bowl. Add dressing and gently toss to coat. Sprinkle with sesame seeds.

Tips

To toast sesame seeds, place up to 3 tbsp (45 mL) seeds in a medium skillet set over medium heat. Cook, shaking the skillet, for 3 to 5 minutes or until seeds are fragrant. Let cool completely before use.

An equal amount of hemp hearts can be used in place of the sesame seeds. They can be added as is or toasted in the same manner as sesame seeds.

If you don't have fresh gingerroot on hand, you can replace it with ½ tsp (2 mL) ground ginger.

✳ Power Ingredient

Bok Choy
Bok choy is packed with vitamins A, C and K. In fact, 1 cup (250 mL) of chopped raw bok choy contains about half of your daily requirements for each of these nutrients. Plus, you'll get healthy levels of folate, vitamin B_6, calcium, iron and potassium. Bok choy is also a very good source of several carotenoids, especially beta carotene, which has been well studied as a dietary antioxidant that may reduce the risk of lung and bladder cancers, as well as macular degeneration.

Moroccan Carrot Salad

Bold spices and tart lemon are wonderful foils to the gentle sweetness of carrots and coconut. Fresh cilantro and dried currants round out this striking salad.

Makes 6 side-dish servings

Tip

You can increase the health benefits you receive from garlic by letting it stand for about 15 minutes after mincing it. Researchers at the American Institute for Cancer Research found that when chopped, minced or crushed garlic was allowed to stand before it was cooked or combined with acidic ingredients (such as vinegar or lemon juice in a salad dressing), more of its cancer-fighting compounds were preserved.

3	cloves garlic, mashed or minced	3
1 tsp	ground cumin	5 mL
1 tsp	sweet smoked paprika	5 mL
¼ tsp	ground cinnamon	1 mL
¼ tsp	fine sea salt	1 mL
⅛ tsp	cayenne pepper (optional)	0.5 mL
3 tbsp	melted virgin coconut oil	45 mL
2 tbsp	freshly squeezed lemon juice	30 mL
4 cups	coarsely shredded carrots (about 1 lb/500 g)	1 L
¾ cup	packed fresh cilantro or flat-leaf (Italian) parsley leaves, chopped	175 mL
⅓ cup	unsweetened shredded or flaked coconut	75 mL
¼ cup	dried currants or raisins	60 mL

1. In a small bowl, whisk together garlic, cumin, paprika, cinnamon, salt, cayenne (if using), coconut oil and lemon juice.

2. In a large bowl, combine carrots, cilantro, coconut and currants. Add dressing and gently toss to coat. Let stand for at least 30 minutes at room temperature to blend the flavors or for up to 1 hour.

Variations

Moroccan Carrot, Orange and Mint Salad: Omit the cumin and paprika and increase the cinnamon to 1 tsp (5 mL). Add 1 tbsp (15 mL) finely grated orange zest and 1 tbsp (15 mL) coconut nectar or coconut sugar to the dressing. Replace the lemon juice with orange juice. In the salad, replace the cilantro with mint.

Turkish Carrot Yogurt Salad: Reduce the lemon juice to 1 tbsp (15 mL) and add 1 cup (250 mL) plain coconut yogurt (store-bought or see recipe, page 49) to the dressing.

Radish and Cucumber Salad

Radishes and cucumbers are available throughout the winter, which means you can make this lively salad as a refreshing counterpoint to hearty dishes all season long.

Makes 4 side-dish servings

Tips

You can replace the fresh tarragon with 1 tsp (5 mL) dried.

A large field cucumber can be used in place of the English cucumber. Peel the cucumber, slice it in half lengthwise and scrape out the seeds with a spoon before slicing crosswise.

An equal amount of finely chopped green onions can be used in place of the chives.

2 tsp	minced fresh tarragon	10 mL
¼ tsp	fine sea salt	1 mL
2 tbsp	melted virgin coconut oil	30 mL
1 tbsp	freshly squeezed lemon juice	15 mL
1	large English cucumber, peeled and sliced	1
1 cup	thinly sliced (crosswise) red radishes	250 mL
3 tbsp	chopped chives	45 mL

1. In a small bowl, whisk together tarragon, salt, coconut oil and lemon juice.

2. In a large bowl, combine cucumber, radishes and chives. Add dressing and gently toss to coat.

☀ Power Ingredient

Radishes

Like other vegetables in the Brassica family (such as cabbage, broccoli and Brussels sprouts), radishes contain two natural compounds, sulforaphane and indole-3, that in animal and lab studies have shown anticancer action. It is thought that these antioxidants may slow or stop the growth of several different types of cancer cells, possibly by prompting the body to make higher levels of detoxifying enzymes. Since these compounds are depleted by cooking, radishes make it easy to reap their nutritional benefits as they are eaten raw. Radishes also provide a significant amount of vitamin C to boost your defenses against everything from common colds to more serious forms of disease.

Sprightly Sprout Salad

The rich, full flavor of coconut oil and toasted coconut flatters the freshness of crunchy fresh vegetables — here, sprouts, carrots and purple cabbage.

Makes 6 side-dish servings

Tip

An equal amount of sunflower sprouts can be used in place of the alfalfa sprouts.

2 tbsp	melted virgin coconut oil	30 mL
1½ tbsp	cider vinegar	22 mL
2 tsp	coconut nectar or coconut sugar	10 mL
¼ tsp	fine sea salt	1 mL
2 cups	shredded purple cabbage	500 mL
2 cups	shredded carrots	500 mL
2 cups	alfalfa sprouts	500 mL
¼ cup	minced chives	60 mL
⅓ cup	unsweetened flaked or shredded coconut, toasted	75 mL

1. In a small bowl, whisk together coconut oil, vinegar, coconut nectar and salt.

2. In a large bowl, combine cabbage, carrots, alfalfa sprouts and chives. Add dressing and gently toss to coat. Sprinkle with coconut.

✳ Power Ingredient

Alfalfa Sprouts

A star in 1970s sandwiches, alfalfa sprouts are once again garnering attention. A good source of protein and B vitamins, alfalfa sprouts also contain compounds that new research indicates may help to reduce both total cholesterol and low-density lipoprotein (LDL, or "bad") cholesterol, without affecting high-density lipoprotein (HDL, or "good") cholesterol levels. Additionally, alfalfa sprouts are one of the most concentrated sources of vitamin K found in nature. Vitamin K is essential for normal platelet function, helping to prevent excessive bleeding and bruising.

Swiss Chard Salad with Grapefruit Coconut Dressing

Earthy, grassy chard finds harmony with a sophisticated grapefruit coconut dressing. Golden raisins and a hint of coconut sugar lend just the right balance of sweetness.

2 tbsp	melted virgin coconut oil	30 mL
1 tbsp	coconut nectar	15 mL
	or coconut sugar	
1 tbsp	finely grated grapefruit zest	15 mL
1 tbsp	freshly squeezed grapefruit juice	15 mL
1 tsp	cider vinegar	5 mL
1/4 tsp	fine sea salt	1 mL
1	large bunch red Swiss chard, ribs removed, leaves thinly sliced crosswise (about 5 cups/1.25 L)	1
3 tbsp	golden raisins, chopped	45 mL
1/4 cup	unsweetened flaked coconut, toasted	60 mL

1. In a small bowl, whisk together coconut oil, coconut nectar, grapefruit zest, grapefruit juice, vinegar and salt.

2. In a large bowl, combine Swiss chard and raisins. Add dressing and gently toss to coat. Let stand for 10 minutes to blend the flavors. Sprinkle with coconut.

❋ Power Ingredient

Raisins
Raisins are a great plant-based source of iron. A mere 2 tbsp (30 mL) delivers 10% of men's and 5% of women's daily recommended intake. Raisins also contain vitamin C and polyphenolic phytonutrients that have antioxidant properties. In addition, raisins provide significant amounts of vitamin A, beta carotene and carotenoid, all of which are essential for healthy eyes.

Brussels Sprouts Slaw

Brussels sprouts look like tiny cabbages; as such, they are ideal for a fresh slaw. Their natural nuttiness pairs perfectly with the fresh lemon coconut dressing.

Tips

Trim the root end from Brussels sprouts and cut off any loose, thick outer leaves, then rinse well to remove any grit that may have gathered under loose leaves.

If using a mandolin to slice the Brussels sprouts, leave the stem ends on, hold each sprout by the stem end and slice crosswise instead of lengthwise.

1½ lbs	Brussels sprouts, trimmed	750 g
2 tbsp	melted virgin coconut oil	30 mL
1 tsp	finely grated lemon zest	5 mL
2 tbsp	freshly squeezed lemon juice	30 mL
1 tsp	Dijon mustard	5 mL
¼ tsp	fine sea salt	1 mL
¼ tsp	freshly cracked black pepper	1 mL
⅓ cup	unsweetened flaked or shredded coconut, toasted	75 mL
¼ cup	hemp hearts or sunflower seeds, toasted	60 mL

1. Using a very sharp knife, very thinly slice Brussels sprouts lengthwise. Use your fingers to separate the leaves and place in a large bowl.

2. In a small bowl, whisk together coconut oil, lemon zest, lemon juice, mustard, salt and pepper.

3. Finely chop coconut until it has the texture of grated Parmesan cheese.

4. Add coconut and hemp hearts to Brussels sprouts. Add dressing and gently toss to coat.

✳ Power Ingredient

Brussels Sprouts
Like nearly all vegetables, Brussels sprouts are naturally low in fat and calories. But unlike most vegetables, Brussels sprouts have significant levels of protein, accounting for more than a quarter of their calories. But that's the mere tip of the nutritional iceberg: Brussels sprouts are loaded with vitamin A, vitamin C, folate, potassium and calcium, plus they have 3 to 5 grams of fiber per 1 cup (250 mL).

Cranberry Orange Muffins (page 120)

Vanilla Coconut Baked Doughnuts (page 110)

Crunchy, Colorful Thai Cabbage Slaw (page 137)

Cauliflower "Couscous" and Date Salad (page 142)

Gingered Carrot and Coconut Soup (page 158)

Moroccan Sweet Potato, Butter Bean and Coconut Tagine (page 180)

Green Thai Curry with Spinach and Sweet Potatoes (page 191) with Cauliflower "Rice" (page 248)

Acorn Squash with Coconut
Chickpea Stuffing (page 205)

Crunchy, Colorful Thai Cabbage Slaw

This fresh, crunchy slaw has just the right balance of sweet and tart. Leftovers are terrific tucked into sandwiches the next day.

Makes 6 side-dish servings

Tip

An equal amount of thickly sliced or shredded green or purple cabbage can be used in place of the napa cabbage.

1 tbsp	grated gingerroot	15 mL
¼ tsp	cayenne pepper	1 mL
¼ tsp	fine sea salt	1 mL
3 tbsp	cider vinegar	45 mL
2 tbsp	melted virgin coconut oil	30 mL
1 tbsp	coconut nectar or coconut sugar	15 mL
6 cups	sliced napa cabbage (about 1 small head)	1.5 L
1 cup	shredded carrots	250 mL
1 cup	thinly sliced green onions	250 mL
¼ cup	packed fresh basil leaves, chopped	60 mL
¼ cup	packed fresh cilantro or mint leaves, chopped	60 mL

1. In a small bowl, whisk together ginger, cayenne, salt, vinegar, coconut oil and coconut nectar.

2. In a large bowl, combine cabbage, carrots, green onions, basil and cilantro. Add dressing and gently toss to coat. Cover and refrigerate for at least 30 minutes, until chilled, or for up to 2 hours.

✳ Power Ingredient

Cabbage

Cabbage is rich in phytonutrients, which may inhibit the growth of cancerous tumors and seem to have particular benefit in offering protection from colon, lung and hormone-based cancers, such as breast cancer, probably by increasing the metabolism of estrogen. Cabbage is also rich in vitamins C and E, folate, fiber and minerals, and is a source of B vitamins, vitamin K, iron and beta carotene. Its juice is a traditional remedy for peptic ulcers, and its indoles can help lower LDL ("bad") cholesterol.

Massaged Kale, Apple and Sunflower Salad

At first glance, your family and guests will think this is spinach salad. The trick to the tender, bright green kale leaves is a vigorous massage, which breaks down the cellular structure of the leaves. The result proves how versatile kale can be, cooked or raw.

Tip

Use a tart-sweet apple, such as Gala, Braeburn or Golden Delicious, for the best flavor in this salad.

3 tbsp	melted virgin coconut oil	45 mL
1 tbsp	cider vinegar	15 mL
1½ tsp	coconut nectar or coconut sugar	7 mL
1 tsp	Dijon mustard	5 mL
¼ tsp	fine sea salt	1 mL
1	large bunch kale, stems and ribs removed, leaves torn into bite-size pieces (about 8 cups/2 L)	1
1	large tart-sweet apple, halved and very thinly sliced crosswise	1
½ cup	thinly sliced green onions	125 mL
3 tbsp	roasted or toasted sunflower seeds	45 mL
3 tbsp	unsweetened flaked or shredded coconut, toasted	45 mL

1. In a large bowl, whisk together coconut oil, vinegar, coconut nectar, mustard and salt.

2. Add kale to bowl. With clean hands, firmly massage and crush the leaves to work in the dressing. Massage until the volume of leaves is reduced by about half and the leaves appear a little darker and somewhat shiny.

3. Add apple and green onions, gently tossing to coat. Sprinkle with sunflower seeds and coconut.

Down Island Potato Salad

This take on potato salad has all the comfort of traditional versions, but with decidedly Caribbean flair from the coconut milk.

Tip

An equal amount of Dijon mustard can be used in place of the coarse-grain mustard.

2½ lbs	red-skinned potatoes (unpeeled), cut into ¼-inch (0.5 cm) thick rounds	1.25 kg
½ cup	well-stirred coconut milk (full-fat)	125 mL
3 tbsp	coarse-grain mustard	45 mL
2 tsp	cider vinegar	10 mL
	Fine sea salt and freshly ground black pepper	
1	red bell pepper, finely chopped	1
1¼ cups	diced celery	300 mL
½ cup	chopped green onions	125 mL

1. Place potatoes in a large pot and cover with cold water. Bring to a boil over medium–high heat. Boil for 9 to 11 minutes or until tender. Drain and let cool completely.

2. In a small bowl, whisk together coconut milk, mustard and vinegar. Season with salt and pepper to taste.

3. In a large bowl, combine cooled potatoes, red pepper, celery and green onions. Add dressing and gently toss to coat.

✳ Power Ingredient

Potatoes
White potatoes get a bad rap from many camps, but they are a nutritious and frugal food worth including in your diet. One medium potato contains just 110 calories per serving, has more potassium than a banana, provides almost half the daily value of vitamin C and contains no fat, sodium or cholesterol. Potatoes are also a good source of vitamin B_6, a water-soluble vitamin that plays important roles in carbohydrate and protein metabolism.

Coconut Roasted Sweet Potato Salad

The natural sweetness of sweet potatoes plays well with lime juice and coconut, especially in this luscious salad. Paprika is the wild card, adding an unexpected depth of flavor and contrast.

Makes 6 side-dish servings

Tip
......

The sweet potatoes can be roasted, cooled and refrigerated in an airtight container for up to 2 days before you prepare the salad.

- Preheat oven to 400°F (200°C)
- Large rimmed baking sheet, greased with coconut oil

3	large sweet potatoes (about 3 lbs/1.5 kg), peeled and cut into 1-inch (2.5 cm) cubes	3
4 tbsp	melted virgin coconut oil, divided	60 mL
1 tsp	fine sea salt, divided	5 mL
1 tsp	hot smoked paprika	5 mL
1/4 cup	freshly squeezed lime juice	60 mL
3 tbsp	coconut nectar or coconut sugar	45 mL
1/2 cup	thinly sliced green onions	125 mL
1/2 cup	packed fresh cilantro leaves, chopped	125 mL
1/2 cup	unsweetened flaked or shredded coconut, toasted	125 mL

1. Place sweet potatoes on prepared baking sheet. Sprinkle with half the coconut oil and half the salt. Gently toss to coat, then spread out in a single layer. Roast in preheated oven for 20 to 25 minutes or until golden brown and tender. Let cool to room temperature in pan. Transfer to a large bowl.

2. In a small bowl, whisk together paprika, the remaining salt, the remaining coconut oil, lime juice and coconut nectar. Add to sweet potatoes, along with green onions and cilantro, gently tossing to coat. Sprinkle with coconut.

✳ Power Ingredient

Smoked Paprika
Smoked paprika is a potent source of vitamin A. Also known as retinol, vitamin A is important for good eyesight, healthy skin, normal immune function, bone formation and wound healing.

Grape and Mint Cauliflower "Tabbouleh"

According to my Lebanese friend, tabbouleh is mostly about the herbs — the greener the salad, the better — so she gives her unequivocal thumbs up to swapping cauliflower for the traditional bulgur.

Tips

An equal amount of ground cumin can be used in place of the coriander.

Fresh flat-leaf (Italian) parsley or cilantro leaves can be used in place of the mint.

Storage Tip

Refrigerate the finished salad in an airtight container for up to 2 days.

• Food processor

1	small to medium head cauliflower, leaves trimmed	1
¾ cup	chopped green onions	175 mL
1 tsp	ground coriander	5 mL
½ tsp	fine sea salt	2 mL
¼ tsp	freshly cracked black pepper	1 mL
¼ cup	melted virgin coconut oil	60 mL
2 tsp	finely grated lime zest	10 mL
2 tbsp	freshly squeezed lime juice	30 mL
1 tbsp	coconut nectar or coconut sugar	15 mL
2 cups	red seedless grapes, halved	500 mL
1 cup	packed fresh mint leaves, chopped	250 mL

1. Cut or break cauliflower into large florets. Place half the florets in food processor and process until they are the texture and size of coarse bulgur. Transfer to a large bowl. Repeat with the remaining cauliflower.

2. To the cauliflower, add green onions, coriander, salt, pepper, coconut oil, lime zest, lime juice, coconut nectar, grapes and mint, gently tossing to combine.

Cauliflower "Couscous" and Date Salad

Middle Eastern ingredients — cardamom, coconut, lime and chickpeas — bring a mosaic of tastes, textures and scents to this salad.

Makes 6 main-dish servings

Tips

Plump, tender Medjool dates are the most commonly available dates in the U.S. and Canada, but any other variety of soft, fresh dates may be used in their place.

To toast sesame seeds, place up to 3 tbsp (45 mL) seeds in a medium skillet set over medium heat. Cook, shaking the skillet, for 3 to 5 minutes or until seeds are fragrant. Let cool completely before use.

Storage Tip

Refrigerate the finished salad in an airtight container for up to 2 days.

- Food processor

1	small to medium head cauliflower, leaves trimmed	1
3 tbsp	virgin coconut oil	45 mL
1 tsp	ground cardamom	5 mL
1 tsp	ground cumin	5 mL
1 tbsp	finely grated lime zest	15 mL
3 tbsp	freshly squeezed lime juice	45 mL
	Sea salt and freshly ground black pepper	
1	can (14 to 19 oz/398 to 540 mL) chickpeas, drained and rinsed	1
1 cup	thinly sliced green onions	250 mL
½ cup	chopped pitted dates	125 mL
3 tbsp	toasted sesame seeds (see tip, at left)	45 mL

1. Cut or break cauliflower into large florets. Place half the florets in food processor and process until they are the texture and size of couscous. Transfer to a large bowl. Repeat with the remaining cauliflower.

2. In a small skillet, melt coconut oil over low heat. Add cardamom and cumin; cook, stirring, for 1 minute or until fragrant. Remove from heat and whisk in lime zest and lime juice. Season to taste with salt and pepper.

3. To the cauliflower, add chickpeas, green onions and dates. Add dressing and gently toss to coat. Sprinkle with sesame seeds.

Warm Mushroom and Edamame Salad

Warm mushrooms contribute meaty robustness to each bite of this beautiful, filling salad.

Tips

To toast sesame seeds, place up to 3 tbsp (45 mL) seeds in a medium skillet set over medium heat. Cook, shaking the skillet, for 3 to 5 minutes or until seeds are fragrant. Let cool completely before use.

An equal amount of toasted hemp hearts (toasted in the same manner as sesame seeds) can be used in place of the sesame seeds.

3 tbsp	virgin coconut oil, divided	45 mL
12 oz	cremini or white mushrooms, sliced	375 g
2 cups	frozen shelled edamame, thawed	500 mL
1 cup	sugar snap peas, trimmed and sliced in half on the diagonal	250 mL
1	small red bell pepper, sliced	1
2 tsp	cider vinegar	10 mL
	Fine sea salt and freshly cracked black pepper	
1 tbsp	toasted sesame seeds (see tip, at left)	15 mL

1. In a large skillet, melt 1 tbsp (15 mL) coconut oil over low heat. Add mushrooms and increase heat to medium-high. Cook, stirring, for 6 to 8 minutes or until tender. Transfer to a bowl.

2. In the same skillet, heat the remaining oil over low heat. Add edamame, sugar snap peas and red pepper. Increase heat to medium-high and cook, stirring, for 5 to 7 minutes or until edamame are bright green and tender. Transfer to bowl with mushrooms.

3. Add vinegar to mushroom mixture and toss to coat. Season to taste with salt and pepper. Sprinkle with sesame seeds.

Lentil and Pomegranate Salad

Make a note to prepare this dish in autumn, when pomegranates are plentiful. The green lentils and pomegranate arils make this look like a salad of gems.

Makes 6 main-dish servings

Tips

Dried brown lentils may be used if green lentils are unavailable.

To remove pomegranate seeds from the fruit, score the pomegranate around the circumference and place it in a large bowl of water. Break the pomegranate open underwater to free the white seed sacs. The seeds will sink to the bottom of the bowl, and the membrane will float to the top. Strain out the seeds and put them in a separate bowl. You can refrigerate or freeze any remaining seeds for another use.

For variety, try replacing the pomegranate seeds with 1 cup (250 mL) halved red grapes or 1/2 cup (125 mL) dried cranberries or chopped dried cherries.

4 cups	water, divided	1 L
1 cup	dried green lentils, rinsed	250 mL
2 tsp	finely grated lemon zest	10 mL
2 tbsp	freshly squeezed lemon juice	30 mL
3 tbsp	melted virgin coconut oil	45 mL
1 tbsp	coconut nectar or coconut sugar	15 mL
1/2 tsp	fine sea salt	2 mL
3/4 cup	pomegranate seeds	175 mL
3/4 cup	packed fresh flat-leaf (Italian) parsley leaves, chopped	175 mL
1/3 cup	unsweetened flaked or shredded coconut, toasted	75 mL

1. In a medium saucepan, bring water to a boil over high heat. Add lentils, reduce heat and simmer for about 30 minutes or until tender but not mushy. Drain and let cool completely.

2. In a small bowl, whisk together lemon zest, lemon juice, coconut oil, coconut nectar and salt. Add to lentils, along with pomegranate seeds, gently tossing to coat. Cover and let stand at room temperature for 20 to 30 minutes to blend the flavors. Add parsley and coconut, gently tossing to combine.

✳ Power Ingredient

Pomegranates
Pomegranates are as rich in nutrients as they are taste and color. They have historically been used as a heart tonic and blood builder, but it is their polyphenol content that makes this fruit so lauded. Polyphenols are antioxidants that boost the ability to reduce inflammation, protect against heart disease, normalize blood pressure and prevent prostate cancer.

Papaya, Basil and White Bean Salad

Papaya has a full, musky flavor that breathes new life into this almost effortless salad.

Tips

When choosing a papaya, look for skin that is turning from green to yellow. It is normal for some of the skin to appear bruised. You should be able to press your thumb into the flesh, but there should still be some resistance. If the papaya is too soft or mushy, or if it has a pronounced sweet perfume, it is overripe. As with bananas, you can buy a green-skinned papaya and leave it on the countertop; it will ripen in about 1 to 3 days.

To prepare the papaya for the salad, rinse off the skin to remove dust and dirt, then place it on a cutting board and slice it in half lengthwise. Scoop out the seeds with a spoon, then return the halves to the cutting board, skin side up. Use a sharp knife to peel off the skin and dice the papaya.

1 tsp	finely grated lime zest	5 mL
1 tbsp	freshly squeezed lime juice	15 mL
2 tbsp	melted virgin coconut oil	30 mL
2 tsp	coconut nectar or coconut sugar	10 mL
1 tsp	Dijon mustard	5 mL
1	can (14 to 19 oz/398 to 540 mL) white beans, drained and rinsed	1
1	large red bell pepper, chopped	1
1½ cups	diced papaya (about 1 medium)	375 mL
½ cup	packed fresh basil leaves, thinly sliced	125 mL
3 tbsp	unsweetened flaked or shredded coconut, toasted	45 mL

1. In a small bowl, whisk together lime zest, lime juice, coconut oil, coconut nectar and mustard.

2. In a large bowl, combine beans, red pepper, papaya and basil. Add dressing and gently toss to coat. Sprinkle with coconut.

✳ Power Ingredient

White Beans

White beans are a good source of protein and are one of the best bean sources of calcium: ½ cup (125 mL) provides about 14% of a day's recommended intake. White beans are also very rich in magnesium, potassium, iron and zinc, and are a very good source of B vitamins and folate. Their soluble fiber helps lower cholesterol and prevent blood sugar levels from rising too rapidly after a meal, making them a good choice for dieters, as well as people with diabetes, insulin resistance and hypoglycemia.

Arugula, Apricot and Crispy Chickpea Salad

This dish is a welcome departure from run-of-the-mill green salads. Garam masala, fresh lemon (both the juice and zest) and sweet chunks of dried apricot give bitter arugula multidimensional flavor, while crispy chickpeas give croutons a run for their money.

Makes 6 side-dish servings

Tip

An equal amount of tender watercress sprigs, baby spinach leaves or mesclun can be used in place of the arugula.

- Preheat oven to 450°F (230°C)
- Large rimmed baking sheet, greased with coconut oil

1	can (14 to 19 oz/398 to 540 mL) chickpeas, drained, rinsed and patted dry	1
1½ tsp	garam masala	7 mL
¼ tsp	fine sea salt, divided	1 mL
3 tbsp	virgin coconut oil, divided	45 mL
2 tsp	finely grated lemon zest	10 mL
2 tbsp	freshly squeezed lemon juice	30 mL
6 cups	packed arugula leaves	1.5 L
½ cup	chopped dried apricots or golden raisins	125 mL
¼ cup	unsweetened flaked or shredded coconut, toasted	60 mL

1. In a medium bowl, combine chickpeas, garam masala, half the salt and 1 tbsp (15 mL) coconut oil. Spread in a single layer on prepared baking sheet. Roast in preheated oven for 10 to 15 minutes or until chickpeas are golden brown and crisp. Let cool completely in pan.

2. In a small bowl, whisk together the remaining salt, lemon zest, lemon juice and the remaining oil.

3. In a large bowl, combine chickpeas, arugula and apricots. Add dressing and gently toss to coat. Sprinkle with coconut.

For even more crunch, replace the toasted coconut with an equal amount of toasted green pumpkin seeds (pepitas) or sunflower seeds.

Variation

Island Chickpea Salad: Replace the garam masala with an equal amount of salt-free jerk seasoning and replace the lemon zest and lemon juice with equal amounts of lime zest and lime juice.

✳ Power Ingredient

Arugula
Arugula, also known as rocket, is a peppery green from the Brassica family. Despite its slightly bitter flavor, it was considered an aphrodisiac in ancient Rome and was often combined with other aphrodisiac herbs, such as lavender and chicory, to create "love potions." Arugula is a great source of folate, copper, iron and vitamins A and C, and is one of the best vegetable sources of vitamin K, which boosts both bone and brain health. Like many of its close relatives, it is a rich source of certain phytochemicals that have been shown to combat cancer-causing elements in the body. Arugula's various phytochemicals also improve intercellular activity and communication (which enhances cellular function and productivity), help protect the skin from the effects of ultraviolet rays, cleanse the blood, improve distribution of oxygen in the blood, boost energy levels and support good skin health.

Watercress Salad with Oranges and Black Beans

Lip-smackingly delicious, this salad is at once refreshing and hearty. The coconut orange dressing complements the richness of black beans and extends the clean assertiveness of watercress.

Tips

A 15-ounce (426 mL) can of mandarin oranges, drained, can be used in place of the orange segments. Zest and juice 1 medium navel orange to yield the zest and juice needed.

An equal amount of arugula or chopped Belgian endive can be used in place of the watercress.

3	large navel oranges	3
2 tbsp	melted virgin coconut oil	30 mL
2 tsp	coconut nectar or coconut sugar	10 mL
1 tsp	Dijon mustard	5 mL
1/2 tsp	fine sea salt	2 mL
1/8 tsp	freshly ground black pepper	0.5 mL
1	can (14 to 19 oz/398 to 540 mL) black beans, drained and rinsed	1
4 cups	packed tender watercress	1 L
1	firm-ripe Hass avocado, diced	1

1. Finely grate 2 tsp (10 mL) orange zest into a glass measuring cup.

2. Using a sharp knife, cut remaining peel and pith from oranges. Working over a large bowl, cut between membranes to release segments. You should have about 1½ cups (375 mL) of segments.

3. Squeeze any remaining juice from orange membranes to measure 3 tbsp (45 mL). Add to measuring cup with zest, along with coconut oil, coconut nectar, mustard, salt and pepper, whisking until blended.

4. Add black beans and dressing to the orange segments, gently tossing to coat (this can be done up to 4 hours ahead, but see tip, opposite). Just before serving, gently toss in watercress and avocado.

Tip

If you are planning to chill the salad for several hours before serving, omit the coconut oil in step 3 and add it just before serving in step 4 (otherwise, it will harden in the refrigerator).

✳ Power Ingredient

Watercress
Watercress is a powerhouse of nutrients — even if eaten in small quantities — and provides good amounts of vitamins C and K, potassium and calcium. It is a great source of carotenes and lutein, for eye health. Watercress is rich in a variety of plant chemicals that can help prevent or minimize cancers, including phenylethyl isothiocyanate, which can help block the action of cells linked with lung cancer. Watercress is also said to detoxify the liver and cleanse the blood, and its benzyl oils are powerful antibiotics. It can help improve night blindness and the light sensitivity associated with porphyria.

Minted Fruit Salad

Fragrant mint and tropical coconut meet a bevy of berries and diced fruit in this refreshing salad. It is equally fitting as side dish or dessert.

Makes 6 side-dish servings

Tips

This salad is best served within 1 to 2 hours of being prepared.

Serve the salad atop plain coconut yogurt (store-bought or see recipe, page 49).

1½ cups	quartered hulled strawberries	375 mL
1½ cups	blackberries	375 mL
1 cup	fresh pineapple chunks	250 mL
1 cup	diced kiwifruit	250 mL
1 cup	loosely packed mint leaves, chopped	250 mL
2 tbsp	melted virgin coconut oil	30 mL
1 tbsp	freshly squeezed lemon juice	15 mL
1 tbsp	coconut nectar or coconut sugar	15 mL
½ cup	unsweetened flaked coconut, toasted	125 mL

1. In a large bowl, gently toss strawberries, blackberries, pineapple, kiwis, mint, coconut oil, lemon juice and coconut nectar. Just before serving, sprinkle with coconut.

✳ Power Ingredient

Pineapple
Pineapple is packed with fiber to benefit digestion and vitamin C to aid your immune system, but it's the fruit's high level of bromelain that has garnered a significant amount of scientific research. Bromelain, an enzyme found in the juice and stem of pineapples, has been used medicinally since ancient times to help reduce inflammation, lessen hay fever symptoms, slow blood clotting and even enhance the absorption of antibiotics. Clinical evidence supports bromelain's role in reducing inflammation, but a study published in the journal *Cellular and Molecular Life Sciences* goes even further, suggesting that bromelain can be used to control the growth of tumors and malignant cells.

Soups, Stews and Chilis

Cantaloupe Coconut Soup with Basil Syrup

Cantaloupe is a unique flavor, so it makes sense to combine it with ingredients that complement — fresh basil and coconut milk — rather than compete.

Tips

Cantaloupes vary in sweetness, so adjust the amount of coconut sugar (more or less) to taste.

An equal amount of honeydew melon can be used in place of the cantaloupe.

- Blender or food processor
- Fine-mesh sieve

Soup

1	large ripe cantaloupe (about 4 lbs/2 kg), cut into chunks	1
2 tbsp	coconut sugar	30 mL
1/2 tsp	fine sea salt	2 mL
1/3 cup	well-stirred coconut milk (full-fat)	75 mL
4 tsp	freshly squeezed lemon juice	20 mL

Basil Syrup

1/2 cup	coconut sugar	125 mL
1/2 cup	coconut water or water	125 mL
1/4 cup	packed fresh basil leaves	60 mL
1 tsp	freshly squeezed lemon juice	5 mL

1. *Soup:* In blender, working in batches, purée cantaloupe, coconut sugar, salt, coconut milk and lemon juice until smooth. Press through sieve into a large bowl. Stir to combine. Cover and refrigerate for at least 1 hour, until cold, or for up to 24 hours.

2. *Syrup:* In a small saucepan, bring coconut sugar and coconut water to a boil over high heat. Cook, stirring, for 5 to 6 minutes or until sugar is dissolved and syrup is slightly thickened. Remove from heat and stir in basil. Transfer to a small bowl, cover and refrigerate for at least 2 hours, until cold, or for up to 2 days.

3. In blender, combine basil mixture and lemon juice; purée until smooth.

4. Stir soup, divide among bowls and drizzle with basil syrup.

Tips

An equal amount of fresh mint can be used in place of the basil.

An equal amount of freshly squeezed lime juice can be used in place of the lemon juice in both the soup and the syrup.

✳ Power Ingredient

Cantaloupe
Cantaloupe is known for its beauty-boosting benefits, including clearing up acne and helping prevent wrinkles. One cup (250 mL) of chopped cantaloupe delivers 100% of the daily values of vitamins A and C. The orange flesh is packed with beta carotene, which converts to vitamin A in the body and helps promote clear skin by thinning the outer layer of dead skin cells that can clog pores and cause blemishes.

Chilled Avocado, Mint and Coconut Soup

This cooling soup is refreshing way to treat your body as a temple.

Tip

An equal amount of fresh cilantro or basil leaves can be used in place of the mint.

- Food processor or blender

2	small ripe Hass avocados, pitted and peeled	2
1	green onion, coarsely chopped	1
½	large English cucumber, peeled and coarsely chopped	½
¼ cup	fresh mint leaves	60 mL
1½ cups	coconut water	375 mL
½ cup	well-stirred coconut milk (full-fat)	125 mL
1 tbsp	freshly squeezed lemon juice	15 mL
1 tsp	fine sea salt	5 mL
	Additional fresh mint leaves	

1. In food processor, working in batches, purée avocados, green onion, cucumber, mint, coconut water, coconut milk, lemon juice and salt until smooth. Transfer to a large bowl. Stir to combine. Cover and refrigerate for at least 1 hour, until cold, or for up to 4 hours.

2. Stir soup, divide among bowls and garnish with mint leaves.

Five-Spice Beet Soup with Coconut Swirl

This crimson and white soup is as gorgeous to behold as it is satisfying to eat.

Tips

Six or 7 medium beets will yield the amount of diced beets needed for this recipe.

The beets can be cooked on the stovetop instead of in the microwave. Combine beets and coconut water in a medium saucepan set over medium-high heat. Bring to a boil, then reduce heat, cover and simmer for 20 to 25 minutes or until beets are very tender.

When puréeing the soup in a food processor or blender, fill the bowl or jug no more than halfway full at a time.

Storage Tip

Store the cooled soup in an airtight container in the refrigerator for up to 2 days or in the freezer for up to 6 months. Thaw overnight in the refrigerator or in the microwave using the Defrost function. Warm soup in a medium saucepan over medium-low heat.

- Food processor, blender or immersion blender

4 cups	diced peeled beets	1 L
2 cups	coconut water	500 mL
1 tbsp	virgin coconut oil	15 mL
2 cups	chopped onions	500 mL
1½ tsp	Chinese five-spice blend	7 mL
2 cups	ready-to-use gluten-free vegetable broth, divided	500 mL
½ cup	well-stirred coconut milk (full-fat)	125 mL

1. In a medium microwave-safe bowl, combine beets and coconut water. Cover loosely and microwave on High for 15 to 20 minutes or until beets are very tender.

2. In a medium saucepan, melt coconut oil over low heat. Add onions, increase heat to medium–high and cook, stirring, for 6 to 8 minutes or until softened.

3. Stir in beet mixture, five-spice blend and 1 cup (250 mL) broth; bring to a boil. Reduce heat to low, cover and simmer for 5 minutes.

4. Working in batches, transfer soup to food processor (or use immersion blender in pan) and purée until smooth. Return soup to pan (if necessary) and whisk in the remaining broth. Warm over medium heat, stirring, for 1 minute.

5. Ladle soup into bowls. Drizzle with coconut milk and use the tip of a knife to swirl the milk into the soup.

Broccoli Bisque

This coconut creamy bisque is full of alkalizing, anti-inflammatory phytonutrients called sulforaphanes, which work to support optimum health and protect against disease.

Makes 6 servings

Tips

For best results, use a vegetable peeler to peel the thick outer layer off the broccoli stems before chopping.

When puréeing soup in a food processor or blender, fill the bowl or jug no more than halfway full at a time.

Storage Tip

Store the cooled soup in an airtight container in the refrigerator for up to 2 days or in the freezer for up to 6 months. Thaw overnight in the refrigerator or in the microwave using the Defrost function. Warm soup in a medium saucepan over medium-low heat.

- Food processor, blender or immersion blender

2 tbsp	virgin coconut oil	30 mL
1½ cups	chopped onions	375 mL
¾ cup	chopped celery	175 mL
2	cloves garlic, minced	2
1½ tsp	dried thyme	7 mL
	Freshly ground black pepper	
1½ lbs	broccoli (florets and peeled stems), coarsely chopped	750 g
5½ cups	ready-to-use gluten-free vegetable broth	1.375 L
¾ cup	well-stirred coconut milk (full-fat)	175 mL
2 tsp	freshly squeezed lemon juice	10 mL
	Fine sea salt	

1. In a large pot, melt coconut oil over low heat. Add onions and celery; increase heat to medium-high and cook, stirring, for 5 to 6 minutes or until softened. Add garlic, thyme and ¼ tsp (1 mL) pepper; cook, stirring, for 30 seconds.

2. Stir in broccoli and broth; bring to a boil. Reduce heat and simmer, stirring occasionally, for 8 to 10 minutes or until broccoli is tender.

3. Working in batches, transfer soup to food processor (or use immersion blender in pot) and purée until smooth. Return soup to pot (if necessary) and whisk in coconut milk and lemon juice. Warm over medium heat, stirring, for 1 minute. Season to taste with salt and pepper.

Cabbage Soup with Cilantro and Lemongrass

If you haven't thought of cabbage as comfort food before, this soup will change your mind. Lemongrass, ginger, sweet potatoes and coconut milk become the perfect cool-weather dinner — hearty without being heavy.

Makes 6 servings

Tips

If lemongrass is unavailable, use 1 tbsp (15 mL) finely grated lemon zest in its place.

An equal amount of gluten-free soy sauce can be used in place of the liquid amino acids.

Storage Tip

Store the cooled soup in an airtight container in the refrigerator for up to 1 day. Warm soup in a medium saucepan over medium-low heat.

2	stalks lemongrass	2
2 tbsp	virgin coconut oil	30 mL
1 tbsp	minced gingerroot	15 mL
6 cups	water	1.5 L
3 cups	cubed peeled sweet potatoes (½-inch/1 cm cubes)	750 mL
⅓ cup	liquid coconut amino acids	75 mL
1 tbsp	Asian hot sauce (such as Sriracha)	15 mL
6 cups	thinly sliced savoy cabbage (about 1 head)	1.5 L
2 cups	packed fresh cilantro leaves	500 mL
1 cup	well-stirred coconut milk (full-fat)	250 mL
1 tbsp	freshly squeezed lime juice	15 mL
	Fine sea salt and freshly ground black pepper	

1. Trim off top third and outer leaves of lemongrass stalks and discard. Lightly smash remaining stalks and cut into 2-inch (10 cm) lengths.

2. In a large saucepan, melt coconut oil over low heat. Add lemongrass and ginger; increase heat to medium-high and cook, stirring, for 1 minute or until fragrant.

3. Stir in water and bring to a boil. Add sweet potatoes, amino acids and hot sauce. Reduce heat to low, cover and simmer, stirring occasionally, for 20 to 25 minutes or until sweet potatoes are tender. Discard lemongrass pieces.

4. Stir in cabbage, cover and simmer, stirring once or twice, for 4 to 5 minutes or until cabbage is wilted.

5. Stir in cilantro, coconut milk and lime juice until cilantro is wilted. Season to taste with salt and pepper.

Gingered Carrot and Coconut Soup

Here, fresh ginger adds gentle heat to a lush soup. Fresh mint and lime juice take the dish from good to grand.

Tip

When puréeing the soup in a food processor or blender, fill the bowl or jug no more than halfway full at a time.

Storage Tip

Store the cooled soup in an airtight container in the refrigerator for up to 2 days or in the freezer for up to 6 months. Thaw overnight in the refrigerator or in the microwave using the Defrost function. Warm soup in a medium saucepan over medium-low heat.

• Food processor, blender or immersion blender

1 tbsp	virgin coconut oil	15 mL
1 cup	chopped onion	250 mL
1 lb	carrots, chopped (about 4 cups/1 L)	500 g
1	1-inch (5 cm) piece gingerroot, chopped	1
1 tsp	fine sea salt	5 mL
3½ cups	coconut water	875 mL
1 cup	well-stirred coconut milk (full-fat)	250 mL
1 tbsp	coconut sugar	15 mL
1 tbsp	freshly squeezed lime juice	15 mL
¼ cup	minced fresh mint	60 mL

Suggested Accompaniments

Plain coconut yogurt

Lime wedges

Toasted unsweetened flaked coconut

1. In a large saucepan, melt coconut oil over low heat. Add onions and increase heat to medium–high; cook, stirring, for 5 to 6 minutes or until softened.

2. Stir in carrots, ginger, salt and coconut water; bring to a boil. Reduce heat and simmer, stirring occasionally, for 25 to 30 minutes or until carrots are very soft.

3. Working in batches, transfer soup to food processor (or use immersion blender in pan) and purée until smooth. Return soup to pan (if necessary) and whisk in coconut milk, sugar and lime juice. Warm over medium heat, stirring, for 1 minute.

4. Ladle soup into bowls and sprinkle with mint. Serve with any of the suggested accompaniments, as desired.

30-Clove Garlic and Coconut Soup

You'll be amazed that a soup this simple can taste so spectacular — not to mention that 2 heads of garlic can yield such a refined, mellow flavor.

Tip

When puréeing soup in a blender or food processor, fill the jug or bowl no more than halfway full at a time.

Storage Tip

Store the cooled soup in an airtight container in the refrigerator for up to 2 days or in the freezer for up to 6 months. Thaw overnight in the refrigerator or in the microwave using the Defrost function. Warm soup in a medium saucepan over medium-low heat.

- Preheat oven to 375°F (190°C)
- 2 large squares foil
- Blender, food processor or immersion blender

2	medium-large heads garlic, halved crosswise	2
1 tbsp	melted virgin coconut oil	15 mL
1	small yellow-fleshed potato (about 6 oz/175 g), peeled and chopped	1
4 cups	ready-to-use gluten-free vegetable broth	1 L
2/3 cup	well-stirred coconut milk (full-fat)	150 mL
1/2 tsp	white or cider vinegar	2 mL
	Fine sea salt and freshly ground black pepper	

1. Place halved garlic heads on squares of foil, cut sides up, and drizzle with coconut oil. Wrap tightly in foil. Place on a baking sheet and roast in preheated oven for 40 to 45 minutes or until tender. Let cool, then squeeze garlic from skin and set aside. Discard skins.

2. In a large saucepan, combine roasted garlic, potato and broth. Bring to a boil over high heat. Reduce heat and simmer, stirring occasionally, for 15 to 20 minutes or until potatoes are tender.

3. Working in batches, transfer soup to blender (or use immersion blender in pan) and purée until smooth. Return soup to pan (if necessary) and whisk in coconut milk and vinegar. Warm over medium heat, stirring, for 1 minute. Season to taste with salt and pepper.

Roasted Cauliflower Soup with Indian Spices

Cauliflower roasts beautifully, the hot oven concentrating its natural sweetness. A judicious array of Indian flavors — coconut, garam masala and lime — keeps the flavor of the soup lively.

Makes 8 servings

Tips

Garam masala (*garam* meaning "hot," referring to the intensity of the spices, not heat from chiles, and *masala* meaning a mixture of spices) is a blend of ground spices common in North Indian and other South Asian cuisines. A typical blend includes peppercorns, cinnamon, cumin, cardamom and cloves.

When puréeing soup in a food processor or blender, fill the bowl or jug no more than halfway full at a time.

- Preheat oven to 400°F (200°C)
- Large rimmed baking sheet, lined with foil and sprayed with nonstick cooking spray
- Food processor, blender or immersion blender

6 cups	cauliflower florets (about 1 large head)	1.5 L
2 tbsp	melted virgin coconut oil, divided	30 mL
	Fine sea salt	
2 cups	chopped onions	500 mL
1½ tbsp	garam masala	22 mL
5 cups	water	1.25 L
1¼ cups	well-stirred coconut milk (full-fat)	300 mL
1½ tbsp	freshly squeezed lime juice	22 mL
	Freshly ground black pepper	
¼ cup	minced fresh chives	60 mL
	Toasted unsweetened shredded or flaked coconut (optional)	

1. On prepared baking sheet, toss cauliflower with half the coconut oil and 2 tsp (10 mL) salt. Spread out in a single layer. Roast in preheated oven for 30 to 35 minutes, stirring occasionally, until golden brown and tender.

2. Meanwhile, in a large pot, heat the remaining oil over low heat. Add onions, increase heat to medium-high and cook, stirring, for 6 to 8 minutes or until softened.

3. Stir in roasted cauliflower, garam masala, 2 tsp (10 mL) salt and water; bring to a boil. Reduce heat and simmer, stirring occasionally, for 20 minutes or until cauliflower is very soft.

Store the cooled
soup in an airtight
container in the
refrigerator for up to
2 days or in the freezer
for up to 6 months.
Thaw overnight
in the refrigerator
or in the microwave
using the Defrost
function. Warm soup
in a medium saucepan
over medium-low heat.

4. Working in batches, transfer soup to food processor (or use immersion blender in pot) and purée until smooth. Return soup to pot (if necessary) and whisk in coconut milk and lime juice. Warm over medium heat, stirring, for 1 minute. Season to taste with salt and pepper.

5. Ladle soup into bowls and sprinkle with chives and coconut, if desired.

✳ Power Ingredient

Limes
Researchers have found that limes contain compounds that may work against carcinogenic cells. Specifically, the antioxidant flavonoid and limonoid content of lime juice may be capable of slowing or stopping the spread of some types of cancer cells. Though the exact mechanism is unknown, scientists have observed that antioxidant limonoids also cause cancer cell death. Lime limonoids destroy more free radicals than either green tea or dark chocolate.

Lemony Leek and Artichoke Soup

Leeks are a sublime soup component, swooning into velvety goodness as they break down.

Tip

When puréeing soup in a blender or food processor, fill the jug or bowl no more than halfway full at a time.

- Blender, food processor or immersion blender

1 tbsp	melted virgin coconut oil	15 mL
2	large leeks (white part only), chopped	2
2	cloves garlic, minced	2
1	yellow-fleshed potato (about 8 oz/ 250 g), peeled and chopped	1
1	package (8 oz/250 g) frozen artichokes	1
4 cups	ready-to-use gluten-free vegetable broth	1 L
1/2 cup	well-stirred coconut milk (full-fat)	125 mL
1 tbsp	freshly squeezed lemon juice	15 mL
	Fine sea salt and freshly ground pepper	

1. In a large saucepan, melt coconut oil over low heat. Add leeks, increase heat to medium–high and cook, stirring, for 5 to 6 minutes or until softened. Add garlic and cook, stirring, for 1 minute.

2. Stir in potato, artichokes and broth; bring to a boil. Reduce heat and simmer, stirring occasionally, for 15 to 20 minutes or until vegetables are tender.

3. Working in batches, transfer soup to blender (or use immersion blender in pan) and purée until smooth. Return soup to pan (if necessary) and whisk in coconut milk and lemon juice. Warm over medium heat, stirring, for 1 minute. Season to taste with salt and pepper.

Storage Tip

Store the cooled soup in an airtight container in the refrigerator for up to 2 days or in the freezer for up to 6 months. Thaw overnight in the refrigerator or in the microwave using the Defrost function. Warm soup in a medium saucepan over medium-low heat.

✳ Power Ingredient

Leeks

The humble leek has a long history. It has been cultivated since the time of the ancient Egyptians, and Hippocrates, the ancient Greek physician and the "father of medicine," prescribed it as a cure for nosebleeds. The Romans considered the leek a superior vegetable, and Emperor Nero ate so many he gained the nickname Porophagus (leek eater). The leek is also associated with the Welsh Saint David. During the Middle Ages, when Saint David was alive, the leek was seen as a healthy and virtuous plant. It was, to the Welsh, the original health food, high in fiber and good for purging the blood, keeping colds at bay and healing wounds. Indeed, leeks contain significant amounts of the flavonoid kaempferol, a compound that multiple studies suggest reduces the risk of developing chronic diseases, most notably cancer. Leeks also appear to support the cardiovascular system by protecting blood vessel linings. Leeks are an excellent source of vitamin A — which aids vision and supports the immune system — and bone-building vitamin K and manganese.

Cream of Wild Mushroom Soup

This is an ideal soup to perk yourself up during the midwinter doldrums, and not just because of the inviting flavor and velvety texture. In the absence of sunlight or supplements, eating mushrooms is a good way to up your vitamin D levels.

Tip

When puréeing soup in a blender or food processor, fill the jug or bowl no more than halfway full at a time.

Storage Tip

Store the cooled soup in an airtight container in the refrigerator for up to 2 days or in the freezer for up to 6 months. Thaw overnight in the refrigerator or in the microwave using the Defrost function. Warm soup in a medium saucepan over medium-low heat.

- Blender, food processor or immersion blender

1 oz	dried porcini mushrooms	30 g
1/3 cup	boiling water	75 mL
1 tbsp	virgin coconut oil	15 mL
1 1/2 cups	chopped onions	375 mL
2	cloves garlic, minced	2
1/4 tsp	ground nutmeg	1 mL
1 lb	mixed wild and/or cultivated mushrooms	500 g
4 cups	ready-to-use gluten-free vegetable broth	1 L
1/2 cup	well-stirred coconut milk (full-fat)	125 mL
	Fine sea salt and freshly cracked black pepper	
2 tbsp	minced fresh chives	30 mL

1. In a small cup, combine porcini mushrooms and boiling water. Let steep for 5 minutes.

2. Meanwhile, in a large saucepan, melt coconut oil over low heat. Add onions, increase heat to medium-high and cook, stirring, for 6 to 8 minutes or until softened. Add garlic and nutmeg; cook, stirring, for 1 minute. Add wild mushrooms and porcini mushrooms and their liquid; cook, stirring, for 5 to 6 minutes or until mushrooms are slightly softened.

3. Stir in broth and bring to a boil. Reduce heat and simmer, stirring occasionally, for 15 to 20 minutes or until mushrooms are very tender.

4. Working in batches, transfer soup to blender (or use immersion blender in pan) and purée until smooth. Return soup to pan (if necessary) and whisk in coconut milk. Warm over medium heat, stirring, for 1 minute. Season to taste with salt and pepper.

5. Ladle soup into bowls and sprinkle with chives.

Spiced Tomato Coconut Soup

This soup is wonderfully warming, and the spicy heat from the cayenne will wake up your taste buds.

Tip

When puréeing soup in a food processor or blender, fill the bowl or jug no more than halfway full at a time.

Storage Tip

Store the cooled soup in an airtight container in the refrigerator for up to 2 days or in the freezer for up to 6 months. Thaw overnight in the refrigerator or in the microwave using the Defrost function. Warm soup in a medium saucepan over medium-low heat.

- Food processor, blender or immersion blender

3 tbsp	virgin coconut oil	45 mL
2 cups	chopped onions	500 mL
2 tsp	ground cumin	10 mL
1½ tsp	ground coriander	7 mL
	Fine sea salt	
¼ tsp	cayenne pepper	1 mL
2	cans (each 28 oz/796 mL) whole tomatoes, with juice	2
6 cups	water	1.5 L
1⅓ cups	well-stirred coconut milk (full-fat)	325 mL
	Freshly ground black pepper	
	Lemon wedges	

1. In a large pot, melt coconut oil over low heat. Add onions, increase heat to medium-high and cook, stirring, for 5 to 6 minutes or until softened. Add cumin, coriander, 1 tsp (5 mL) salt and cayenne; cook, stirring, for 30 seconds.

2. Stir in tomatoes, breaking them up with the back of the spoon. Add water and bring to a boil. Reduce heat and simmer, stirring occasionally, for about 20 minutes to blend the flavors.

3. Working in batches, transfer soup to food processor (or use immersion blender in pot) and purée until smooth. Return soup to pot (if necessary) and whisk in coconut milk. Warm over medium heat, stirring, for 1 minute. Season to taste with salt and black pepper.

4. Ladle soup into bowls and serve with lemon wedges.

Spring Vegetable Soup with Coconut Broth

Don't thumb your nose at frozen peas — they are wonderfully tasty and nutritious, not to mention frugal, convenient and versatile.

4 cups	coconut water	1 L
2 tsp	finely grated lemon zest	10 mL
	Fine sea salt	
1 tsp	dried thyme	5 mL
1 lb	asparagus, trimmed and sliced diagonally into ¼-inch (1 cm) pieces, tips intact	500 g
1	zucchini, diced	1
¾ cup	frozen petite peas	175 mL
2 tbsp	minced fresh chives	30 mL
1 tbsp	freshly squeezed lemon juice	15 mL
	Freshly cracked black pepper	

1. In a large pot, combine coconut water, lemon zest, ¾ tsp (3 mL) salt and thyme. Bring to a boil over medium–high heat. Reduce heat to low, cover and simmer, stirring occasionally, for 15 minutes.

2. Stir in asparagus, zucchini and peas; simmer, uncovered, for 3 to 5 minutes or until vegetables are tender. Stir in chives and lemon juice. Season to taste with salt and pepper.

✻ Power Ingredient

Peas
Peas contain a unique assortment of health-protective phytonutrients. One of these, a polyphenol called coumestrol, has recently come to the forefront of research into stomach cancer protection. New research indicates that daily consumption of green peas, along with other legumes, may reduce the risk of stomach cancer. Peas also contain vitamin K, which activates osteocalcin, a protein needed to bind calcium to the bone matrix. Sugar snap peas, an accidental hybrid that occurred in the 1960s, are high in vitamin C and fiber.

Smoked Paprika Pumpkin Soup

Sipping this seductive, smoky soup is a delicious way to benefit your complexion. Pumpkin is an excellent source of vitamin E, an antioxidant that contributes to healthy skin. For even more vitamin E, be sure to add the garnish of green pumpkin seeds.

2	cans (each 15 oz/425 mL) pumpkin purée (not pie filling)	2
2 tbsp	coconut sugar	30 mL
2½ tsp	hot smoked paprika	12 mL
5 cups	ready-to-use gluten-free vegetable broth	1.25 L
1 cup	well-stirred coconut milk (full-fat)	250 mL
1½ tsp	cider vinegar	7 mL
	Fine sea salt and freshly cracked black pepper	
	Lightly salted roasted green pumpkin seeds (pepitas) (optional)	

1. In a large pot, combine pumpkin, coconut sugar, paprika and broth. Bring to a boil over medium-high heat. Reduce heat and simmer, stirring occasionally, for 20 minutes.

2. Reduce heat to low and whisk in coconut milk and vinegar. Simmer, stirring occasionally, for 5 minutes. Season to taste with salt and pepper.

3. Ladle soup into bowls and sprinkle with pumpkin seeds, if desired.

Sweet Potato Bisque with Cardamom

Coconut milk and jalapeño add sweetness and spice to this silky sweet potato soup, but it's the cardamom that really pulls all the flavors together.

Makes 6 servings

Tip

When puréeing the soup in a food processor or blender, fill the bowl or jug no more than halfway full at a time.

Storage Tip

Store the cooled soup in an airtight container in the refrigerator for up to 2 days or in the freezer for up to 6 months. Thaw overnight in the refrigerator or in the microwave using the Defrost function. Warm soup in a medium saucepan over medium-low heat.

- Food processor, blender or immersion blender

2 lbs	sweet potatoes, peeled and shredded	1 kg
1	small jalapeño pepper, seeded and chopped	1
¾ cup	chopped green onions, divided	175 mL
1¼ tsp	ground cardamom	6 mL
4 cups	ready-to-use gluten-free vegetable broth	1 L
1 cup	well-stirred coconut milk (full-fat)	250 mL
2 tsp	cider or white vinegar	10 mL
	Fine sea salt and freshly ground black pepper	

1. In a large saucepan, combine sweet potatoes, jalapeño, ½ cup (125 mL) green onions, cardamom and broth. Bring to a boil over medium-high heat. Reduce heat and simmer, stirring occasionally, for 25 to 30 minutes or until sweet potatoes are very soft.

2. Working in batches, transfer soup to food processor (or use immersion blender in pan) and purée until smooth. Return soup to pan (if necessary) and whisk in coconut milk and vinegar. Warm over medium heat, stirring, for 1 minute. Season to taste with salt and pepper.

3. Ladle soup into bowls and sprinkle with the remaining green onions.

Hot-and-Sour Coconut Soup

This riff on a favorite Thai soup tickles your taste buds with the hot-sour (as well as salty-sweet) combination of flavors for which Southeast Asian food is known.

Makes 4 servings

Tips

An equal amount of gluten-free soy sauce can be used in place of the liquid amino acids.

White or cremini mushrooms can be used in place of the shiitake mushrooms.

If you don't have fresh gingerroot on hand, you can use 1½ tsp (7 mL) ground ginger in its place.

Storage Tip

Store the cooled soup in an airtight container in the refrigerator for up to 2 days. Warm soup in a medium saucepan over medium-low heat.

1 tbsp	grated gingerroot	15 mL
1 tbsp	coconut sugar	15 mL
¾ tsp	freshly ground black pepper	3 mL
4 cups	coconut water	1 L
3 tbsp	liquid coconut amino acids	45 mL
8 oz	shiitake mushrooms, stems removed, caps sliced	250 g
1½ tbsp	potato starch	22 mL
2 tbsp	unseasoned rice vinegar or cider vinegar	30 mL
2	green onions, thinly sliced	2
1¼ cups	diced drained soft or firm tofu	300 mL

1. In a large pot, combine ginger, coconut sugar, pepper, coconut water and amino acids. Bring to a boil over medium–high heat. Stir in mushrooms. Reduce heat to low, cover and simmer, stirring occasionally, for 5 to 8 minutes or until mushrooms are tender.

2. In a small bowl, whisk together potato starch and vinegar. Stir into soup and simmer, stirring, until thickened, about 1 minute. Stir in green onions and tofu. Cover and let stand for 2 minutes or until tofu is warmed through. Serve immediately.

✳ Power Ingredient

Ginger
For thousands of years, ginger has been considered a healthy food, and recent research has borne this out. The main active compounds are terpenes and gingerols, which have anticancer properties and have been shown to destroy colon, ovarian and rectal cancer cells. Gingerols also have a powerful anti-inflammatory action, and ginger has been shown to improve pain and swelling in up to 75% of people with arthritis, as well as improving mobility. In addition, ginger may ease migraine tension and has long been used as a remedy for nausea and to aid digestion, relaxing the intestines and helping to eliminate flatulence.

Shirataki Coconut Pho

In this redesigned Vietnamese classic, shirataki noodles join meaty tofu, and coconut water gives the spicy broth a subtle undercurrent of sweetness.

Tips

Shirataki noodles — a grain-free, no-carb, super-low-calorie Japanese pasta made from the ground root of the konjac plant — are increasingly available in the refrigerator section of supermarkets and Asian markets. They have a slightly unpleasant smell and slimy texture when they are first removed from the package. Rinsing them in cold water for 1 minute resolves both issues.

An equal amount of gluten-free soy sauce can be used in place of the liquid amino acids.

Storage Tip

Prepare soup through step 2 and let cool. Store in an airtight container in the refrigerator for up to 2 days. Warm soup in a medium saucepan over medium-low heat. Continue with step 3.

1	package (8 oz/250 g) shirataki noodles	1
2 tbsp	finely grated gingerroot	30 mL
1 tbsp	coconut sugar	15 mL
6 cups	coconut water	1.5 L
3 tbsp	liquid coconut amino acids	45 mL
8 oz	drained firm or extra-firm tofu, cut into ½-inch (1 cm) cubes	250 g
2 tbsp	freshly squeezed lime juice	30 mL
1 cup	mung bean sprouts	250 mL
1 cup	packed fresh basil leaves, sliced	250 mL
½ cup	packed fresh cilantro leaves	125 mL
½ cup	chopped green onions	125 mL
¼ cup	unsweetened flaked or shredded coconut, toasted	60 mL
1	Thai red chile pepper, thinly sliced crosswise (optional)	1

1. In a mesh sieve, drain noodles. Rinse under cold water for 1 minute. Drain and set aside.

2. In a large saucepan, combine ginger, coconut sugar, coconut water and amino acids. Bring to a boil over medium–high heat. Add noodles and tofu; cook for 2 minutes to allow noodles and tofu to absorb flavors. Stir in lime juice.

3. Using tongs, divide noodles and tofu among four soup bowls. Ladle hot soup broth over top. Top with bean sprouts, basil, cilantro, green onions, coconut and chile (if using).

Masoor Dal Soup

Aromatic, lentil-based dal is often served as an accompaniment or side dish. Here, I've transformed it into a soul-satisfying soup that easily stands on its own.

Makes 8 servings

Tip

If you don't have an immersion blender, you can use a stand blender to blend the soup. At the end of step 3, transfer a batch of soup to the blender, filling no more than halfway, and purée until smooth. Return purée to pan. Continue to purée batches of soup until partially or entirely smooth.

Storage Tip

Store the cooled soup in an airtight container in the refrigerator for up to 2 days or in the freezer for up to 6 months. Thaw overnight in the refrigerator or in the microwave using the Defrost function. Warm soup in a medium saucepan over medium-low heat.

- Immersion blender (see tip, at left)

2 tbsp	virgin coconut oil	30 mL
2 cups	chopped onions	500 mL
1 cup	chopped carrots	250 mL
1 tbsp	medium or hot curry powder	15 mL
2 tsp	garam masala	10 mL
1 cup	dried red lentils, rinsed	250 mL
4 cups	ready-to-use gluten-free vegetable broth	1 L
1¼ cups	well-stirred coconut milk (full-fat)	300 mL
1 tbsp	freshly squeezed lime juice	15 mL
¼ cup	packed fresh mint or cilantro leaves, roughly chopped	60 mL
	Toasted unsweetened flaked or shredded coconut (optional)	

1. In a large saucepan, melt coconut oil over low heat. Add onions, increase heat to medium-high and cook, stirring, for 6 to 8 minutes or until softened. Add carrots, curry powder and garam masala; cook, stirring, for 1 minute.

2. Stir in lentils and broth; bring to a boil. Reduce heat to medium-low, cover, leaving lid ajar, and simmer, stirring occasionally, for 25 to 30 minutes or until lentils are falling apart. Using immersion blender, blend soup until partially or entirely smooth.

3. Stir in coconut milk and lime juice; simmer, stirring occasionally, for 3 to 4 minutes to blend the flavors. Stir in mint.

4. Ladle soup into bowls and sprinkle with coconut, if desired.

Hoppin' John Soup

Hoppin' John is a traditional dish in the American South, believed to predispose the eater to good fortune if eaten first thing in the New Year. Black-eyed peas pack this spicy soup with plenty of folate, while onions infuse it with vitamin C.

Tip

Two 14- to 19-oz (398 to 540 mL) cans of black-eyed peas, drained and rinsed, may be used in place of the frozen peas. Reduce the simmering time in step 2 to 20 minutes.

Storage Tip

Store the cooled soup in an airtight container in the refrigerator for up to 2 days or in the freezer for up to 6 months. Thaw overnight in the refrigerator or in the microwave using the Defrost function. Warm soup in a medium saucepan over medium-low heat.

- Food processor, blender or immersion blender

2 tbsp	virgin coconut oil	30 mL
1½ cups	chopped onions	375 mL
1	red bell pepper, chopped	1
¾ cup	chopped celery	175 mL
1 tsp	dried thyme	5 mL
1 tsp	hot smoked paprika	5 mL
½ tsp	fine sea salt	2 mL
2	packages (each 10 oz/300 g) frozen black-eyed peas	2
5 cups	water	1.25 L
1	can (10 oz/284 mL) diced tomatoes with chiles, with juice	1
⅔ cup	well-stirred coconut milk (full-fat)	150 mL
½ cup	chopped green onions	125 mL

1. In a large saucepan, melt coconut oil over low heat. Add onions, red pepper and celery; increase heat to medium–high and cook, stirring, for 6 to 8 minutes or until softened. Add thyme, paprika and salt; cook, stirring, for 30 seconds.

2. Stir in peas and water; bring to a boil. Reduce heat to low, cover and simmer, stirring occasionally, for 35 to 40 minutes or until peas are very tender. Stir in tomatoes.

3. Transfer 2 cups (500 mL) of the soup solids and ½ cup (125 mL) of the soup liquid to food processor and purée until smooth (or, using immersion blender in pan, pulse soup in three or four quick spurts to partially blend it, leaving it chunky). Return purée to pan (if necessary) and stir in coconut milk. Simmer, stirring, for 2 to 3 minutes to blend the flavors.

4. Ladle soup into bowls and sprinkle with green onions.

Black Bean Coconut Soup

Don't be fooled by the short ingredients list; this spicy soup has a surprisingly complex flavor (which becomes even more pronounced on day two).

Tip

If you only have sweet smoked paprika, add ⅛ tsp (0.5 mL) cayenne pepper.

Storage Tip

Store the cooled soup in an airtight container in the refrigerator for up to 2 days or in the freezer for up to 6 months. Thaw overnight in the refrigerator or in the microwave using the Defrost function. Warm soup in a medium saucepan over medium-low heat.

2	cans (each 14 to 19 oz/ 398 to 540 mL) black beans, drained and rinsed	2
1	can (10 oz/284 mL) diced tomatoes with chiles, with juice	1
1 tbsp	ground cumin	15 mL
1 tsp	chipotle chile powder or hot smoked paprika	5 mL
	Fine sea salt	
2 cups	coconut water	500 mL
2 tbsp	freshly squeezed lime juice, divided	30 mL
	Freshly ground black pepper	
½ cup	well-stirred coconut milk (full-fat)	125 mL

Suggested Accompaniments

Chopped green onions

Toasted unsweetened flaked or shredded coconut

1. In a medium saucepan, mash one can of beans. Add the remaining beans, tomatoes, cumin, chile powder, ¾ tsp (3 mL) salt and coconut water. Bring to a boil over medium–high heat. Reduce heat and simmer, stirring occasionally, for 25 to 30 minutes or until thickened. Stir in 1 tbsp (15 mL) lime juice and season to taste with salt and pepper.

2. In a small bowl, whisk together coconut milk and the remaining lime juice until blended. Season to taste with salt.

3. Ladle soup into bowls and drizzle with coconut milk mixture. Serve with any of the suggested accompaniments, as desired.

Persian Coconut Soup with Split Peas, Chickpeas and Herbs

In the depths of winter, there's nothing like the bewitching combination of coconut and lime to transport you mentally to an exotic (and warm!) locale. This soup, with its hearty mix of split peas and chickpeas offset by fresh green onions and pungent garlic, should do the trick.

Makes 6 servings

Tips
....

Dried yellow lentils or green split peas may be used in place of the yellow split peas.

Freshly squeezed lemon juice can be used in place of the lime juice.

To toast sesame seeds, place up to 3 tbsp (45 mL) seeds in a medium skillet set over medium heat. Cook, shaking the skillet, for 3 to 5 minutes or until seeds are fragrant. Let cool completely before use.

4 tbsp	virgin coconut oil, divided	60 mL
2 cups	chopped onions	500 mL
	Fine sea salt and freshly cracked black pepper	
2/3 cup	dried yellow split peas, rinsed	150 mL
5 cups	water	1.25 L
2	cans (each 14 to 15 oz/398 to 425 mL) chickpeas, drained and rinsed	2
1 cup	chopped green onions, divided	250 mL
2 tbsp	dried dillweed	30 mL
2 cups	well-stirred coconut milk (full-fat)	500 mL
3 tbsp	freshly squeezed lime juice	45 mL
3	cloves garlic, minced	3
1 tbsp	dried mint	15 mL
2 tbsp	toasted sesame seeds (see tip, at left)	30 mL

1. In a large saucepan, melt 1 tbsp (15 mL) coconut oil over low heat. Add onions, 1½ tsp (7 mL) salt and ¼ tsp (1 mL) pepper; increase heat to medium-high and cook, stirring, for 6 to 8 minutes or until onions are softened.

2. Stir in split peas and water; bring to a boil. Reduce heat to medium-low, cover and simmer, stirring occasionally, for 30 minutes. Add chickpeas, ½ cup (125 mL) green onions and dill; cook for 5 to 10 minutes or until split peas are falling apart.

3. Reduce heat to low and whisk in coconut milk. Simmer, stirring often, for 5 minutes to blend the flavors, thinning soup with water if it's too thick. Whisk in lime juice and season to taste with salt and pepper.

Store the cooled soup in an airtight container in the refrigerator for up to 2 days or in the freezer for up to 6 months. Thaw overnight in the refrigerator or in the microwave using the Defrost function. Warm soup in a medium saucepan over medium-low heat.

4. Meanwhile, in a small skillet, melt the remaining oil over medium heat. Add garlic, mint and a pinch of salt. Cook, stirring, for 1 to 2 minutes or until garlic is slightly softened.

5. Ladle soup into bowls, drizzle with garlic oil and sprinkle with sesame seeds and the remaining green onions.

✳ Power Ingredient

Split Peas

Split peas, like other legumes, are rich in soluble fiber, which forms a gel-like substance in the digestive tract that binds cholesterol-containing bile and carries it out of the body. Split peas also contain an isoflavone called daidzein, which acts like weak estrogen in the body. The consumption of daidzein has been linked to a reduced risk of certain health conditions, including breast and prostate cancer. Split peas are particularly rich in potassium, a mineral that can help lower blood pressure and control fluid retention, and may help limit the growth of potentially damaging plaques in the blood vessels.

Mushroom, Edamame and Bok Choy Soup

Lightly simmered bok choy, with its almost bitter leaves and sweet, succulent stems, offers a fine balance of flavor and texture in this easily assembled soup.

Tip

An equal amount of gluten-free soy sauce can be used in place of the liquid amino acids.

3	cloves garlic, minced	3
1½ cups	frozen shelled edamame	375 mL
1 tbsp	ground ginger	15 mL
7 cups	coconut water	1.75 L
2 tbsp	liquid coconut amino acids	30 mL
2 tbsp	unseasoned rice vinegar	30 mL
1 tbsp	toasted sesame oil	15 mL
1 lb	shiitake or white mushrooms, stems removed if necessary, sliced	500 g
6 cups	sliced bok choy	1.5 L
¾ cup	thinly sliced green onions	175 mL
	Fine sea salt and freshly ground black pepper	

1. In a large pot, combine garlic, edamame, ginger, coconut water, amino acids, vinegar and oil. Bring to a boil over medium–high heat. Reduce heat to low, cover and simmer for 10 minutes or until edamame are tender.

2. Stir in mushrooms and simmer, stirring occasionally, for 5 minutes or until mushrooms are tender.

3. Stir in bok choy and green onions; simmer for 3 to 4 minutes or until bok choy is wilted. Season to taste with salt and pepper.

Storage Tip

Store the cooled soup in an airtight container in the refrigerator for up to 2 days. Warm soup in a pot over medium-low heat.

✳ Power Ingredient

Shiitake Mushrooms

All mushrooms are healthful additions to your diet (see box, page 207), but shiitake mushrooms have several unique features that make them worth incorporating into your culinary repertoire. Shiitake mushrooms contain lentinan, a compound that makes our immune system strong, helping to fight off disease and infection. According to the American Cancer Society, lentinan may arrest or slow tumor growth as well, though they note that more clinical trials are needed to understand the mushrooms' efficacy. Shiitake mushrooms also contain a compound called D-eritadenine, which helps lower cholesterol and supports cardiovascular health.

Brazilian Black Bean Stew with Mango

There are lots of black bean soups and stews in the world, but this earthy, satisfying rendition has plenty of Brazilian flair and flavor — mango, cilantro, coconut and sweet potatoes — to make it a standout.

Tip

Regular diced tomatoes may be used in place of the tomatoes with chiles. You'll need about 2½ cups (625 mL) tomatoes with juice for this recipe.

Storage Tip

Store the cooled stew in an airtight container in the refrigerator for up to 2 days or in the freezer for up to 6 months. Thaw overnight in the refrigerator or in the microwave using the Defrost function. Warm stew in a medium saucepan over medium-low heat.

2 tbsp	virgin coconut oil	30 mL
1½ cups	chopped onions	375 mL
1	red bell pepper, chopped	1
4	cloves garlic, minced	4
3 cups	cubed peeled sweet potatoes (½-inch/1 cm cubes)	750 mL
1 tbsp	ground cumin	15 mL
¾ tsp	fine sea salt	3 mL
¼ tsp	cayenne pepper	1 mL
2	cans (each 14 to 19 oz/ 398 to 540 mL) black beans, drained and rinsed	2
2	cans (each 10 oz/284 mL) diced tomatoes with chiles, with juice	2
1½ cups	coconut water	375 mL
1	large ripe mango, diced	1
½ cup	packed fresh cilantro leaves, chopped	125 mL

1. In a large saucepan, melt coconut oil over low heat. Add onions and red pepper; increase heat to medium-high and cook, stirring, for 6 to 8 minutes or until softened. Add garlic, sweet potatoes, cumin, salt and cayenne; cook, stirring, for 2 minutes.

2. Stir in beans, tomatoes and coconut water; bring to a boil. Reduce heat to medium-low, cover, leaving lid ajar, and simmer, stirring occasionally, for 20 to 25 minutes or until sweet potatoes are very tender.

3. Stir in mango and cilantro; simmer, stirring occasionally, for 4 to 5 minutes or until mango is warmed through.

Mustard Green and Kidney Bean Stew

Here is a clear-cut example of a recipe whose sum is far greater than its parts. Bitter greens, sweet onions, creamy kidney beans and earthy cumin come together in one seriously satisfying stew.

Makes 4 servings

Tip

Two pounds (1 kg) of chopped trimmed fresh mustard greens may be used in place of the frozen greens. After adding the greens in step 2, boil, without stirring, for 4 to 5 minutes or until greens are wilted but not yet tender. Continue with step 2.

2 tbsp	virgin coconut oil	30 mL
2	large onions, quartered	2
2	cans (each 14 to 19 oz/ 398 to 540 mL) dark red kidney beans, drained and rinsed	2
2 tsp	ground cumin	10 mL
1 tsp	fine sea salt	5 mL
½ tsp	freshly cracked black pepper	2 mL
1 cup	coconut water	250 mL
2	packages (each 10 oz/300 g) frozen chopped mustard greens	2
1 tsp	red wine vinegar	5 mL

1. In a large pot, melt coconut oil over low heat. Add onions, increase heat to medium–high and cook, stirring occasionally and breaking onions up with spoon, for 8 to 10 minutes or until softened.

2. Stir in beans, cumin, salt, pepper and coconut water; bring to a boil and boil for 2 minutes. Add mustard greens and boil, without stirring, for 2 to 3 minutes or until greens are thawed. Stir to combine. Reduce heat to low, cover and simmer, stirring occasionally, for 10 to 15 minutes or until greens are tender.

Moroccan Sweet Potato, Butter Bean and Coconut Tagine

Butter beans are canned lima beans, and their name is indicative of their buttery taste and texture.

Tips

An equal amount of dark raisins, chopped dried apricots or chopped dates can be used in place of the golden raisins.

An equal amount of white beans (such as Great Northern or cannellini) can be used in place of the butter beans.

2 tbsp	virgin coconut oil	30 mL
1½ cups	chopped onions	375 mL
1	red bell pepper, chopped	1
3 cups	diced peeled sweet potatoes	750 mL
2	cloves garlic, minced	2
2 tsp	sweet smoked paprika	10 mL
1½ tsp	ground cumin	7 mL
1½ tsp	ground cinnamon	7 mL
2	cans (each 14 to 19 oz/ 398 to 540 mL) butter beans, drained and rinsed	2
½ cup	golden raisins	125 mL
1 tsp	fine sea salt	5 mL
2 cups	coconut water	500 mL
1 tsp	finely grated lemon zest	5 mL
2 tbsp	freshly squeezed lemon juice	30 mL
1 cup	well-stirred coconut milk (full-fat)	250 mL
¾ cup	packed fresh cilantro or flat-leaf (Italian) parsley leaves, chopped	175 mL
½ cup	unsweetened flaked or shredded coconut, toasted	125 mL

1. In a large saucepan, melt coconut oil over low heat. Add onions, red pepper and sweet potatoes; increase heat to medium–high and cook, stirring, for 6 to 8 minutes or until onions and red pepper are softened. Add garlic, paprika, cumin and cinnamon; cook, stirring occasionally, for 7 to 10 minutes or until sweet potatoes are beginning to soften.

Store the cooled tagine in an airtight container in the refrigerator for up to 2 days or in the freezer for up to 6 months. Thaw overnight in the refrigerator or in the microwave using the Defrost function. Warm the tagine in a medium saucepan over medium-low heat.

2. Stir in beans, raisins, salt, coconut water, lemon zest and lemon juice; bring to a boil. Reduce heat to medium-low, cover, leaving lid ajar, and simmer, stirring occasionally, for 10 minutes. Stir in coconut milk and simmer for 5 minutes.

3. Ladle tagine into bowls and sprinkle with cilantro and coconut.

✳ Power Ingredient

Sweet Potatoes

Sweet potatoes are renowned for their high levels of fiber, carotenoids (especially beta carotene), copper, manganese, potassium and vitamins C and E. But did you know that they also pack a solid punch of protein? Better still, research geneticists at the USDA Agricultural Research Service report that sweet potatoes contain a particularly high-quality protein, akin to that found in eggs.

High in cancer-fighting antioxidants, sweet potatoes also rank as a top food for combating chronic inflammation (a low-grade, persistent, body-wide inflammatory response triggered by numerous health conditions, including arthritis and long-term obesity) thanks to ample amounts of vitamin A, which the body synthesizes into anti-inflammatory retinoids. In addition, sweet potatoes are rich in vitamin B_6, potassium and a protein called dioscorin. This unique combination of nutrients has led researchers to pronounce sweet potatoes to be beneficial for lowering blood pressure and homocysteine levels, thereby reducing the risk of heart disease.

Zucchini and Petite Pea Tagine

Zucchini is like a sponge, soaking up any flavors in its company. This dish, with an undercurrent of coconut and Moroccan spices, is no exception.

Tip

Other varieties of tender squash, such as yellow crookneck or a small pattypan, may be used in place of the zucchini.

2 tbsp	virgin coconut oil	30 mL
2 cups	chopped onions	500 mL
2 tsp	ground coriander	10 mL
1 tsp	ground cinnamon	5 mL
3	small zucchini, diced	3
1	can (14 to 15 oz/ 398 to 425 mL) diced tomatoes, with juice	1
1	can (14 to 19 oz/398 to 540 mL) chickpeas, drained and rinsed	1
¼ cup	golden or dark raisins	60 mL
1 cup	coconut water	250 mL
1 cup	frozen petite peas, thawed	250 mL
	Cauliflower "Rice" (page 248)	
½ cup	packed fresh mint leaves, chopped	125 mL

1. In a large saucepan, melt coconut oil over low heat. Add onions, increase heat to medium-high and cook, stirring, for 6 to 8 minutes or until softened. Add coriander and cinnamon; cook, stirring, for 30 seconds.

2. Stir in zucchini, tomatoes, chickpeas, raisins and coconut water; bring to a boil. Reduce heat to medium-low, cover and simmer, stirring occasionally, for 10 minutes or until zucchini is tender. Stir in peas and simmer for 1 minute.

3. Serve over Cauliflower "Rice," sprinkled with mint.

Green Chile Chili

With its notes of garlic, cumin and cilantro playing off the gentle spice of jalapeño, this meatless chili combines the best parts of chili and soup.

Makes 8 servings

Storage Tip

Store the cooled chili in an airtight container in the refrigerator for up to 2 days or in the freezer for up to 6 months. Thaw overnight in the refrigerator or in the microwave using the Defrost function. Warm chili in a medium saucepan over medium-low heat.

- Food processor

2	cans (each 12 oz/340 mL) whole tomatillos, with juice	2
1	small jalapeño, seeds and ribs removed	1
1 tbsp	virgin coconut oil	15 mL
2 cups	chopped onions	500 mL
1	red bell pepper, chopped	1
4	cloves garlic, minced	4
1 tbsp	ground cumin	15 mL
1 ½ tsp	ground coriander	7 mL
1 cup	packed fresh cilantro leaves, chopped, divided	250 mL
3	cans (each 14 to 19 oz/ 398 to 540 mL) white beans (such as Great Northern or cannellini), drained and rinsed	3
1½ cups	coconut water or water	375 mL
1¼ cups	well-stirred coconut milk (full-fat)	300 mL
	Fine sea salt and freshly ground black pepper	
	Lime wedges (optional)	

1. In food processor, purée tomatillos and jalapeño. Set aside.

2. In a large pot, melt coconut oil over low heat. Add onions and red pepper; increase heat to medium-high and cook, stirring, for 6 to 8 minutes or until softened. Add garlic, cumin and coriander; cook, stirring, for 1 minute.

3. Stir in tomatillo purée, half the cilantro, beans and coconut water; bring to a boil. Reduce heat to medium-low, cover, leaving lid ajar, and simmer, stirring occasionally, for 15 minutes or until slightly thickened. Stir in coconut milk. Season to taste with salt and black pepper. Simmer for 4 to 5 minutes to blend the flavors.

4. Ladle chili into bowls and sprinkle with the remaining cilantro. Serve with lime wedges on the side, if desired.

Spicy Samosa Chili

Get all of the irresistible flavors of samosas without the dough or deep-frying.

Tip

Regular diced tomatoes may be used in place of the tomatoes with chiles. You'll need about 2½ cups (625 mL) tomatoes with juice for this recipe.

Storage Tip

Store the cooled chili in an airtight container in the refrigerator for up to 2 days or in the freezer for up to 6 months. Thaw overnight in the refrigerator or in the microwave using the Defrost function. Warm chili in a medium saucepan over medium-low heat.

2 tbsp	virgin coconut oil	30 mL
1½ cups	chopped onions	375 mL
1 cup	chopped carrots	250 mL
1 tbsp	medium or hot curry powder	15 mL
2½ tsp	garam masala	12 mL
1 tsp	fine sea salt	5 mL
1	yellow-fleshed potato (about 8 oz/250 g), peeled and cut into ½-inch (1 cm) dice	1
2	cans (each 14 to 19 oz/ 398 to 540 mL) chickpeas, drained and rinsed	2
2	cans (each 10 oz/284 mL) diced tomatoes with chiles, with juice	2
3 tbsp	tomato paste	45 mL
1½ cups	coconut water or water	375 mL
⅔ cup	well-stirred coconut milk (full-fat)	150 mL

Suggested Accompaniments

Fresh lime wedges

Chopped fresh mint or cilantro leaves

Toasted unsweetened flaked or shredded coconut

Plain coconut yogurt

Toasted green pumpkin seeds (pepitas)

1. In a large saucepan, melt coconut oil over low heat. Add onions and carrots; increase heat to medium-high and cook, stirring, for 6 to 8 minutes or until softened. Add curry powder, garam masala and salt; cook, stirring, for 1 minute.

2. Stir in potato, chickpeas, tomatoes, tomato paste and coconut water; bring to a boil. Reduce heat to medium-low, cover, leaving lid ajar, and simmer, stirring occasionally, for 20 to 25 minutes or until potato is tender and chili is slightly thickened. Stir in coconut milk and simmer for 1 minute.

3. Ladle chili into bowls and serve with any of the suggested accompaniments, as desired.

Main Dishes

Spiced Eggplant and Mushroom Ragù

The North African combination of cumin, coriander and cinnamon, and a splash of fresh lemon juice, play up the eggplant's meatiness and the coconut milk's richness.

Tip

The spaghetti squash can also be prepared in the oven. Preheat oven to 325°F (160°C) and lightly spray a small rimmed baking sheet with nonstick cooking spray (preferably olive oil). Cut squash in half lengthwise and remove seeds. Place squash, cut side down, on prepared baking sheet and bake for 35 to 40 minutes or until a knife is easily inserted. Let cool for 5 to 10 minutes, then scoop out pulp and continue with step 4.

3 tbsp	virgin coconut oil, divided	45 mL
1¼ cups	chopped onions	300 mL
1	large eggplant, peeled and coarsely chopped	1
12 oz	mushrooms, quartered	375 g
1½ tsp	ground cumin	7 mL
1 tsp	ground coriander	5 mL
½ tsp	ground cinnamon	2 mL
1	can (14 to 15 oz/ 398 to 425 mL) diced tomatoes, with juice	1
½ cup	well-stirred coconut milk (full-fat)	125 mL
	Fine sea salt	
½ cup	packed fresh cilantro leaves, chopped, divided	125 mL
2 tbsp	freshly squeezed lemon juice	30 mL
	Freshly ground black pepper	
1	spaghetti squash (about 2 lbs/1 kg)	1

1. In a large pot, melt 2 tbsp (30 mL) coconut oil over low heat. Add onions, increase heat to medium-high and cook, stirring, for 5 minutes or until starting to soften. Add eggplant, mushrooms, cumin, coriander and cinnamon; cook, stirring, for 5 minutes.

2. Stir in tomatoes, coconut milk and ½ tsp (2 mL) salt; reduce heat to low, cover and simmer, stirring occasionally, for 15 minutes. Stir in half the cilantro and the lemon juice; simmer, uncovered, stirring occasionally, for 5 minutes to heat through and blend the flavors. Season to taste with salt and pepper.

3. Meanwhile, pierce squash all over with a fork. Place on a paper towel in the microwave. Microwave on Medium-High (70%) for 13 to 15 minutes or until soft. Let cool for 5 to 10 minutes.

Tip
......

Coconut oil can be stored at room temperature, and it has the longest shelf life of any plant oil. The oil will fluctuate from liquid to solid; this is completely normal and does not affect the oil's quality.

4. Cut squash in half lengthwise, remove seeds and scoop out pulp. Transfer pulp to a bowl and, using a fork, rake into strands. Add the remaining coconut oil, tossing to coat. Season to taste with salt and pepper.

5. Divide squash among four plates and top with ragù and the remaining cilantro.

❋ Power Ingredient

Eggplant
Eggplant is one of the healthiest foods around. Low in calories and an excellent source of dietary fiber, eggplant may also help lower cholesterol levels. Eggplant is a very good source of potassium and vitamins B_1 and B_6, and a good source of folate, magnesium, copper, manganese and niacin. Recently, researchers have discovered that eggplant skin contains an anthocyanin flavonoid called nasunin, which is a potent antioxidant and free-radical scavenger that protects cell membranes from damage. Nasunin also helps move excess iron out of the body.

Swiss Chard and Cherry Tomato Casserole

The tangy sweetness of cherry tomatoes contrasts nicely with the grassy-fresh chard, while coconut milk gives a mellowness to the tofu.

Makes 4 servings

Tips

An equal amount of kale, spinach or red Swiss chard may be used in place of the regular Swiss chard.

An equal amount of diced fresh tomatoes or drained canned diced tomatoes can be used in place of the cherry tomatoes.

- Preheat oven to 400°F (200°C)
- 8-inch (20 cm) glass baking dish, greased with coconut oil

1 tbsp	virgin coconut oil	15 mL
1	large bunch Swiss chard, ribs removed, leaves thinly sliced crosswise (about 5 cups/1.25 L)	1
2	cloves garlic, minced	2
1 tsp	fine sea salt, divided	5 mL
1 lb	extra-firm or firm tofu, drained	500 g
¼ cup	nutritional yeast	60 mL
¼ cup	well-stirred coconut milk (full-fat)	60 mL
	Freshly cracked black pepper	
2 cups	cherry or grape tomatoes, halved	500 mL

1. In a large skillet, melt coconut oil over low heat. Add Swiss chard, increase heat to medium-high and cook, stirring, for 5 to 6 minutes or until wilted and tender. Add garlic and cook, stirring, for 1 minute. Remove from heat and press chard against side of pan with a wooden spoon to release juices. Drain and discard juices. Stir in ½ tsp (2 mL) salt. Let cool slightly.

2. Meanwhile, in a medium bowl, mash tofu with a fork until it resembles ricotta cheese. Stir in the remaining salt, nutritional yeast and coconut milk until well blended. Stir in chard mixture until combined. Season to taste with pepper.

3. Transfer tofu mixture to prepared baking dish. Scatter tomatoes evenly over top, then gently press down to smooth top.

4. Bake for 25 to 30 minutes or until casserole is firm and golden brown. Let cool for 15 minutes and serve warm, or let cool completely and serve at room temperature.

Tip

The casserole can be made in a muffin pan for perfectly portioned servings that are great for lunches, too. Grease a 6-cup muffin pan with coconut oil. Prepare the casserole as directed through step 2. Divide tofu mixture among prepared cups and sprinkle with tomatoes. Bake for 17 to 22 minutes or until firm and golden brown. Let cool as directed.

Storage Tip

Store the cooled casserole, covered with plastic wrap or foil, in the refrigerator for up to 2 days.

✳ Power Ingredient

Swiss Chard

Swiss chard is one of the most powerful anti-cancer foods thanks to its combination of nutrients and soluble fiber. For starters, it is an excellent source of vitamins C, E and K, chlorophyll, fiber and several minerals, including potassium, magnesium, iron and manganese. It is a good source of many other nutrients, including protein, vitamin B_6, calcium, thiamine, selenium, zinc, niacin and folate. Swiss chard is closely related to beets and shares the same high concentrations of betacyanins and betaxanthins. Swiss chard also contains antioxidant phenols and flavonols, which multiple research studies indicate may inhibit the growth of some types of cancer cells.

In addition, Swiss chard offers tremendous antioxidant protection in the form of phytonutrients known as carotenoids. Researchers point to three carotenoids in particular — beta carotene, lutein and zeaxanthin — that are abundant in chard and may help maintain eye health as well as reduce the risk of cataracts. Further support comes when the body converts beta carotene to vitamin A, which also helps promote healthy vision, boosts immunity and may even fight cancer. Swiss chard's high vitamin C content provides even more immune support. Vitamin E, another chard superstar, has shown anti-inflammatory effects and helps protect tissue from oxidation damage. And researchers note that the high level of vitamin K in Swiss chard is especially beneficial in the maintenance of bone health.

Potato Masala with Cinnamon and Cilantro

The distinctive, bold flavor of curry powder — an excellent multipurpose spice blend to keep on hand — enlivens the potatoes and coconut milk in this dish.

Tip

To toast coconut, preheat oven to 300°F (150°C). Spread coconut in a thin, even layer on an ungreased baking sheet. Bake for 15 to 20 minutes, stirring every 5 minutes, until golden brown and fragrant. Transfer to a plate and let cool completely.

2 tbsp	virgin coconut oil	30 mL
1½ cups	chopped onions	375 mL
2 tbsp	mild curry powder	30 mL
1¼ tsp	ground cinnamon	6 mL
¾ cup	well-stirred coconut milk (full-fat)	175 mL
2 lbs	yellow-fleshed potatoes (such as Yukon gold), peeled and cut into 1-inch (2.5 cm) cubes	1 kg
1¼ cups	coconut water	300 mL
1 tsp	fine sea salt	5 mL
1⅓ cups	frozen petite peas, thawed	325 mL
⅓ cup	unsweetened flaked coconut, toasted (see tip, at left)	75 mL
½ cup	packed fresh cilantro leaves, chopped	125 mL

1. In a large saucepan, melt coconut oil over low heat. Add onions, increase heat to medium–high and cook, stirring occasionally, for 5 to 6 minutes or until softened. Add curry powder and cinnamon; cook, stirring, for 30 seconds. Add coconut milk and cook, stirring, for 1 minute or until thickened.

2. Add potatoes, reduce heat and boil gently, stirring often, for 10 minutes or until potatoes are barely tender.

3. Stir in coconut water and salt, scraping up any brown bits from bottom of pan. Increase heat to medium–high and bring to a boil. Reduce heat to medium–low, cover and simmer, stirring occasionally, for 16 to 20 minutes or until potatoes are tender.

4. Stir in peas and simmer, uncovered, for 1 minute.

5. Serve sprinkled with toasted coconut and cilantro.

Green Thai Curry with Spinach and Sweet Potatoes

This grain-, gluten- and meat-free riff on Thai green curry tickles your taste buds with the hot-sour-salty-sweet foursome of flavors for which Southeast Asian food is known. Serve over Cauliflower "Rice" (page 248).

Serve over Cauliflower "Rice" (page 248).

Makes 4 servings

Tips
....

If you can only find a 19-oz (540 mL) can of chickpeas, use about three-quarters of the can (about 1½ cups/375 mL drained).

Most Thai curry pastes are naturally vegan and gluten-free. Still, read the label before purchase to be certain.

1 tbsp	virgin coconut oil	15 mL
1	large onion, thinly sliced	1
2 tbsp	Thai green curry paste	30 mL
2 lbs	sweet potatoes, peeled and cut into 1-inch (2.5 cm) chunks	1 kg
1½ cups	coconut water or water	375 mL
	Fine sea salt	
1	can (14 to 15 oz/398 to 425 mL) chickpeas, drained and rinsed	1
1	can (14 oz/398 mL) coconut milk (full-fat), well-stirred	1
8 cups	packed baby spinach (about 6 oz/175 g)	2 L
2 tbsp	freshly squeezed lime juice	30 mL
	Cayenne pepper	

1. In a large saucepan, melt coconut oil over low heat. Add onion, increase heat to medium–high and cook, stirring, for 6 to 8 minutes or until softened. Add curry paste and cook, stirring, for 30 seconds.

2. Stir in sweet potatoes, coconut water and 1 tsp (5 mL) salt; bring to a boil. Reduce heat and simmer, stirring occasionally, for 12 minutes.

3. Stir in chickpeas and coconut milk; reduce heat and simmer, stirring occasionally, for 3 to 7 minutes or until sweet potatoes are tender.

4. Stir in spinach and lime juice; simmer for 1 to 2 minutes or until spinach is wilted. Season to taste with salt and cayenne.

Coconut Squash Pizza

Hankering for a great pizza? Here's your recipe. In the crust, butternut squash bolsters the coconut flour and chickpea flour with great flavor and enough substance to support any and all of your favorite toppings.

Makes one 10-inch (25 cm) crust

Tip

......

An equal amount of pumpkin purée (not pie filling) or mashed cooked sweet potato can be used in place of the squash.

- Preheat oven to 400°F (200°C)
- Food processor
- Large pizza pan or baking sheet, greased with coconut oil

¾ cup	chickpea flour	175 mL
½ cup	coconut flour	125 mL
¼ cup	potato starch	60 mL
1 tbsp	gluten-free baking powder	15 mL
½ tsp	fine sea salt	2 mL
1 cup	canned butternut squash purée or thawed frozen winter squash purée	250 mL
1 tbsp	melted virgin coconut oil	15 mL

Suggested Toppings

Marinara sauce

Vegan basil pesto

Hummus

Shredded or grated vegan "cheese"

Vegan "Parmesan Cheese" (see recipe, opposite)

Chopped, thinly sliced or coarsely shredded vegetables (zucchini, red onion, carrots, broccoli, cauliflower)

Leftover grilled or roasted vegetables, coarsely chopped

Pitted ripe or brine-cured black olives, sliced or chopped

1. In food processor, combine chickpea flour, coconut flour, potato starch, baking powder and salt. Pulse to combine. Add squash and coconut oil; pulse until a cohesive dough forms.

2. Press out dough on prepared pan, pressing to a 10-inch (25 cm) circle. Top with any of the suggested toppings.

3. Bake in preheated oven for 20 to 25 minutes or until crust is set and golden brown at the edges.

Vegan "Parmesan Cheese"

Nutritional yeast sounds nothing like cheese, but tasting is believing: it has a distinctive, cheese-like flavor and is the secret ingredient in all kinds of vegan "cheese" sauces. Blending it with hemp hearts gives it the appearance and texture of Parmesan cheese, making it a fantastic option for sprinkling on everything from salads to soups to pizza.

Makes 1 cup (250 mL)

Tip

Consider adding ¼ tsp (1 mL) garlic powder and/or onion powder, and/or ½ tsp (2 mL) dried basil or dried Italian seasoning, for an instant flavor boost.

- Food processor

½ cup	nutritional yeast	125 mL
½ cup	hemp hearts or sunflower seeds	125 mL
¼ tsp	fine sea salt	1 mL

1. In food processor, combine yeast, hemp hearts and salt. Process until hemp hearts are finely ground and mixture has the texture of finely grated Parmesan cheese.
2. Store in an airtight container in the refrigerator for up to 2 months.

✳ Power Ingredient

Winter Squash
Winter squash varieties, such as acorn, butternut and delicata squash, have particularly high levels of carotenoids, which are antioxidants that the body can convert into vitamin A. A tremendous body of research supports the ability of these carotenoids to prevent free-radical damage to cells, as well as cancer.

✳ Power Ingredient

Butternut Squash
Butternut squash is teeming with vitamins and other goodies, including vitamin C, magnesium, vitamin A, fiber, folate, copper, vitamin B_{12}, potassium and phosphorus, not to mention high fiber and very few calories.

Roasted Vegetable Pizza

A chickpea flour crust cradles a bevy of vegetables that are spiffed up with salt, hot pepper flakes and a sprinkle of cheesy nutritional yeast.

Makes 6 servings

Tip

Consider the vegetables suggested here as a starting-off point; you can use an equal amount of your favorite vegetables, such as bell peppers, broccoli, fennel and mushrooms, in their place.

- Preheat oven to 450°F (230°C)
- Large roasting pan, lined with foil or parchment paper

	Farinata (page 102)	
1	small red onion, cut into 1-inch (2.5 cm) chunks	1
12 oz	cremini or button mushrooms, trimmed and thickly sliced	375 g
12 oz	asparagus, trimmed and cut into 1-inch (2.5 cm) pieces	375 g
¾ tsp	fine sea salt	3 mL
½ tsp	hot pepper flakes	2 mL
2 tbsp	melted virgin coconut oil	30 mL
2 cups	cherry or grape tomatoes	500 mL
2 tbsp	nutritional yeast (optional)	30 mL

1. Prepare Farinata according to recipe instructions (but do not cut into wedges).

2. In a large bowl, combine red onion, mushrooms, asparagus, salt, hot pepper flakes and coconut oil. Spread in a single layer in prepared roasting pan. Roast in preheated oven for 18 to 21 minutes, stirring occasionally, until mushrooms and onions begin to brown. Add tomatoes and roast for 7 to 10 minutes or until tomatoes begin to burst and shrivel.

3. Spoon vegetables on top of Farinata and sprinkle with nutritional yeast, if using. Cut into wedges and serve.

Lentils with Roasted Cauliflower, Green Olives and Currants

The caramelized nuttiness of roasted cauliflower, the briny bite of green olives and a hint of sweetness from dried currants are all anchored by the rustic flavor of lentils.

Makes 4 servings

Tip

An equal amount of chopped pitted brine-cured black olives (such as kalamata) may be used in place of the green olives.

- Preheat oven to 450°F (230°C)
- Large rimmed baking sheet, lined with parchment paper

1 cup	dried brown lentils, rinsed	250 mL
2 cups	coconut water	500 mL
	Fine sea salt and freshly ground black pepper	
6 cups	roughly chopped cauliflower florets (about 1 medium head)	1.5 L
2 tbsp	melted virgin coconut oil	30 mL
1 cup	packed fresh flat-leaf (Italian) parsley leaves, coarsely chopped	250 mL
1/3 cup	chopped pitted green olives	75 mL
1/4 cup	dried currants or chopped raisins	60 mL

1. In a large saucepan, combine lentils and coconut water. Bring to a boil over medium–high heat. Reduce heat and simmer, stirring occasionally, for 40 to 45 minutes or until very tender. Season to taste with salt and pepper.

2. Meanwhile, on prepared baking sheet, toss cauliflower with 1/4 tsp (1 mL) salt and coconut oil; spread out in a single layer. Roast in preheated oven for 20 to 25 minutes, stirring once or twice, until golden brown and tender.

3. To the cauliflower (still on baking sheet), add parsley, olives and currants, tossing to combine.

4. Divide lentils among shallow bowls and top with cauliflower mixture.

Broccoli Rabe Kootu

Kootu is a South Indian stew-like dish made with lentils and a host of different vegetables. Broccoli rabe stars in this version.

Tip

An equal amount of brown lentils can be used in place of the red lentils. Simmer the brown lentils for 35 to 40 minutes or until very tender.

2 tbsp	virgin coconut oil	30 mL
3 cups	chopped onions	750 mL
3	cloves garlic, minced	3
1 tbsp	garam masala	15 mL
	Fine sea salt	
⅔ cup	well-stirred coconut milk (full-fat)	150 mL
1 cup	dried red lentils, rinsed	250 mL
3 cups	water	750 mL
1 lb	broccoli rabe, trimmed and roughly chopped	500 g
1 tbsp	freshly squeezed lime juice	15 mL
	Freshly ground black pepper	

1. In a large pot, melt coconut oil over low heat. Add onions, garlic, garam masala and 1 tsp (5 mL) salt; increase heat to medium-low, cover and cook, stirring occasionally, for 20 minutes. Add coconut milk and cook, stirring, for 10 minutes or until onions are tender. Remove from heat.

2. In a medium saucepan, combine lentils and water. Bring to a boil over medium–high heat. Reduce heat and simmer for about 22 minutes or until very tender but not mushy. Drain and add to onion mixture.

3. Meanwhile, in a large pot of boiling salted water, cook broccoli rabe, stirring occasionally, for 3 to 4 minutes or until tender–crisp. Drain and add to onion mixture.

4. Place onion mixture over medium heat and cook, stirring, for 5 minutes to blend the flavors. Stir in lime juice and season to taste with salt and pepper.

Tips

The broccoli rabe can be replaced with 3 cups (750 mL) chopped broccoli florets.

An equal amount of freshly squeezed lemon juice can be used in place of the lime juice.

Variation

Spicy Cauliflower Kootu: Replace the broccoli rabe with 3 cups (750 mL) chopped cauliflower florets. Replace the garam masala with 2 tsp (10 mL) hot curry powder and 1 tsp (5 mL) ground ginger.

* Power Ingredient

Broccoli Rabe

Also known as rapini or broccoletti, broccoli rabe is a leafy green vegetable and a member of the Brassicaceae (mustard) family. It has a taste similar to mustard greens — nutty, slightly bitter and mildly pungent — and is a great source of the vitamins A, C and K and minerals such as potassium, calcium and iron. It is also a rich source of glucosinolates, which the body converts to cancer-fighting sulforaphanes and indoles.

Bell Peppers Stuffed with Mushrooms and Lentils

This riff on stuffed peppers will bowl you over with its depth of flavor and its incredible ease of preparation. The containers are as nutritious as the filling.

Makes 6 servings

Tip

If you can only find a 19-oz (540 mL) can of lentils, use about three-quarters of the can (about 1½ cups/375 mL drained).

- Preheat oven to 350°F (180°C)
- 13- by 9-inch (33 by 23 cm) glass baking dish

6	red or green bell peppers	6
2 tbsp	virgin coconut oil	30 mL
1 lb	cremini or button mushrooms, chopped	500 g
1 cup	packed fresh cilantro or flat-leaf (Italian) parsley leaves, chopped	250 mL
2 tsp	ground cumin	10 mL
1	can (14 to 15 oz/398 to 425 mL) lentils, rinsed and drained	1
1	can (14 to 15 oz/398 to 425 mL) fire-roasted tomatoes, with juice	1
⅓ cup	well-stirred coconut milk (full-fat)	75 mL
	Fine sea salt and freshly ground black pepper	
½ cup	unsweetened flaked coconut	125 mL

1. Cut ½ inch (1 cm) of each top off bell peppers, keeping stems intact; set tops aside. Pull out and discard seeds and membranes.

2. In a large skillet, melt coconut oil over low heat. Add mushrooms, increase heat to medium–high and cook, stirring, for 4 to 5 minutes or until tender. Add cilantro and cumin; cook, stirring, for 1 minute. Add lentils and tomatoes; cook, stirring, for 3 minutes. Stir in coconut milk and season to taste with salt and pepper.

3. Divide lentil mixture evenly among bell peppers. Top each with 2 tbsp (30 mL) coconut. Place stuffed peppers in baking dish, tucking tops beside peppers.

4. Bake in preheated oven for 25 to 30 minutes or until peppers are soft. Serve, replacing pepper tops on each stuffed pepper.

Tips

A can of beans, such as chickpeas, white beans or pinto beans, can be used in place of the lentils.

Regular diced tomatoes can be used in place of the fire-roasted tomatoes.

Variations

Mexican Stuffed Peppers: Replace the lentils with an equal-size can of black beans. Add 1 tsp (5 mL) chili powder with the cumin.

Italian White Bean Stuffed Peppers: Replace the lentils with an equal-size can of white beans. Use an equal amount of flat-leaf (Italian) parsley in place of the cilantro and replace the cumin with an equal amount of dried Italian seasoning. Replace the flaked coconut with ¼ cup (60 mL) Vegan "Parmesan Cheese" (page 193).

✳ Power Ingredient

Tomatoes

Tomatoes are one of the best sources of the carotenoid pigment lycopene, a compound that multiple studies suggest can help prevent a variety of cancers. Tomatoes are an exception to the rule that cooking food reduces or destroys valuable micronutrients: lycopene is better absorbed when it has been heated, either during processing or cooking, as the heat turns the molecule into more useful isomers. Tomatoes provide significant amounts of bone-strengthening vitamin K, and some research suggests that lycopene also supports bone health. Many studies link tomatoes with heart benefits, and although the mechanisms are not yet clear, the antioxidant vitamins C and E in tomatoes, along with lycopene, appear to slow down the processes that eventually cause heart disease.

Stuffed Poblano Chiles

Poblano chiles are a Latin American staple, and after savoring their mild, almost fruity heat in this easy supper, you may soon make them a regular feature in your own kitchen.

Makes 4 servings

Tips

If you can only find a 19-oz (540 mL) can of beans, use about three-quarters of the can (about 1½ cups/375 mL drained).

An equal amount of black or red beans can be used in place of the pinto beans.

- Preheat oven to 350°F (180°C)
- 9-inch (23 cm) square glass baking dish

⅔ cup	well-stirred coconut milk (full-fat)	150 mL
3 tbsp	nutritional yeast	45 mL
2 tbsp	freshly squeezed lime juice, divided	30 mL
	Fine sea salt	
2 tbsp	virgin coconut oil	30 mL
1	red bell pepper, chopped	1
2 tsp	ground cumin	10 mL
2½ tsp	Asian chile-garlic sauce	10 mL
1	can (14 to 15 oz/398 to 425 mL) pinto beans, drained, rinsed and coarsely mashed	1
½ cup	packed fresh cilantro leaves, chopped	125 mL
4	poblano chile peppers, cut in half lengthwise and seeded	4
2 cups	canned tomato purée	500 mL

1. In a small bowl, combine coconut milk, nutritional yeast and 1 tbsp (15 mL) lime juice. Season to taste with salt. Set aside.

2. In a large skillet, melt coconut oil over low heat. Add red pepper, cumin, ¾ tsp (3 mL) salt and chile–garlic sauce; increase heat to medium–high and cook, stirring, for 5 to 6 minutes or until pepper is slightly softened. Remove from heat and stir in beans, cilantro and the remaining lime juice.

If you do not have Asian chile-garlic sauce, you can use a combination of 2 cloves minced garlic and ¼ tsp (1 mL) cayenne pepper in its place.

Two cups (500 mL) mild salsa can be used in place of the tomato purée.

The filling for the poblanos can be prepared up to 24 hours in advance. Store it in an airtight container in the refrigerator, then proceed with steps 3 and 4 when ready to bake.

3. Place poblano halves, cut side up, in baking dish. Divide bean mixture evenly among poblano halves. Pour tomato purée into pan (do not pour on top of poblanos).

4. Cover and bake in preheated oven for 15 minutes. Spoon coconut milk mixture on top of poblanos. Bake, uncovered, for 15 to 20 minutes or until tomato purée is bubbling and poblanos are softened. Serve, spooning tomato purée over poblanos.

❋ Power Ingredient

Poblano Peppers

The long, slightly heart-shaped appearance of poblano peppers hints at their health benefits. Research suggests that poblano peppers may act as a thinning agent, improving heart health by helping to dissolve fibrin, an insoluble protein that builds up in your blood vessels and may cause blood clots.

Stuffed Portobellos

Woodsy, meaty portobello mushrooms make a substantial base for sumptuous spinach filling enlivened by sun-dried tomatoes and brine-cured olives.

Tip

Extra-large portobello mushrooms work best in this dish to accommodate the volume of filling. If they are unavailable, use 8 regular portobello mushrooms in their place.

- Preheat oven to 500°F (260°C)
- Large rimmed baking sheet, lined with foil and greased with coconut oil

4	extra-large portobello mushrooms	4
2 tbsp	melted virgin coconut oil, divided	30 mL
2 tsp	balsamic vinegar	10 mL
2 tbsp	coconut flour	30 mL
½ cup	coconut water or water	125 mL
6 cups	packed baby spinach, roughly torn (about 6 oz/175 g)	1.5 L
2 tbsp	nutritional yeast	30 mL
3 tbsp	chopped drained oil-packed sun-dried tomatoes	45 mL
3 tbsp	chopped pitted brine-cured black olives (such as kalamata)	45 mL
	Fine sea salt and freshly cracked black pepper	

1. Remove stems from mushrooms. Chop stems and set aside. Using a spoon, gently scoop out black gills on underside of mushroom caps. Discard gills. Place mushroom caps, hollow side down, on prepared baking sheet. Brush 1 tbsp (15 mL) oil and the vinegar over tops of mushrooms. Bake in preheated oven for 5 to 7 minutes or until tender.

2. Meanwhile, in a small bowl, combine coconut flour and coconut water; let stand for 5 minutes.

An equal amount of trimmed kale or Swiss chard can be used in place of the spinach.

If you do not like olives, omit them and increase the sun-dried tomatoes to 6 tbsp (90 mL).

3. In a large skillet, heat the remaining oil over low heat. Add spinach and mushroom stems, increase heat to medium-high and cook, stirring, for 1 to 2 minutes or until wilted. Add coconut flour mixture, nutritional yeast, sun-dried tomatoes and olives; cook, stirring, for 1 to 2 minutes to heat through and blend the flavors. Season to taste with salt and pepper.

4. Turn mushrooms over on baking sheet and fill caps with spinach mixture. Bake for 7 to 10 minutes or until filling is golden brown.

✳ Power Ingredient

Portobello Mushrooms
Portobello mushrooms are rich in a range of nutrients including selenium, B vitamins, copper and potassium, but one of its lesser known star nutrients is conjugated linolenic acid, or CLA. CLA benefits multiple mechanisms in the body, from boosting metabolism to increasing lean muscle tissue. Beyond its lean and trim functions, CLA has fascinating therapeutic uses as well. CLA lessens the production of estrogen, and is therefore protective against breast cancer. In addition, it reduces damage to the aorta of the heart, so it's protective against cardiovascular disease, and reduces inflammation in the body.

Caribbean-Spiced Stuffed Sweet Potatoes

Drawing inspiration from the Caribbean islands, this satisfying dish makes dinner easy, exotic and enticing in one fell swoop.

Makes 2 servings

Tip
......

If you can only find a 19-oz (540 mL) can of beans, use about three-quarters of the can (about 1½ cups/ 375 mL drained).

- Preheat oven to 425°F (220°C)
- Rimmed baking sheet

2	sweet potatoes (each about 12 oz/375 g)	2
1	can (14 to 15 oz/398 to 425 mL) black beans, drained and rinsed	1
1 tsp	Jamaican jerk seasoning	5 mL
½ cup	chunky chipotle salsa	125 mL
½ cup	well-stirred coconut milk (full-fat)	125 mL
1 tsp	freshly squeezed lime juice	5 mL
2 tbsp	packed fresh cilantro leaves, chopped	30 mL

1. Prick sweet potatoes all over with a fork and place on baking sheet. Bake in preheated oven for about 1 hour or until tender.

2. Meanwhile, in a medium saucepan, combine beans, jerk seasoning, salsa and coconut milk. Bring to a boil over medium-high heat. Reduce heat and simmer, stirring occasionally, for 5 to 10 minutes to blend the flavors. Stir in lime juice and cilantro.

3. Transfer sweet potatoes to dinner plates and let cool for 5 minutes. Slit each lengthwise, press to open, then spoon bean mixture into the center.

✳ Power Ingredient

Black Beans
Like many other legumes, black beans are a superb source of the cholesterol-lowering dietary fiber that benefits cardiovascular health. One cup (250 mL) supplies nearly three-quarters of the daily value for fiber. They also contain good amounts of iron, which helps to increase energy throughout the day. And their dark skin is indicative of their high level of antioxidants, particularly anthocyanins, which have been shown to improve brain function.

Acorn Squash with Coconut Chickpea Stuffing

This beautiful dish is loaded with protein, antioxidants and incredible flavor.

Tips

Delicata squash may be used in place of the acorn squash.

If you can only find a 19-oz (540 mL) can of chickpeas, use about three-quarters of the can (about 1½ cups/375 mL drained).

An equal amount of raisins, coarsely chopped, may be used in place of the currants.

- Preheat oven to 350°F (180°C)
- Large rimmed baking sheet

2	acorn squash (each about 1 lb/500 g), halved lengthwise and seeded	2
2 tbsp	melted virgin coconut oil, divided	30 mL
	Fine sea salt	
1	can (14 to 15 oz/398 to 425 mL) chickpeas, drained, rinsed and coarsely mashed	1
⅓ cup	dried currants	75 mL
½ cup	well-stirred coconut milk (full-fat)	125 mL
3 cups	packed baby spinach, roughly chopped	750 mL
¾ cup	unsweetened flaked coconut, toasted	175 mL
½ cup	packed fresh mint leaves, chopped	125 mL
1 tbsp	freshly squeezed lemon juice	15 mL
	Freshly cracked black pepper	

1. Lightly brush cut sides of squash with 1 tbsp (15 mL) coconut oil. Sprinkle with ½ tsp (2 mL) salt. Place cut side down on baking sheet. Bake in preheated oven for 40 to 45 minutes or until tender.

2. In a large skillet, melt the remaining oil over low heat. Add chickpeas, increase heat to medium-high and cook, stirring, for 4 to 5 minutes or until heated through. Add currants and coconut milk; cook, stirring, for 1 minute. Remove from heat and add spinach, coconut, mint and lemon juice, gently tossing to combine. Season to taste with salt and pepper.

3. Fill squash cavities with chickpea mixture.

Mushroom Shepherd's Pie

Taking inspiration from the shepherd's pie my mother made (and I loved) throughout my childhood, I developed this newfangled vegetarian "pie."

Makes 6 servings

Tip
......

If you can only find a 19-oz (540 mL) can of chickpeas, use about three-quarters of the can (about 1½ cups/ 375 mL drained).

- Preheat oven to 400°F (200°C)
- 8-cup (2 L) glass baking dish, greased with coconut oil

1½ lbs	sweet potatoes, peeled and cut into chunks	750 g
1 cup	well-stirred coconut milk (full-fat), divided	250 mL
1 tbsp	virgin coconut oil	15 mL
1½ cups	chopped onions	375 mL
1 lb	cremini or button mushrooms, halved (or quartered if large)	500 g
3	cloves garlic, minced	3
2 tsp	dried thyme	10 mL
1	can (14 to 15 oz/398 to 425 mL) diced tomatoes, drained	1
1	can (14 to 15 oz/398 to 425 mL) chickpeas, drained, rinsed and coarsely mashed	1
	Fine sea salt and freshly cracked black pepper	

1. Place sweet potatoes in a large pot of cold water and bring to a boil over medium-high heat. Boil for 15 to 20 minutes or until very tender. Drain. Return sweet potatoes to the pot, along with ½ cup (125 mL) coconut milk; mash until smooth. Season to taste with salt and pepper.

2. Meanwhile, in a large saucepan, melt coconut oil over low heat. Add onions, increase heat to medium-high and cook, stirring, for 5 minutes or until starting to brown. Add mushrooms, garlic and thyme; cook, stirring, for 5 minutes or until mushrooms release their liquid.

An equal amount of white beans (such as Great Northern or cannellini) can be used in place of the chickpeas.

An equal amount of crumbled dried rosemary can be used in place of the thyme.

3. Stir in tomatoes, chickpeas and the remaining coconut milk; bring to a boil. Reduce heat to low, cover and simmer, stirring occasionally, for 5 minutes. Remove from heat and season to taste with salt and pepper.

4. Spoon mushroom mixture into prepared baking dish. Spread mashed sweet potatoes on top.

5. Bake in preheated oven for 15 to 20 minutes or until heated through and topping is browned.

✳ Power Ingredient

Mushrooms

Fresh mushrooms have multiple health benefits. They are an excellent source of potassium, a mineral that helps lower elevated blood pressure and reduces the risk of stroke. They also provide 20% to 40% of the daily value of copper, a mineral that has cardio-protective properties. Mushrooms are the only vegetarian food source of vitamin D and are a good source of B vitamins, which provide energy by breaking down proteins, fats and carbohydrates, and play a key role in the nervous system. As if that is not enough, the beta glucans in mushrooms appear to boost immunity and help resistance against allergies, while the selenium and ergothioneine may help protect our cells from damage that causes chronic disease.

Recent research is shedding light on potential benefits that mushrooms can have for your skin. Thanks to their anti-inflammatory properties, mushrooms can help improve acne, rosacea and eczema. They are also rich in antioxidants that protect your skin against wrinkles and discoloration caused by environmental damage.

Okra and Black-Eyed Pea Jambalaya

This take on jambalaya — a traditional favorite from the Southern United States — is my idea of easy living.

Tips

If you can only find a 19-oz (540 mL) can of black-eyed peas, use about three-quarters of the can (about 1½ cups/375 mL drained).

A can of black or white beans can be used in place of the black-eyed peas.

2 tbsp	virgin coconut oil, divided	30 mL
1 lb	fresh or thawed frozen okra, trimmed and cut into ½-inch (1 cm) slices	500 g
	Fine sea salt and freshly ground black pepper	
1	large green bell pepper, chopped	1
1¼ cups	chopped onions	300 mL
4	cloves garlic, minced	4
2 tsp	dried thyme	10 mL
¼ tsp	cayenne pepper	1 mL
1	can (14 to 15 oz/398 to 425 mL) diced tomatoes, with juice	1
1	can (14 to 15 oz/398 to 425 mL) black-eyed peas, drained and rinsed	1
1 cup	packed fresh cilantro or flat-leaf (Italian) parsley leaves, chopped, divided	250 mL
½ cup	well-stirred coconut milk (full-fat)	125 mL
	Cauliflower "Rice" (page 248)	

1. In a large saucepan, melt half the coconut oil over low heat. Add okra, increase heat to medium–high and cook, stirring, for 12 to 15 minutes or until browned. Transfer to a plate and season to taste with salt and black pepper.

2. In the same pan, melt the remaining oil over low heat. Add green pepper and onions; increase heat to medium–high and cook, stirring, for 6 to 8 minutes or until softened. Add garlic, thyme and cayenne; cook, stirring, for 30 seconds.

A red bell pepper can be used in place of the green bell pepper.

The amount of cayenne pepper specified here adds a very subtle amount of heat; adjust (more or less) according to your preference.

For a lighter jambalaya, replace the coconut milk with an equal amount of coconut water.

3. Stir in tomatoes, peas, half the cilantro and coconut milk; reduce heat to medium-low, cover, leaving lid ajar, and simmer, stirring once or twice, for 10 minutes. Return okra to the pan and simmer for 3 minutes to heat through and blend the flavors. Season to taste with salt and pepper.

4. Serve over Cauliflower "Rice," sprinkled with the remaining cilantro.

✳ Power Ingredient

Black-Eyed Peas

Like other legumes, black-eyed peas are high in fiber and protein, as well as potassium, vitamin E and iron. Black-eyed peas also contain zinc, an essential trace mineral that has significant health benefits. The average adult needs only 8 to 11 milligrams of zinc per day, and you can find more than 3 milligrams in 1 cup (250 mL) of black-eyed peas. Zinc can help reduce the risk of macular degeneration and protect against night blindness, boosts the immune system and can help fight influenza and heal wounds. The zinc in black-eyed peas also has antioxidant properties, helping to protect your cells from free radicals, which contribute to several health problems and can speed up the aging process.

Split Pea Dal with Lime and Coconut

Distinctive flavors of India — cumin, curry powder, ginger and pepper — combine with velvety yellow split peas and creamy coconut milk in this sensational comfort-food dish. Fresh lime brightens the flavor of dish.

Makes 4 servings

Tip

An equal amount of red or yellow lentils may be used in place of the split peas. Reduce the cooking time to 20 to 25 minutes.

2 cups	dried yellow split peas, rinsed	500 mL
5 cups	water	1.25 L
2 tbsp	virgin coconut oil	30 mL
4	cloves garlic, minced	4
2 cups	chopped onions	500 mL
2 tbsp	curry powder	30 mL
1 tbsp	ground cumin	15 mL
1 tbsp	ground ginger	15 mL
¼ tsp	cayenne pepper	1 mL
	Fine sea salt	
1 cup	well-stirred coconut milk (full-fat)	250 mL
3 tbsp	freshly squeezed lime juice	45 mL
	Freshly ground black pepper	

Suggested Accompaniments

Coconut Flax Tortillas (page 100), warmed

Diced cucumber

Fresh cilantro leaves

1. In a medium saucepan, combine split peas and water. Bring to a boil over medium–high heat. Reduce heat to low, cover, leaving lid ajar, and simmer for 45 to 50 minutes or until split peas are tender. Remove from heat.

2. Meanwhile, in a large skillet, melt coconut oil over low heat. Add garlic, onions, curry powder, cumin, ginger and cayenne; increase heat to medium and cook, stirring, for 8 to 10 minutes or until onions are softened.

3. Stir in split peas and any remaining cooking liquid, 1 tsp (5 mL) salt and coconut milk; cook, stirring, for 5 to 8 minutes to blend the flavors. Remove from heat and stir in lime juice; season to taste with salt and pepper.

4. Serve with any of the suggested accompaniments, as desired.

Black-Eyed Pea Tacos with Pineapple Slaw

It is said that eating black-eyed peas on New Year's Day will bring good luck, but this legume is so versatile, delicious and nutritious, it's worth adding to your diet all year long.

Makes 4 servings

Tips

In place of fresh pineapple, you can use diced canned pineapple (canned in juice, not syrup) or thawed frozen pineapple.

If you can only find 19-oz (540 mL) cans of black-eyed peas, you will need about 1½ cans (about 3 cups/ 750 mL drained).

3 tbsp	virgin coconut oil, divided	45 mL
½ cup	unsweetened flaked coconut	125 mL
2 cups	shredded coleslaw mix (shredded cabbage and carrots)	500 mL
1 cup	diced fresh pineapple	250 mL
¼ cup	packed fresh mint leaves	60 mL
1 tbsp	freshly squeezed lime juice	15 mL
	Fine sea salt and freshly ground black pepper	
2	cans (14 to 15 oz/398 to 425 mL) black-eyed peas, drained and rinsed	2
1½ tsp	chipotle chile powder	7 mL
8	Coconut Flax Tortillas (page 100), warmed	8

1. In a large skillet, melt 2 tbsp (30 mL) coconut oil over low heat. Add coconut, increase heat to medium-high and cook, stirring, for 2 to 4 minutes or until coconut is golden brown.

2. Transfer coconut to a large bowl and add coleslaw mix, pineapple, mint and lime juice; toss to combine. Season to taste with salt and pepper. Set aside.

3. In the same skillet, melt the remaining oil over low heat. Add peas and chile powder; increase heat to medium-high and cook, stirring, for 2 to 3 minutes or until peas are warmed through.

4. Fill tortillas with peas and coleslaw mix.

Chipotle Black Bean Tacos

Long on flavor and short on preparation time, this superfast, superfood spin on a fast-food favorite provides ample amounts of lean protein, fiber and antioxidants, all with about 10 minutes of effort from start to finish.

Makes 4 servings

Tips
....

If you can only find 19-oz (540 mL) cans of beans, you will need about 1½ cans (about 3 cups/750 mL drained).

A can of pinto or white beans can be used in place of the black beans.

1 tbsp	virgin coconut oil	15 mL
2	cans (each 14 to 15 oz/ 398 to 425 mL) black beans, drained and rinsed	2
1¼ cups	chipotle salsa	300 mL
1 tsp	ground cumin	5 mL
½ cup	plain coconut yogurt (store-bought or see recipe, page 49)	125 mL
1 tbsp	freshly squeezed lime juice	15 mL
8	Coconut Flax Tortillas (page 100), warmed	8
2 cups	shredded coleslaw mix (shredded cabbage and carrots)	500 mL
½ cup	packed fresh cilantro leaves	125 mL

1. In a large skillet, melt coconut oil over low heat. Add beans and salsa, partially mashing beans with a fork. Increase heat to medium and cook, stirring, for 4 to 5 minutes or until heated through.

2. Meanwhile, in a small bowl, whisk together cumin, coconut yogurt and lime juice.

3. Fill tortillas with bean mixture, coleslaw mix, cilantro and dollops of lime yogurt.

✳ Power Ingredient

Cilantro
Cilantro has a reputation for being high on the list of healing herbs. In research studies, when cilantro was added to the diet of diabetic mice, it helped stimulate their secretion of insulin and lowered their blood sugar. The leaves contain the compound dodecenal, which tests show is twice as effective at killing salmonella bacteria as some antibiotics. In addition, eight other antibiotic compounds were isolated from the plant. Cilantro has also been shown to lower "bad" cholesterol and increase "good" cholesterol. It is a good source of several nutrients, including potassium and calcium, and contains high levels of lutein and zeaxanthin, which help protect our eyes and eyesight.

Black Bean Coconut Burgers

Black beans are a natural choice for vegan burgers because of their satisfying, meaty texture. They rival red meat burgers on multiple nutrition counts, too: both provide high amounts of protein, iron and other vitamins. However, while red meats are high in saturated fat, cholesterol and an array of potentially health-threatening additives, beans are full of heart-healthy fiber.

Makes 4 servings

Tips

If you can only find 19-oz (540 mL) cans of beans, you will need about 1½ cans (about 3 cups/750 mL drained).

The moisture content of canned beans can vary. If the patty mixture appears too wet, add a small amount of additional coconut flour; if too dry, add a small amount more coconut milk.

- Food processor

¼ cup	packed fresh cilantro leaves	60 mL
¼ cup	coconut flour	60 mL
3 tbsp	ground flax seeds (flaxseed meal)	45 mL
2 tsp	ground cumin	10 mL
1 tsp	dried oregano	5 mL
¼ tsp	cayenne pepper	1 mL
⅓ cup	well-stirred coconut milk (full-fat)	75 mL
2	cans (each 14 to 15 oz/ 398 to 425 mL) black beans, drained and rinsed, divided	2
1 tbsp	virgin coconut oil	15 mL

1. In food processor, combine cilantro, coconut flour, flax seeds, cumin, oregano, cayenne, coconut milk and half the beans; pulse until a chunky purée forms.

2. Transfer purée to a medium bowl and stir in the remaining beans. Form into four ¾-inch (2 cm) thick patties.

3. In a large skillet, melt coconut oil over low heat. Add patties, increase heat to medium and cook for 4 minutes. Turn patties over and cook for 3 to 5 minutes or until crispy on the outside and hot in the center.

Sunflower Seed Patties

A bite of these patties, fragrant with lemon zest and smoky with spices, is very comforting despite the modern assemblage of ingredients.

Makes 4 servings

Tips

If you can only find a 19-oz (540 mL) can of beans, use about three-quarters of the can (about 1½ cups/ 375 mL drained).

The moisture content of canned beans can vary. If the patty mixture appears too wet, add a small amount of additional coconut flour; if too dry, add a small amount more coconut water.

- Food processor

3	cloves garlic, coarsely chopped	3
1	can (14 to 15 oz/398 to 425 mL) red kidney beans, drained and rinsed	1
¾ cup	lightly salted roasted sunflower seeds	175 mL
½ cup	packed fresh Italian (flat-leaf) parsley leaves	125 mL
¼ cup	coconut flour	60 mL
2 tsp	finely grated lemon zest	10 mL
1 tsp	hot smoked paprika or chipotle chile powder	5 mL
½ tsp	fine sea salt	2 mL
½ cup	coconut water or water	125 mL
1 tbsp	virgin coconut oil	15 mL

1. In food processor, combine garlic, beans, sunflower seeds, parsley, coconut flour, lemon zest, paprika, salt and coconut water; pulse until blended but still chunky. Let stand for 5 minutes. Form into four ¾-inch (2 cm) thick patties.

2. In a large skillet, melt coconut oil over low heat. Add patties, increase heat to medium and cook for 4 minutes. Turn patties over and cook for 3 to 5 minutes or until crispy on the outside and hot in the center.

> ✳ **Power Ingredient**
>
> **Parsley**
> Parsley is rich in a flavonoid known as apigenin, which research indicates may reduce certain cancers, such as skin, breast and prostate cancer. The essential oils in parsley leaves may also help to suppress overstimulated immune responses, which makes parsley a crucial player in the fight against allergies, as well as autoimmune and persistent inflammatory disorders.

Butter Beans in Tapenade Coconut Broth

Creamy butter beans, enhanced with lemon and a briny olive and coconut broth, hold their own as the **star of this simple and slightly spicy supper.**

Tips

If you can only find a 19-oz (540 mL) can of beans, use about three-quarters of the can (about 1½ cups/ 375 mL drained).

A can of white beans can be used in place of the butter beans.

2	cloves garlic, thinly sliced	2
1	can (14 to 15 oz/398 to 425 mL) diced tomatoes with Italian seasonings, with juice	1
½ tsp	hot pepper flakes	2 mL
½ tsp	fine sea salt	2 mL
1⅓ cups	coconut water	325 mL
1	can (14 to 15 oz/398 to 425 mL) butter beans, drained and rinsed	1
⅓ cup	chopped pitted brine-cured black olives (such as kalamata)	75 mL
1 tsp	finely grated lemon zest	5 mL
1 tbsp	freshly squeezed lemon juice	15 mL
½ cup	packed fresh flat-leaf (Italian) parsley leaves, chopped	125 mL

1. In a large skillet, combine garlic, tomatoes, hot pepper flakes, salt and coconut water. Bring to a boil over medium-high heat. Reduce heat and simmer, stirring occasionally, for 2 minutes.

2. Add beans, reduce heat to low, cover and simmer for 7 to 8 minutes or until beans are heated through and flavors are blended. Stir in olives, lemon zest and lemon juice.

3. Serve sprinkled with parsley.

✳ Power Ingredient

Butter Beans
Butter beans' high levels of soluble fiber help absorb water in the stomach to form a gel that decreases the metabolism rate of the bean's carbohydrates, preventing blood sugar levels from rapidly spiking after a meal.

Great Northern Beans with Fennel and Orange

Fennel's flavorful charms shine in this bright mélange; eating the dish will make you glow.

Tips

If you can only find 19-oz (540 mL) cans of beans, you will need about 1½ cans (about 3 cups/750 mL drained).

An equal amount of canned chickpeas or lentils can be used in place of the white beans.

Dark raisins can be used in place of the golden raisins.

2 tbsp	virgin coconut oil	30 mL
2 cups	chopped fennel (about 1 large bulb), fronds reserved	500 mL
½ tsp	fine sea salt	2 mL
2	cans (14 to 15 oz/398 to 425 mL) Great Northern or other white beans, drained and rinsed	2
¼ cup	golden raisins, chopped	60 mL
1½ tsp	ground cumin	7 mL
2 tsp	finely grated orange zest	10 mL
½ cup	coconut water	125 mL
⅓ cup	green pumpkin seeds (pepitas), toasted	75 mL

1. In a large skillet, melt coconut oil over low heat. Add fennel and salt; increase heat to medium-high and cook, stirring, for 5 to 6 minutes or until fennel is tender-crisp.

2. Stir in beans, raisins, cumin, orange zest and coconut water; cook, stirring, for 5 to 6 minutes or until beans are heated through.

3. Chop enough of the reserved fennel fronds to measure ¼ cup (60 mL). Stir fennel fronds into beans.

4. Serve sprinkled with pumpkin seeds.

Tips

An equal amount of toasted sunflower seeds or hemp hearts can be used in place of the green pumpkin seeds.

Don't toss the long green stalks from the fennel bulb! They make wonderful flavor additions to soups, broths and stews. Leave the pieces large, so they are easy to fish out when the recipe is finished cooking (the stalks themselves are fairly tough).

Variation

Smoked Paprika Chickpeas with Fennel and Mint: Replace the white beans with an equal amount of chickpeas. Add 1½ tsp (7 mL) smoked paprika with the cumin. Add 2 tbsp (30 mL) chopped fresh mint with the pumpkin seeds.

✳ Power Ingredient

Green Pumpkin Seeds

Green pumpkin seeds, also called pepitas, are a nutritious snack. Even in small servings, they provide a significant amount of zinc and iron. Zinc is an antioxidant mineral that boosts the immune system and, for men, improves fertility and protects against prostate enlargement and cancer. Iron is important for healthy blood cells and energy levels. Their high iron and zinc content makes pumpkin seeds a particularly significant food for vegetarians. The seeds also contain sterols, which can help remove LDL ("bad") cholesterol from the body and inhibit the development of breast, colon and prostate cancer cells. In addition, pumpkin seeds contain omega-3 fats, vitamin E, folate and magnesium, all of which can help maintain heart health.

Edamame Shirataki Noodles

Shirataki noodles are made from the ground root of the konjac plant, which happens to be rich in glucomannan, a compound that works to fill you up so you don't feel hungry. Its secret is soluble fiber, which makes you feel full without being bloated.

Makes 4 servings

Tips

Shirataki noodles — a grain-free, no-carb, super-low-calorie Japanese pasta — are increasingly available in the refrigerator section of supermarkets and Asian markets. They have a slightly unpleasant smell and slimy texture when they are first removed from the package. Rinsing them in cold water for 1 minute resolves both issues.

An equal amount of gluten-free soy sauce can be used in place of the liquid amino acids.

8 oz	shirataki fettuccine noodles	250 g
1½ cups	frozen shelled edamame, thawed	375 mL
1¼ cups	coconut water	300 mL
2 tbsp	virgin coconut oil	30 mL
12 oz	button or cremini mushrooms, quartered	375 g
2 cups	shredded coleslaw mix (shredded cabbage and carrots)	500 mL
2 tsp	Asian chile-garlic sauce	10 mL
2 tsp	coconut sugar	10 mL
3 tbsp	liquid coconut amino acids	45 mL
2 tsp	rice vinegar	10 mL

1. Drain noodles and rinse under cold water for 1 minute. Drain and set aside.

2. In a large skillet, combine edamame and coconut water. Bring to a boil over medium-high heat. Boil for 5 to 6 minutes, stirring occasionally, until almost all of the liquid is absorbed and edamame are just tender. Transfer to a bowl.

3. In the same skillet, melt coconut oil over low heat. Add mushrooms, increase heat to medium-high and cook, stirring, for 5 to 6 minutes or until mushrooms release their liquid. Add coleslaw mix and chile-garlic sauce; cook, stirring, for 3 to 4 minutes or until coleslaw is softened.

4. In a small cup, combine coconut sugar, amino acids and vinegar. Add to skillet, along with noodles and edamame; toss gently to combine. Cook, stirring, for 3 to 4 minutes to blend the flavors.

Chimichurri Tempeh and Spaghetti Squash

Chimichurri, a quick blended sauce of olive oil, fresh herbs, acid (such as lemon juice or vinegar) and a touch of heat, is the national condiment of both Uruguay and Argentina.

Tips

The spaghetti squash can also be prepared in the oven. Preheat oven to 325°F (160°C) and lightly spray a small rimmed baking sheet with nonstick cooking spray (preferably olive oil). Cut squash in half lengthwise and remove seeds. Place squash, cut side down, on prepared baking sheet and bake for 35 to 40 minutes or until a knife is easily inserted. Let cool for 5 to 10 minutes, then scoop out pulp and continue with step 4.

An equal amount of cilantro leaves can be used in place of the parsley.

- Blender or food processor

1	spaghetti squash (about 2 lbs/1 kg)	1
2	cloves garlic	2
1 cup	packed fresh flat-leaf (Italian) parsley leaves	250 mL
1/4 tsp	hot pepper flakes	1 mL
4 tbsp	melted virgin coconut oil, divided	60 mL
2 tbsp	red wine vinegar	30 mL
	Fine sea salt and freshly ground black pepper	
1	red bell pepper, sliced	1
8 oz	gluten-free tempeh, cut into 1-inch (2.5 cm) cubes	250 g

1. Pierce squash all over with a fork. Place on a paper towel in the microwave. Microwave on Medium-High (70%) for 13 to 15 minutes or until soft. Let cool for 5 to 10 minutes.

2. Meanwhile, in blender, combine garlic, parsley, hot pepper flakes, 3 tbsp (45 mL) coconut oil and vinegar; purée until smooth. Season to taste with salt and black pepper.

3. In a large nonstick skillet, heat the remaining oil over low heat. Add red pepper, increase heat to medium-high and cook, stirring, for 5 minutes. Add tempeh and cook, stirring, for 1 to 2 minutes or until pepper is softened.

4. Cut squash in half, remove seeds and scoop out pulp. Transfer pulp to a bowl and, using a fork, rake into strands. Stir in half the chimichurri (parsley mixture).

5. Divide squash among four bowls and top with tempeh mixture. Drizzle with the remaining chimichurri.

Tempeh with Red Pepper and Coconut Harissa

Tempeh, made with fermented soybeans, is a great option for anyone who has difficulty digesting tofu and other plant-based proteins. The fermentation process greatly reduces the oligosaccharides that can make beans hard to digest and creates an enzyme that allows for increased absorption of minerals such as zinc, iron and calcium.

Makes 4 servings

Tip

For a less spicy dish, use an equal amount of sweet smoked paprika in place of the hot smoked paprika.

- Preheat broiler, with rack set 4 to 6 inches (10 to 15 cm) from the heat source
- Blender
- Broiler pan, greased with coconut oil

Red Pepper and Coconut Harissa

1	clove garlic	1
1	jar (8 oz/227 mL) roasted red bell peppers, drained	1
¾ tsp	hot smoked paprika	3 mL
½ tsp	ground cumin	2 mL
¼ tsp	ground coriander	1 mL
¼ cup	well-stirred coconut milk (full-fat)	60 mL
	Fine sea salt and freshly cracked black pepper	
1 tbsp	virgin coconut oil	15 mL
1 lb	gluten-free tempeh, cut into ½-inch (1 cm) strips	500 g

1. *Harrisa:* In blender, combine garlic, roasted peppers, paprika, cumin, coriander and coconut milk; purée until smooth. Season to taste with salt and pepper. Set aside.

2. In a large skillet, melt coconut oil over low heat. Add tempeh, increase heat to medium-high and cook, stirring, for 2 to 3 minutes or until browned.

3. Serve tempeh with harissa.

Coconut Za'atar Kale, Tempeh and "Rice"

Za'atar is a multipurpose Middle Eastern spice blend featuring thyme leaves, sesame seeds and sumac.

Tips

To toast sesame seeds, place up to 3 tbsp (45 mL) seeds in a medium skillet set over medium heat. Cook, shaking the skillet, for 3 to 5 minutes or until seeds are fragrant. Let cool completely before use.

Sumac is available at Middle Eastern grocers and from online spice purveyors. If you can't find it, omit it from the za'atar blend and increase the lemon juice in the tempeh mixture to 4 tsp (20 mL).

- Steamer basket

Coconut Za'atar

¼ cup	unsweetened flaked coconut, toasted	60 mL
2 tbsp	toasted sesame seeds (see tip, at left)	30 mL
1 tsp	minced fresh thyme	5 mL
1 tsp	ground sumac (see tip, at left)	5 mL
½ tsp	fine sea salt	2 mL

Sautéed Kale and Tempeh

1	large bunch kale, tough stems and center ribs removed, leaves very thinly sliced crosswise (about 6 cups/1.5 L)	1
2 tbsp	virgin coconut oil	30 mL
2	cloves garlic, minced	2
¼ tsp	hot pepper flakes	1 mL
8 oz	gluten-free tempeh, crumbled	250 g
1 tbsp	freshly squeezed lemon juice	15 mL

Cauliflower "Rice" (page 248)

1. *Coconut Za'atar:* In a small bowl, combine coconut, sesame seeds, thyme, sumac and salt.

2. *Kale and Tempeh:* Place kale in a steamer basket set over a large pot of boiling water. Cover and steam for 8 to 10 minutes or until tender.

3. In a large skillet, melt coconut oil over low heat. Add garlic and hot pepper flakes; cook, stirring, for 1 minute. Add tempeh and cook, stirring, for 2 minutes. Add kale, increase heat to medium and cook, stirring occasionally, for 2 to 3 minutes to blend the flavors. Remove from heat and stir in lemon juice.

4. Stir half the za'atar into Cauliflower "Rice." Divide among four shallow bowls or dinner plates and top with tempeh mixture. Sprinkle with the remaining za'atar.

Red Curry Tempeh with Pineapple

Thai curry paste, basil and lime give tempeh instant Southeast Asian bragging rights. Serve the curry over Cauliflower "Rice" (page 248) to soak up all of the wonderful sauce.

(page 248)

Makes 4 servings

Tip

Most Thai curry pastes are naturally vegan and gluten-free. Still, read the label before purchase to be certain.

1½ cups	well-stirred coconut milk (full-fat)	375 mL
1½ tbsp	Thai red curry paste	22 mL
1 tbsp	virgin coconut oil	15 mL
1 lb	gluten-free tempeh, cut into ½-inch (1 cm) strips	500 g
2 cups	diced pineapple or mango	500 mL
1 cup	packed fresh basil leaves, chopped	250 mL
1 tbsp	freshly squeezed lime juice	15 mL
	Fine sea salt and freshly ground black pepper	

1. In a small bowl, whisk together coconut milk and curry paste.

2. In a large skillet, melt coconut oil over low heat. Add tempeh, increase heat to medium-high and cook, stirring, for 2 to 3 minutes or until browned. Add coconut milk mixture and pineapple; cook, stirring, for 3 to 4 minutes or until heated through. Stir in basil and lime juice. Season to taste with salt and pepper.

✳ Power Ingredient

Basil
In addition to being a good source of vitamin A, the essential oils in basil leaves contain eugenol, which has an anti-inflammatory effect. A 2002 study by researchers at Purdue University revealed that basil contains a range of essential oils rich in phenolic compounds and a wide array of other natural products, including polyphenols, such as flavonoids and anthocyanins. The herb contains high quantities of (E)-beta caryophyllene (BCP), which may be useful in treating arthritis and inflammatory bowel diseases, according to research conducted at the Swiss Federal Institute of Technology.

Primavera Tofu and Peas

Studded with crisp snap peas and tender petite peas, this substantial tofu dish deserves its billing as a main course.

Makes 4 servings

Tip

One tsp (5 mL) dried tarragon may be used in place of the fresh tarragon.

1 lb	firm or extra-firm tofu, drained and crumbled	500 g
3 tbsp	nutritional yeast	45 mL
¼ cup	plain coconut yogurt (store-bought or see recipe, page 49)	60 mL
8 oz	sugar snap peas, strings removed	250 g
2 tbsp	virgin coconut oil	30 mL
1 cup	frozen petite peas, thawed	250 mL
1 tbsp	chopped fresh tarragon	15 mL
½ tsp	fine sea salt	2 mL
2 tsp	finely grated lemon zest	10 mL
2 tbsp	freshly squeezed lemon juice	30 mL

1. In a small bowl, combine tofu, nutritional yeast and coconut yogurt. Set aside.

2. In a large skillet of boiling water, cook sugar snap peas for 3 to 4 minutes or until tender-crisp. Drain.

3. In the same skillet, melt coconut oil over low heat. Add drained sugar snap peas, petite peas, tarragon and salt; increase heat to medium and cook, stirring, for 2 minutes. Add tofu mixture, lemon zest and lemon juice, gently tossing to combine. Cook, stirring gently, for 2 to 4 minutes or until heated through.

> **✻ Power Ingredient**
>
> *Citrus Zest*
> The oils in the peels of citrus fruits contain powerful compounds that stimulate the body's production of a detoxifying enzyme. The peel also contains more than four times as much fiber as the fruit inside, and more tangeretin and nobiletin — flavonoids with anticancer, antidiabetic and anti-inflammatory properties. A 2004 study on animals suggests that these nutrients may even reduce harmful LDL cholesterol better than some prescription drugs.

Red Lentil Tofu Frittata

A wedge of this hearty frittata — a riff on the egg-filled classic — is clean and bright with flavor, yet still hearty enough to make a satisfying meal.

Makes 6 servings

Tip

......

An equal amount of brown lentils can be used in place of the red lentils. Simmer the brown lentils for 35 to 40 minutes or until very tender.

- 9-inch (23 cm) glass baking dish, greased with coconut oil

½ cup	dried red lentils, rinsed	125 mL
2 cups	water	500 mL
1 lb	extra-firm or firm tofu, drained	500 g
2	cloves garlic, minced	2
3 tbsp	coconut flour	45 mL
1 tbsp	ground cumin	15 mL
¾ tsp	fine sea salt	3 mL
¼ tsp	freshly cracked black pepper	1 mL
½ cup	well-stirred coconut milk (full-fat)	125 mL
1 cup	chopped drained roasted red bell peppers	250 mL
½ cup	packed fresh cilantro or flat-leaf (Italian) parsley leaves, chopped	125 mL

1. In a medium saucepan, combine lentils and water. Bring to a boil over medium-high heat. Reduce heat and simmer for about 20 to 25 minutes or until lentils are very tender but not mushy. Drain and let cool slightly.

2. Preheat oven to 400°F (200°C).

3. Meanwhile, in a medium bowl, mash tofu with a fork until it resembles ricotta cheese. Stir in garlic, coconut flour, cumin, salt, pepper and coconut milk. Add lentils, roasted peppers and cilantro, stirring until combined.

4. Transfer tofu mixture to prepared baking dish, pressing down firmly to smooth top.

5. Bake for 25 to 30 minutes or until firm and golden brown. Let cool slightly and serve warm or let cool completely.

Store leftover frittata in an airtight container in the refrigerator for up to 2 days.

Variation

Mediterranean Red Lentil Tofu Frittata: Replace the cumin with 1 tsp (5 mL) dried oregano and use parsley rather than cilantro.

✳ Power Ingredient

Lentils
Lentils pack a one-two punch of protein and fiber. A large body of clinical evidence indicates that their high levels of fiber may help reduce cholesterol levels and maintain blood sugar. Lentils are also rich in folate. In fact, they contain more of this important B vitamin than any other unfortified plant food. In addition to protecting against coronary artery disease by lowering levels of homocysteine in the blood, folate helps prevent birth defects. And folate coupled with vitamin B_6 (also plentiful in lentils) may help reduce women's risk of developing breast cancer.

Japanese Ginger "Noodle" Bowls

This aromatic one-bowl dinner features a classic combination of Japanese flavors, but the spicy, ginger-infused sauce is what sets the dish apart.

Makes 4 servings

Tips

The spaghetti squash can also be prepared in the oven. Preheat oven to 325°F (160°C) and lightly spray a small rimmed baking sheet with nonstick cooking spray (preferably olive oil). Cut squash in half lengthwise and remove seeds. Place squash, cut side down, on prepared baking sheet and bake for 35 to 40 minutes or until a knife is easily inserted. Let cool for 5 to 10 minutes, then scoop out pulp and continue with step 3.

An equal amount of gluten-free soy sauce can be used in place of the liquid amino acids.

1	spaghetti squash (about 2 lbs/1 kg)	1
2 tbsp	minced gingerroot	30 mL
1 tbsp	coconut sugar	15 mL
1½ cups	coconut water	375 mL
¼ cup	liquid coconut amino acids	60 mL
2 tsp	Asian chile-garlic sauce	10 mL
2 cups	thinly sliced onions	500 mL
8 oz	firm or extra-firm tofu, cut into ½-inch (1 cm) cubes	250 g
1 tbsp	virgin coconut oil	15 mL
	Fine sea salt and freshly ground black pepper	
¼ cup	thinly sliced green onions	60 mL

1. Pierce squash all over with a fork. Place on a paper towel in the microwave. Microwave on Medium-High (70%) for 13 to 15 minutes or until soft. Let cool for 5 to 10 minutes.

2. Meanwhile, in a small saucepan, whisk together ginger, coconut sugar, coconut water, amino acids and chile-garlic sauce. Bring to a boil over medium-high heat. Add onions, reduce heat and simmer, stirring occasionally, for 5 to 7 minutes or until softened. Add tofu and cook, stirring, for 1 to 2 minutes or until heated through.

3. Cut squash in half, remove seeds and scoop out pulp. Transfer pulp to a bowl and, using a fork, rake into strands. Add coconut oil and toss to coat. Season to taste with salt and pepper.

4. Divide squash among four bowls and top with tofu mixture. Sprinkle with green onions.

Side Dishes

Roasted Vegetables

Tips for Perfect Roasted Vegetables

1. Roast in a very hot oven (450°F/230°C). The vegetables cook quickly — many take only 10 to 20 minutes — but still have a chance to brown nicely on the outside by the time they become tender inside.

2. Cut evenly. It's very important to cut the vegetables into pieces of about the same size. Unevenly sized pieces won't roast and brown in the same amount of time, and you'll end up with both over-roasted and under-roasted vegetables.

3. Line the pan. To prevent sticking, line a large rimmed baking sheet or roasting pan with foil; otherwise, when you have to pry stuck vegetables off the baking sheet, all of the delicious caramelization gets left behind on the pan.

4. Toss with coconut oil and sea salt. Use 1 tbsp (15 mL) melted coconut oil and ¼ tsp (1 mL) fine sea salt for every 1 lb (500 g) of vegetables.

5. Spread in a single layer, with lots of room. Spread the vegetables in a single layer so that they are not touching. If they're crowded in the pan, they will steam rather than roast.

6. Gently toss halfway through roasting. For even browning, use a pancake turner or spatula to gently toss or turn the vegetables over halfway through the roasting time

Vegetable	Preparation	Roasting Time at 450°F (230°C)
Asparagus	Trimmed	10 to 15 minutes
Beets, tops trimmed off	Whole, unpeeled, pricked with a fork, then peeled after roasting	1 hour
Bell peppers	1-inch (2.5 cm) wide strips	10 to 12 minutes
Broccoli	Stems trimmed, peeled and sliced into $\frac{1}{4}$-inch (0.5 cm) rounds; florets split into $1\frac{1}{2}$-inch (4 cm) pieces	12 to 15 minutes
Brussels sprouts	Trimmed and quartered lengthwise	20 to 25 minutes
Butternut squash	Peeled and cut into 1-inch (2.5 cm) pieces	20 to 25 minutes
Carrots	Cut into 1-inch (2.5 cm) pieces	30 to 40 minutes
Cauliflower	Cut into $1\frac{1}{2}$-inch (3.5 cm) florets	20 to 30 minutes
Eggplant	Cut into $\frac{1}{2}$-inch (1 cm) thick slices	20 to 25 minutes
Fennel	Trimmed and each bulb cut into 12 wedges	35 to 40 minutes
Green beans	Trimmed	20 to 30 minutes
Onions	Each onion cut into 12 wedges	20 to 30 minutes
Potatoes	Peeled and cut into $1\frac{1}{2}$-inch (4 cm) pieces	35 to 40 minutes
Sweet potatoes	Peeled and cut into $1\frac{1}{2}$-inch (4 cm) pieces	30 to 35 minutes
Turnips	Peeled and each cut into 6 wedges	45 to 50 minutes
Zucchini	Trimmed and cut in half crosswise, then each half quartered	15 to 20 minutes

Olive Orange Asparagus

Orange zest provides bright notes of citrus flavor in this elegant version of steamed asparagus —an easy way to add more zest to your life!

Makes 4 servings

Tip
......

In place of the tapenade, you can use 2 tsp (10 mL) finely chopped briny olives (such as kalamata) plus 1/2 tsp (1 mL) minced garlic.

- Steamer basket

1½ lbs	asparagus, trimmed	750 g
1½ tbsp	virgin coconut oil	22 mL
2 tsp	prepared black olive tapenade	10 mL
1 tsp	finely grated orange zest	10 mL
2 tbsp	freshly squeezed orange juice	30 mL

1. Place asparagus in a steamer basket set over a large pot of boiling water. Cover and steam for 3 to 5 minutes or until tender. Remove with tongs and pat dry with paper towels.

2. In a large skillet, melt coconut oil over low heat. Add tapenade and orange zest; cook, stirring, for 30 seconds. Add asparagus and orange juice, tossing to coat. Cook, stirring, for 2 to 3 minutes or until asparagus is heated through.

> **✳ Power Ingredient**
>
> *Olives*
> If you think olives are merely flavor accents, think again. Olives are mostly fat, but 75% of the fat is oleic acid, a monounsaturated fat that research indicates may lower blood cholesterol levels, promote the development of bones and marrow, help maintain balance in the metabolism and fight oxidization, which lies at the root of many serious diseases. Olives are also a good source of vitamin E and other beneficial phytonutrient compounds, including polyphenols and flavonoids, which appear to have significant anti-inflammatory properties and can delay aging and assist in the restoration of body tissues.

Coconut-Braised Baby Bok Choy

Staggeringly simple, and versatile enough to go with a broad range of dishes, this flavorful, vibrant side is destined to become one of your go-to dishes.

Tip
......

An equal amount of regular bok choy, trimmed and sliced crosswise, may be used in place of the baby bok choy.

2	cloves garlic, minced	2
1/8 tsp	hot pepper flakes	0.5 mL
1 1/2 cups	coconut water	375 mL
1 1/2 lbs	baby bok choy, trimmed	750 g
1/4 tsp	freshly ground black pepper	1 mL
1 tbsp	virgin coconut oil	15 mL

1. In a large skillet, combine garlic, hot pepper flakes and coconut water. Bring to a simmer over medium-high heat. Arrange bok choy evenly in skillet. Reduce heat to medium-low, cover and simmer for about 5 minutes or until tender. Using tongs, transfer bok choy to a serving dish, cover and keep warm.

2. Increase heat to medium-high and boil broth mixture until reduced to about 1/4 cup (60 mL). Stir in black pepper and coconut oil. Pour over bok choy.

Steamed Broccoli with Tahini Coconut Sauce

This easy side dish is as packed with nutrition as it is with flavor. The broccoli is chock full of beta carotene — a powerful antioxidant that the body converts to vitamin A — while tahini is high in vitamin E and vitamins B_1, B_2, B_3, B_5 and B_{15}.

Makes 6 servings

Tips

This simple tahini dressing can be used as a multipurpose salad and vegetable dressing.

An equal amount of cider vinegar may be used in place of the lemon juice.

- Steamer basket

1½ lbs	broccoli (about 1 large bunch), tough stems trimmed off	750 g
1	clove garlic, minced	1
¼ cup	tahini	60 mL
¼ cup	well-stirred coconut milk (full-fat)	60 mL
1 tbsp	freshly squeezed lemon juice	15 mL
	Fine sea salt and freshly cracked black pepper	

1. Cut broccoli into small florets. Use a vegetable peeler to peel the stem, then cut the stem crosswise into ¼-inch (0.5 cm) thick slices. Place in a steamer basket set over a large pot of boiling water. Cover and steam for 5 to 7 minutes or until tender. Transfer to a serving dish.

2. In a small bowl, whisk together garlic, tahini, coconut milk and lemon juice. Season to taste with salt and pepper. Drizzle over broccoli.

✻ Power Ingredient

Broccoli

Broccoli has an abundance of sulforaphanes, which work to support optimum health and protect against disease. It also has an enzyme called myrosinase, which can reduce the risk of developing cancer. However, overcooking broccoli can undermine the beneficial effects of myrosinase, according to researchers at the University of Illinois. Therefore, to really get the most out of this vegetable, eat it raw or lightly steamed.

Chipotle Black Bean Tacos (page 212)

Japanese Ginger "Noodle" Bowls (page 226)

Coconut-Braised Baby Bok Choy (page 231)

Coconut Shortbread (page 254), Jam Thumbprints (page 260)
and No-Bake Hemp Brownie Bites (page 274)

Raspberry Crumble Bars (page 270)

Carrot Cupcakes with Whipped Lemon Coconut Cream (page 280)

Coconut Cream Pie (page 286)

Strawberry Coconut Mousse (page 298)

Shredded Brussels Sprouts Sauté

Miniature royalty of the cruciferous clan, Brussels sprouts strut their stuff in this modern side dish. Crunchy and slightly sweet when cooked quickly, the sprouts are an important part of the vegetable defense against cancer. They are also rich in calcium, folate and fiber.

Tip
......

When selecting Brussels sprouts, pick bright green, evenly shaped, firm heads that feel heavy for their size. Avoid sprouts that feel puffy or somewhat spongy, and any with black spotting or yellow leaves.

1 lb	Brussels sprouts	500 g
2 tbsp	virgin coconut oil	30 mL
½ cup	chopped green onions	125 mL
2 tsp	freshly squeezed lime juice	10 mL
	Fine sea salt and freshly cracked black pepper	

1. Trim ends off Brussels sprouts. Cut sprouts in half and thinly slice lengthwise.

2. In a large skillet, melt coconut oil over low heat. Add Brussels sprouts and green onions; increase heat to medium–high and cook, stirring, for 7 to 8 minutes or until softened but still bright green. Remove from heat and stir in lime juice. Season to taste with salt and pepper.

Carrot Fritters with Minted Yogurt Sauce

These carrot fritters are great on their own, but are positively addictive with the accompanying minted yogurt sauce.

Tips

An equal amount of ground cumin or curry powder can be used in place of the garam masala.

Cilantro, basil or parsley leaves can be used in place of the mint.

The coconut yogurt can be replaced with ⅔ cup (150 mL) well-stirred coconut milk (full-fat) whisked with 1 tbsp (15 mL) lemon juice.

- Preheat oven to 200°F (100°C)
- Small rimmed baking sheet

¼ cup	packed fresh mint leaves, chopped	60 mL
¾ tsp	fine sea salt, divided	3 mL
¾ cup	plain coconut yogurt (store-bought or see recipe, page 49), divided	175 mL
3 tbsp	chickpea flour	45 mL
2 tbsp	coconut flour	30 mL
1½ tsp	garam masala	7 mL
¼ tsp	gluten-free baking powder	1 mL
½ cup	water	125 mL
2 cups	finely shredded carrots	500 mL
1 cup	chopped green onions	250 mL
2 tbsp	virgin coconut oil, divided	30 mL

1. In a small bowl, whisk together mint, a pinch of salt and ½ cup (125 mL) yogurt. Refrigerate until ready to use.

2. In a large bowl, whisk together chickpea flour, coconut flour, garam masala, the remaining salt, baking powder, water and the remaining yogurt. Stir in carrots and green onions. Let batter stand for 5 minutes.

3. In a large skillet, melt half the coconut oil over low heat. Scoop batter into the pan by ¼-cup (60 mL) dollops, flattening them slightly with the back of a spoon. Increase heat to medium–high and cook, turning once, for 2 to 3 minutes per side or until golden brown on both sides and hot in the center. Transfer to baking sheet and keep warm in preheated oven. Repeat with the remaining oil and batter, adjusting heat as necessary between batches.

4. Serve fritters with minted yogurt sauce.

Broiled Eggplant with Coconut Yogurt Sauce

Broiled eggplant and a garlicky yogurt sauce melt into each other in this hearty side dish. Add some coconut flatbread (page 101) on the side.

Add some coconut flatbread (page 101) on the side.

Makes 6 servings

Tip

To mash garlic, working with one clove at a time, place the side of a chef's knife flat against the clove. Place the heel of your hand on the side of the knife and apply pressure so that the clove flattens slightly (this will loosen the peel). Remove and discard the peel, then roughly chop the garlic. Sprinkle a pinch of coarse salt over the garlic. Use the flat part of the knife as before to press the garlic against the cutting board. Repeat until the garlic turns into a fine paste. The mashed garlic is now ready for use in your favorite recipe.

- Preheat broiler, with rack set 4 to 6 inches (10 to 15 cm) from the heat source
- Broiler pan, greased with virgin coconut oil

2	eggplant (each about 1 lb/ 500 g), cut crosswise into ¾-inch (2 cm) slices	2
	Melted virgin coconut oil	
½ tsp	fine sea salt, divided	2 mL
1	clove garlic, mashed (see tip, at left)	1
½ cup	plain coconut yogurt (store-bought or see recipe, page 49)	125 mL
2 tsp	freshly squeezed lemon juice	10 mL
1 tsp	fresh thyme leaves	5 mL

1. Place eggplant on prepared pan and brush with coconut oil. Sprinkle with half the salt. Broil for 15 to 20 minutes, turning occasionally, until very soft.

2. Meanwhile, in a small bowl, combine garlic, the remaining salt, coconut yogurt and lemon juice.

3. Serve eggplant topped with coconut yogurt and sprinkled with thyme.

✳ Power Ingredient

Thyme
Thyme contains a unique volatile oil called thymol, which has historically been used for its antimicrobial qualities. Thymol has been shown to be effective against a host of various bacteria and fungi, making it a favorite choice for respiratory issues such as coughs and chest congestion, as well as a protectant against food-borne illnesses. In addition, research indicates that thymol protects the delicate fatty structures that compose our cells, particularly targeting the kidney, brain and heart. As a result, it may improve memory, protect against cardiovascular disease and promote detoxification.

Lemon Rosemary Glazed Parsnips

The bright and woodsy flavors of lemon and rosemary highlight the concentrated sweetness of the coconut-simmered parsnips to great effect.

Tip

The rosemary can be replaced with 1 tbsp (15 mL) chopped tender-leaf herbs, such as cilantro, mint, basil or parsley.

1 cup	coconut water or water	250 mL
2 tbsp	virgin coconut oil	30 mL
1½ tbsp	coconut nectar or coconut sugar	22 mL
½ tsp	fine sea salt	2 mL
1¼ lbs	parsnips (about 8 medium), cut into ¼-inch (0.5 cm) thick slices	625 g
1½ tsp	minced fresh rosemary leaves	7 mL
1 tsp	freshly squeezed lemon juice	5 mL

1. In a large skillet, combine coconut water, coconut oil, coconut nectar and salt. Bring to a boil over medium-high heat, stirring occasionally. Add parsnips, reduce heat to medium, cover and boil gently for 10 to 12 minutes or until just tender. Using a slotted spoon, transfer parsnips to a dish.

2. Add rosemary to skillet, increase heat to medium-high and return cooking liquid to a boil. Boil, stirring occasionally, until reduced to a glaze (about 2 tbsp/30 mL). Return parsnips to the pan, reduce heat and simmer, stirring, until heated through and coated with glaze. Stir in lemon juice.

Variation

Lemon Rosemary Glazed Carrots: Substitute carrots for the parsnips.

Tip

Consider using an equal combination of parsnips and carrots.

Storage Tip

Leftover glazed parsnips can be stored in an airtight container in the refrigerator for up to 2 days.

❋ Power Ingredient

Parsnips

Parsnips look like pale white cousins of carrots, and like their bright orange relatives, they have the ability to boost serotonin in the brain, which helps you feel happier. Parsnips also contain falcarinols that have strong antibacterial, antimicrobial and antifungal properties, aiding the body in the fight against inflammation. New research suggests that parsnip consumption can help regulate the immune response. Dendritic cells play a key role in the regulation of the immune system. Studies show that the compound falcarindiol, found in parsnips, has the ability to stop dendritic (or immune) cells from reaching maturity. The ability to suppress the immune system gives parsnips great potential to be part of a new therapy for the treatment of autoimmune and allergic diseases.

Stir-Fried Mushrooms with Lemon and Parsley

Elegance comes easily with this simple side dish. Flecks of parsley and a hint of citrus enhance the mushrooms' meaty robustness in each bite.

Makes 4 servings

Tips

An equal amount of gluten-free soy sauce can be used in place of the liquid amino acids.

When selecting mushrooms, choose those with a fresh, smooth appearance, free from major blemishes and with a dry surface. Once home, keep mushrooms refrigerated; they're best when used within a few days of purchase. When ready to use, gently wipe mushrooms with a damp cloth or soft brush to remove dirt. Alternatively, rinse them quickly with cold water, then immediately pat dry with paper towels.

1 tbsp	freshly squeezed lemon juice	15 mL
1½ tsp	liquid coconut amino acids	7 mL
1 tsp	coconut nectar or coconut sugar	5 mL
1 tbsp	virgin coconut oil	15 mL
1 lb	cremini or button mushrooms, quartered	500 g
1	clove garlic, minced	1
⅓ cup	packed fresh flat-leaf (Italian) parsley leaves, chopped	75 mL

1. In a small bowl or cup, combine lemon juice, amino acids and coconut nectar.

2. In a large skillet, melt coconut oil over low heat. Add mushrooms, increase heat to medium-high and cook, stirring, for 7 to 8 minutes or until golden brown. Add lemon juice mixture and garlic; cook, stirring, for 1 to 2 minutes or until sauce is absorbed.

3. Serve sprinkled with parsley.

Sautéed Cherry Tomatoes

This gorgeous side dish delivers a lot of glamour — as well as vitamin C, fiber and carotenoids — for very little work.

Makes 4 servings

Tip

An equal amount of finely chopped fresh mint or cilantro can be used in place of the parsley.

2 tbsp	virgin coconut oil	30 mL
1 tsp	minced garlic	5 mL
1 tbsp	cider vinegar	15 mL
4 cups	cherry or grape tomatoes	1 L
⅛ tsp	fine sea salt	0.5 mL
⅛ tsp	freshly ground black pepper	0.5 mL
1 tbsp	finely chopped fresh flat-leaf (Italian) parsley	15 mL

1. In a large skillet, melt coconut oil over low heat. Add garlic and vinegar; increase heat to medium-high and bring to a simmer.

2. Stir in tomatoes, salt and pepper; simmer, stirring, for 2 to 4 minutes or until tomato skins just begin to split.

3. Serve sprinkled with parsley.

Variation

Smoky Sautéed Cherry Tomatoes: Add ¼ tsp (1 mL) ground cumin with the salt, and replace the black pepper with ½ tsp (2 mL) hot smoked paprika or chipotle chile powder.

Coconut Collard Green Ribbons

Slicing collard greens into super-thin strips allows them to cook quickly while maintaining a bit of crunch. Their glorious emerald hue hints at their tremendous nutritional power.

Makes 4 servings

Tip
.....

If using coconut sugar in place of coconut nectar, stir the vinegar mixture until the sugar dissolves.

1½ lbs	collard greens	750 g
1 tbsp	cider vinegar	15 mL
2 tsp	coconut nectar or coconut sugar	10 mL
2 tbsp	virgin coconut oil	30 mL
3	cloves garlic, minced	3
¼ tsp	fine sea salt	1 mL
⅛ tsp	hot pepper flakes	0.5 mL

1. Using a very sharp knife and working with one collard green leaf at a time, cut away the stems and tough portion of center ribs from all collard greens. Discard stems and ribs. Rinse and spin-dry or pat dry leaves.

2. Stack half the collard leaves and roll them up crosswise into a tight cylinder. Cut the cylinder crosswise into ¼-inch (0.5 cm) thick slices. Repeat with the remaining leaves. Toss the collard ribbons to uncoil them. Set aside.

3. In a small bowl, whisk together vinegar and coconut nectar. Set aside.

4. In a large skillet, melt coconut oil over low heat. Add garlic, salt and hot pepper flakes; cook, stirring, for 1 minute. Add collard ribbons, increase heat to medium-high and cook, tossing, for 1 to 2 minutes or until collard ribbons are coated with oil and just wilted. Add the vinegar mixture and gently toss to coat.

✻ Power Ingredient

Collard Greens
Collard greens are an excellent source of vitamins B_6 and C, carotenes, chlorophyll and manganese. They are also a very good source of fiber and several minerals, including iron, copper and calcium, and a good source of vitamins B_1, B_2 and E.

Quick Sautéed Kale

Coconut oil, sea salt and red wine vinegar—this recipe is proof that it takes minimal ingredients and time to produce a spectacular dish.

Makes 4 servings

Tip
......

Unlike other greens, kale stems are so tough they are virtually inedible. Hence, they, along with the tougher part of the center rib, must be removed before cooking. To do so, lay a leaf upside down on a cutting board and use a paring knife to cut a V shape along both sides of the rib, cutting it and the stem free from the leaf.

- Steamer basket

1 lb	kale, tough stems and ribs removed, leaves cut into ¼-inch (0.5 cm) wide strips (about 8 cups/2 L)	500 g
1 tbsp	virgin coconut oil	15 mL
¼ tsp	fine sea salt	1 mL
1 tbsp	red wine vinegar	15 mL

1. Place kale in a steamer basket set over a large pot of boiling water. Cover and steam for 8 to 10 minutes or until tender.

2. In a large skillet, melt coconut oil over low heat. Add kale and salt; increase heat to medium-high and cook, stirring occasionally, for 1 to 2 minutes or until heated through. Remove from heat and stir in vinegar.

✳ Power Ingredient

Kale

Kale's impressive concentration of nutrients strengthens the immune system and fights viruses and bacteria. Kale has heaps of fiber — 5 grams in 1 cup (250 mL) — and sulfur, both of which aid with digestion and promote liver health. Fiber also lowers cholesterol. The vitamin C in kale hydrates your body and increases your metabolism, leading to weight loss and healthy blood sugar levels.

Spicy Sautéed Spinach

Here, the triple zing of garlic, mustard seeds and hot pepper flakes enhances the fresh, grassy flavor of the spinach. The entire quick, satisfying dish is bolstered by the nuanced flavor of coconut oil.

Makes 6 servings

Tip

For a heartier side dish, add a 14- to 19-oz (398 to 540 mL) can of white beans or chickpeas, drained and rinsed, along with the spinach.

2 tbsp	virgin coconut oil	30 mL
3	cloves garlic, thinly sliced lengthwise	3
2 tsp	yellow mustard seeds	10 mL
½ tsp	hot pepper flakes	2 mL
2	packages (each 10 oz/300 g) baby spinach	2
¼ tsp	fine sea salt	1 mL

1. In a large pot, melt coconut oil over low heat. Add garlic, mustard seeds and hot pepper flakes; increase heat to medium–high and cook, stirring, for 1 minute or until green onions are softened and mustard seeds begin to pop.

2. Add spinach and salt; cook, tossing with tongs, for 2 to 3 minutes or until spinach is wilted but still bright green.

✳ Power Ingredient

Spinach

Spinach contains more than a dozen different flavonoid compounds, all of which act as powerful anti-inflammatory and anticancer agents. Researchers have found that eating spinach may decrease the incidence of several types of cancer, including breast cancer in women. Spinach is also loaded with vitamin C, folate and beta carotene, as well as vitamin K, which is essential for bone health. Just 1 cup (250 mL) of sautéed spinach provides over 1000% of the recommended daily value of vitamin K.

Calabrese Swiss Chard

Earthy, grassy Swiss chard makes a gorgeous, incredibly tasty side dish.

Tip

An equal amount of kale or mustard greens can be used in place of the Swiss chard.

1½ lbs	Swiss chard (about 1 large bunch)	750 g
1½ tbsp	virgin coconut oil	22 mL
3	cloves garlic, minced	3
3 tbsp	dried currants or coarsely chopped raisins	45 mL
¼ tsp	fine sea salt	1 mL
¼ tsp	hot pepper flakes	1 mL
1 tbsp	red wine vinegar	15 mL

1. Trim stems and center ribs from Swiss chard, then cut stems and ribs crosswise into 1-inch (2.5 cm) pieces. Stack chard leaves, roll them up crosswise into a tight cylinder and cut the cylinder crosswise into 1-inch (2.5 cm) thick slices.

2. In a large, heavy pot, melt coconut oil over low heat. Add garlic and cook, stirring, for 1 to 2 minutes or until golden. Stir in chard stems and ribs; increase heat to medium, cover and cook, stirring occasionally, for 8 to 10 minutes or until stems are tender.

3. Add half the chard leaves and cook, stirring, for 1 minute or until slightly wilted. Add the remaining chard leaves, currants, salt and hot pepper flakes; cover and cook, stirring occasionally, for 4 to 6 minutes or until leaves are tender. Stir in vinegar.

4. Using a slotted spoon, transfer Swiss chard mixture to plates or a serving bowl.

Crispy Coconut French Fries

Giving the vitamin-C-packed potato wedges a bath in hot water removes some of their starch, allowing them to become brown and crispy like oil-cooked fries while maintaining their superfood status.

Makes 6 servings

Tip

Coconut oil can be stored at room temperature, and it has the longest shelf life of any plant oil. The oil will fluctuate from liquid to solid; this is completely normal and does not affect the oil's quality.

- Preheat oven to 475°F (240°C)
- Large rimmed baking sheet, lined with parchment paper

1 1/2 lbs	russet potatoes, peeled and cut lengthwise into 3-inch (7.5 cm) long by 1/4-inch (0.5 cm) thick sticks	750 g
	Hot water	
2 tbsp	virgin coconut oil	30 mL
3/4 tsp	fine sea salt	3 mL
1/2 tsp	freshly cracked black pepper	2 mL

1. Place potatoes in a large bowl and add enough hot (not boiling) water to cover. Let stand for 10 minutes. Drain, pat dry and return to dry bowl.

2. Meanwhile, in a small skillet, melt coconut oil over low heat.

3. Pour oil over potatoes, tossing to coat. Add salt and pepper, tossing to coat. Spread in a single layer on prepared baking sheet.

4. Bake in preheated oven for 18 to 20 minutes or until golden on the bottom. Turn potatoes over and bake for 10 minutes or until golden and crisp. Serve immediately.

Variations

Garlicky French Fries: In step 2, add 4 cloves coarsely chopped garlic to melted oil. Cook, stirring, for 2 to 3 minutes or until garlic is golden. Using a slotted spoon, transfer garlic to a small bowl and set aside. Prepare fries as directed; sprinkle reserved garlic over finished fries.

Sweet Potato Fries: Preheat oven to 425°F (225°C). Use sweet potatoes instead of russet potatoes and skip step 1. Bake for 20 minutes. Gently turn sweet potatoes over and bake for 12 to 17 minutes or until crisp.

Parsnip Fries: Preheat oven to 400°F (200°C). Use parsnips instead of russet potatoes and skip step 1. Bake for 15 minutes. Gently turn parsnips over and bake for 12 to 17 minutes or until crisp.

Mashed Sweet Potatoes

These velvety sweet potatoes will make you glow with pleasure, in part from the high levels of carotenoids, which are beneficial to a healthy complexion.

Makes 6 servings

Tip

The sweet potatoes can also be mashed using a hand masher.

2 lbs	sweet potatoes, peeled and diced	1 kg
1/3 cup	well-stirred coconut milk (full-fat)	75 mL
2 tsp	coconut sugar	10 mL
1/4 tsp	fine sea salt	1 mL
1/4 tsp	freshly ground black pepper	1 mL

1. Place sweet potatoes in a medium saucepan and cover with water. Bring to a boil over high heat. Reduce heat and boil for 8 minutes or until tender. Drain, reserving 1/4 cup (60 mL) of the cooking water.

2. In a large bowl, using an electric mixer on medium speed, beat sweet potatoes and coconut milk until smooth, adding some of the reserved cooking water if mixture is too thick. Beat in coconut sugar, salt and pepper.

Variation

Winter Spice Sweet Potatoes: Increase the coconut sugar to 1 tbsp (15 mL) and replace the black pepper with 2 tsp (10 mL) pumpkin pie spice.

Lemon Basil Edamame Mash

Fresh lemon balances the richness of coconut and sweetness of basil in this springtime mash-up.

Tip

Frozen baby lima beans may be used in place of the edamame.

- Food processor

2 cups	frozen shelled edamame	500 mL
1	clove garlic	1
½ cup	packed fresh basil leaves	125 mL
½ tsp	fine sea salt	2 mL
½ cup	well-stirred coconut milk (full-fat)	125 mL
1 tsp	finely grated lemon zest	5 mL
2 tbsp	freshly squeezed lemon juice	30 mL

1. In a medium saucepan of boiling water, cook edamame for 4 to 6 minutes or until tender. Drain.

2. In food processor, combine hot edamame, garlic, basil, salt, coconut milk, lemon zest and lemon juice; pulse until blended into a thick purée.

✳ Power Ingredient

Edamame

Rich in minerals and disease-preventing plant chemicals, edamame (fresh soybeans) are among the few plant sources of complete protein, making them an ideal food for vegetarians. Soybeans have been cultivated in China for over 10,000 years and are an excellent source of calcium, B vitamins, potassium, zinc and magnesium. They are a very good source of iron, although this iron can only be absorbed by the body if consumed with foods rich in vitamin C. Soy is rich in plant chemicals that offer protection from diseases, including breast and prostate cancers and heart disease. A regular intake of soybeans can also reduce menopausal symptoms.

Coconut Cauliflower Purée

Although cauliflower is an excellent source of vitamins C and K, everyone will be too busy licking their plates to care.

Makes 6 servings

Tip

Frozen cauliflower florets (about two 1-lb/500 g bags) may be used in place of the fresh cauliflower. Increase the steaming time by 2 to 3 minutes.

- Steamer basket
- Food processor

6	cloves garlic	6
1	head cauliflower (2 to 2½ lbs/ 1 to 1.25 kg), broken into florets	1
½ tsp	fine sea salt	2 mL
⅛ tsp	freshly ground black pepper	0.5 mL
¾ cup	well-stirred coconut milk (full-fat)	175 mL
1 tbsp	freshly squeezed lemon juice	15 mL

1. Place garlic and cauliflower in a steamer basket set over a large pot of boiling water. Cover and steam for 7 to 9 minutes or until cauliflower is tender. Reserve steaming water.

2. In food processor, combine half the hot cauliflower mixture, salt, pepper, coconut milk and lemon juice; purée until smooth. Add the remaining cauliflower mixture and purée until smooth, adding a bit of the steaming water as needed to moisten.

Cauliflower "Rice"

This grain-free version of rice is endlessly versatile. Use it almost anywhere you would use rice: as a side dish, in salads, in fried "rice" or as the base for stews, stir-fries or curries.

Makes 4 servings

Tip

Instead of using a food processor, grate the cauliflower florets using the large holes of a cheese grater.

- Food processor

1	small to medium head cauliflower, ends trimmed	1
2 tbsp	virgin coconut oil	30 mL
	Fine sea salt and freshly cracked black pepper	

1. Cut or break cauliflower into large florets. Place half the florets in food processor and process until the size and texture of rice. Transfer to a large bowl and repeat with the remaining cauliflower.

2. In a large skillet, melt coconut oil over low heat. Add cauliflower, increase heat to medium and cook, stirring, for 4 to 5 minutes or until just tender. Season to taste with salt and pepper.

✳ Power Ingredient

Cauliflower

Cauliflower is rich in vitamin C — 1 cup (250 mL) will give you nearly your entire day's worth. Vitamin C stimulates the production of bone-building cells (osteoblasts) while suppressing the cells that destroy bone (osteoclasts). This is the mechanism behind the findings of a 2010 study published in the *Journal of Biological Chemistry*, which showed that vitamin C reduces fracture rates and increases bone mass. Vitamin C is also vital to the production of collagen, a protein-based connective tissue in bones and cartilage. And vitamin C is a powerful antioxidant: it helps convert toxins into water-soluble substances that can be flushed out of the body.

In addition to vitamin C, cauliflower is a good source of vitamin K, fiber and folate, and contains a decent amount of selenium (another antioxidant), calcium and vitamin A. And, like most other veggies, it has few calories, little sodium and no fat or cholesterol. It also contains powerful cancer-fighting phytochemicals called glucosinolates. Clinical studies indicate that regular intake of cauliflower may reduce the risk of several types of cancer.

Jamaican Peas and Cauliflower "Rice"

Coconut oil, allspice and thyme, together with cauliflower "rice" and dark red kidney beans, give this oh-so-easy side dish its down-island flavor.

Makes 6 servings

Tip

Instead of using a food processor, grate the cauliflower florets using the large holes of a cheese grater.

- Food processor

1	small to medium head cauliflower, ends trimmed	1
3 tbsp	virgin coconut oil	45 mL
2	cloves garlic, minced	2
1/2 tsp	ground allspice	2 mL
1 tsp	dried thyme	5 mL
1/2 tsp	fine sea salt	2 mL
1/2 tsp	hot pepper sauce	2 mL
1	can (14 to 19 oz/398 to 540 mL) dark red kidney beans, drained and rinsed	1
1/2 cup	chopped green onions	125 mL

1. Cut or break cauliflower into large florets. Place half the florets in food processor and process until the size and texture of rice. Transfer to a large bowl and repeat with the remaining cauliflower.

2. In a large skillet, melt coconut oil over low heat. Add garlic and allspice; cook, stirring, for 1 minute or until fragrant. Add cauliflower, thyme, salt and hot pepper sauce. Increase heat to medium-high and cook, stirring, for 3 to 4 minutes or until cauliflower is softened.

3. Stir in beans and green onions; cook, stirring, for 2 to 3 minutes or until beans are warmed through.

✳ Power Ingredient

Red Kidney Beans
Dark red kidney beans are high in good-quality protein and minerals. An average portion contains at least a quarter of a day's iron needs, to help prevent anemia and increase energy levels, while the zinc content helps boost the immune system and maintain fertility. The high amount of insoluble fiber helps prevent colon cancer, and the total fiber content helps people with diabetes or insulin resistance regulate blood sugar levels.

Coconut "Bacon"

Yes, you read the title correctly: coconut "bacon"! The crispy, smoky-sweet crunch and flavor of bacon is made with ease (no flying grease) and a short list of ingredients. Use it any way you would traditional bacon: on salads, in sandwiches, as a soup topper or simply nibbled out of hand.

Tips

An equal amount of gluten-free soy sauce can be used in place of the liquid amino acids.

Be sure to use large-flake coconut pieces to best capture the texture of traditional bacon.

Storage Tip

Store cooled "bacon" in an airtight container at room temperature for up to 2 months.

- Large rimmed baking sheet, lined with parchment paper

1 tbsp	liquid smoke	15 mL
1 tbsp	liquid coconut amino acids	15 mL
1 tbsp	coconut nectar or coconut sugar	15 mL
½ tsp	smoked or sweet paprika (optional)	2 mL
1¾ cups	unsweetened large-flake coconut	425 mL

1. In a medium bowl, combine liquid smoke, amino acids, coconut nectar and paprika (if using). Add coconut, tossing to coat evenly. Let stand for 20 minutes to absorb flavors.

2. Preheat oven to 325°F (160°C). Spread coconut evenly in a single layer on prepared baking sheet.

3. Bake, stirring every 5 minutes, for 20 to 25 minutes or until coconut appears dry and crispy. Immediately transfer coconut to a clean, dry bowl and let cool completely.

Cookies and Cakes

Not-Nutty Butter Cookies

Here, tahini — ground sesame seed paste — stands in for peanut butter with great flair and flavor.

Makes 28 cookies

Tip

An equal amount of smooth sunflower seed butter can be used in place of the tahini.

- Preheat oven to 350°F (180°C)
- 2 large baking sheets, lined with parchment paper

1 cup	coconut flour	250 mL
1½ tsp	gluten-free baking powder	7 mL
¼ tsp	fine sea salt	1 mL
¾ cup	well-stirred coconut milk (full-fat)	175 mL
2 tbsp	ground flax seeds (flaxseed meal)	30 mL
½ cup	well-stirred tahini	125 mL
¼ cup	coconut sugar	60 mL
1 tbsp	gluten-free vanilla extract	15 mL

1. In a small bowl, whisk together coconut flour, baking powder and salt.

2. In a medium bowl, whisk together coconut milk and flax seeds; let stand for 5 minutes to thicken. Stir in tahini, coconut sugar and vanilla until blended.

3. Add the flour mixture to the tahini mixture, stirring until combined (dough will be very stiff).

4. Roll dough into 1-inch (2.5 cm) balls. Place balls 2 inches (5 inches) apart on prepared baking sheets. Using the tines of a fork, flatten each cookie slightly, making a cross-hatch pattern.

5. Bake, one sheet at a time, in preheated oven for 7 to 9 minutes or until just set at the center and edges are golden brown. Let cool on pan on a wire rack for 5 minutes, then transfer to the rack to cool completely.

Storage Tip

Store the cooled cookies in an airtight container in the refrigerator for up to 1 week or in the freezer for up to 3 months.

❋ Power Ingredient

Tahini

Tahini provides four nutrients that support your immune system: zinc, selenium, iron and copper. Even a small amount of zinc improves the strength of your immune system because it's needed for the normal development and functioning of white blood cells, which destroy germs. Selenium is needed for the proper functioning of enzymes responsible for regulating the immune response and for creating antioxidants and antibodies. Iron and copper are both components of enzymes that produce white blood cells and maintain the immune system. Just 1 tbsp (15 mL) of tahini has 26% of the recommended daily intake of copper and 9% to 12% of zinc, iron and selenium. You also get 6% of the phosphorus you require daily. Beyond boosting bone and tooth health, phosphorous helps remove waste from the kidneys.

Coconut Shortbread

This modern, good-health twist on slice-and-bake cookies is perfect for so many occasions because the dough can be made and chilled a day ahead (or frozen for weeks ahead), until you are ready to slice and bake.

Tip

The wrapped dough can be placed in an airtight container and frozen for up to 3 months. Thaw in the refrigerator for 4 to 6 hours before slicing and baking.

- Waxed paper, parchment paper or foil
- Large baking sheet, lined with parchment paper

½ cup + 1 tbsp	chickpea flour	140 mL
⅓ cup	coconut flour	75 mL
4 tsp	potato starch	20 mL
⅛ tsp	fine sea salt	0.5 mL
½ cup	softened (not melted) virgin coconut oil	125 mL
⅓ cup	coconut sugar	75 mL
2 tbsp	well-stirred coconut milk (full-fat)	30 mL
2 tsp	gluten-free vanilla extract	10 mL

1. In a large bowl, whisk together chickpea flour, coconut flour, potato starch and salt.

2. In a medium bowl, using an electric mixer, beat coconut oil and coconut sugar on medium speed for 1 to 2 minutes or until blended and smooth. Scrape sides and bottom of bowl with a spatula. Add coconut milk and vanilla; beat for 1 minute, until blended and smooth.

3. Using a wooden spoon, stir flour mixture into coconut oil mixture until blended.

4. Transfer dough to a large piece of waxed paper. Roll dough into a cylinder about 2 inches (5 cm) in diameter. Tightly wrap in paper, twisting the ends to seal. Refrigerate for at least 1 hour, until very firm, or for up to 24 hours.

5. Preheat oven to 350°F (180°C). Unwrap dough and slice crosswise into $\frac{1}{4}$-inch (0.5 cm) thick slices. Place cookies 1 inch (2.5 cm) apart on prepared baking sheet.

6. Bake for 12 to 16 minutes or until golden brown and just barely set at the center. Transfer cookies to a wire rack to cool completely.

Snickerdoodles

Snickerdoodles are an old-fashioned favorite, and this grain-free version will renew — and perhaps even double — everyone's affection.

Makes about 36 cookies

Storage Tip

Store the cooled cookies in a cookie tin at room temperature for up to 3 days or freeze in an airtight container for up to 3 months.

- Preheat oven to 350°F (180°C)
- 2 large baking sheets, lined with parchment paper

$2/3$ cup	chickpea flour	150 mL
$1/2$ cup	coconut flour	125 mL
$1/3$ cup	potato starch	75 mL
$1\frac{1}{2}$ tsp	gluten-free baking powder	7 mL
$1/4$ tsp	fine sea salt	1 mL
$1\frac{1}{4}$ cups	coconut sugar, divided	300 mL
2 tbsp	psyllium husk	30 mL
$1/2$ cup	well-stirred coconut milk (full-fat)	125 mL
$1/2$ cup	melted virgin coconut oil	125 mL
2 tsp	gluten-free vanilla extract	10 mL
$1\frac{1}{2}$ tbsp	ground cinnamon	22 mL

1. In a large bowl, whisk together chickpea flour, coconut flour, potato starch, baking powder and salt.

2. In a medium bowl, whisk together $3/4$ cup (175 mL) coconut sugar, psyllium, coconut milk, coconut oil and vanilla until well blended. Let stand for 5 minutes to thicken.

3. Add the coconut milk mixture to the flour mixture and stir until just blended.

4. On a large plate, combine remaining the coconut sugar and cinnamon.

5. Roll dough into 1-inch (2.5 cm) balls. Roll balls in cinnamon sugar to coat. Place balls 2 inches (5 cm) apart on prepared baking sheets. Press each ball down with your fingertips to flatten slightly.

6. Bake, one sheet at a time, in preheated oven for 10 to 12 minutes or until cookies look dry on top and are lightly browned on the bottom. Let cool on pan on a wire rack for 5 minutes, then transfer to the rack to cool completely.

Cardamom Lime Cookies

Inspired by Indian dessert flavors, these cookies fill your senses and leave you longing for more. A healthy portion of freshly grated lime zest really makes them sing.

Makes 20 cookies

Tips

Lemon or orange zest can be used in place of the lime zest.

The lime zest can be replaced with 1 tsp (5 mL) gluten-free vanilla extract.

Storage Tip

Store the cooled cookies in an airtight container in the refrigerator for up to 1 week or in the freezer for up to 3 months.

- Preheat oven to 350°F (180°C)
- 2 large baking sheets, lined with parchment paper

⅔ cup	coconut flour	150 mL
⅓ cup	potato starch	75 mL
1 tsp	ground cardamom	5 mL
½ tsp	gluten-free baking powder	2 mL
¼ tsp	baking soda	1 mL
¼ tsp	fine sea salt	1 mL
½ cup	coconut sugar	125 mL
3 tbsp	psyllium husk	45 mL
½ cup	well-stirred coconut milk (full-fat)	125 mL
¼ cup	melted virgin coconut oil	60 mL
¼ cup	tahini or smooth sunflower seed butter	60 mL
1 tbsp	finely grated lime zest	15 mL

1. In a large bowl, whisk together coconut flour, potato starch, cardamom, baking powder, baking soda and salt.

2. In a small bowl, whisk together coconut sugar, psyllium, coconut milk, coconut oil, tahini and lime zest until well blended. Let stand for 5 minutes to thicken.

3. Add the coconut milk mixture to the flour mixture and stir until just blended (dough will be thick).

4. Drop dough by tablespoonfuls (15 mL) onto prepared baking sheets, spacing them 2 inches (5 cm) apart. Flatten slightly with your fingertips.

5. Bake, one sheet at a time, in preheated oven for 14 to 16 minutes or until just set at the edges (centers will be slightly soft). Let cool on pan on a wire rack for 5 minutes, then transfer to the rack to cool completely.

Apple Coconut Cookies

Coconut sugar has a deep caramel profile that, when combined with fresh apple, results in an autumnal treat reminiscent of caramel apples. Ground cinnamon in the batter clinches it.

Makes 18 small cookies

Tip

An equal amount of tahini can be used in place of the sunflower seed butter.

Storage Tip

Store the cooled cookies in an airtight container in the refrigerator for up to 1 week or in the freezer for up to 3 months.

- Preheat oven to 350°F (180°C)
- Large baking sheet, lined with parchment paper

2 tbsp	psyllium husk	30 mL
½ cup	coconut water or water	125 mL
¼ cup	coconut sugar	60 mL
⅓ cup	melted virgin coconut oil	75 mL
2 tbsp	smooth sunflower seed butter	30 mL
½ cup	chickpea flour	125 mL
¼ cup	coconut flour	60 mL
1 tbsp	potato starch	15 mL
1 tsp	gluten-free baking powder	5 mL
1 tsp	ground cinnamon	5 mL
½ tsp	baking soda	2 mL
½ tsp	fine sea salt	2 mL
⅔ cup	shredded peeled tart-sweet apple (such as Gala or Braeburn)	150 mL

1. In a medium bowl, whisk together psyllium and coconut water. Let stand for 5 minutes to thicken. Whisk in coconut sugar, coconut oil and sunflower seed butter until well blended.

2. In a large bowl, whisk together chickpea flour, coconut flour, potato starch, baking powder, cinnamon, baking soda and salt.

3. Add the coconut water mixture to the flour mixture and stir until just blended. Stir in apple.

4. Roll heaping teaspoons (5 mL) of dough into balls. Place balls 2 inches (5 cm) apart on prepared baking sheet. Flatten balls slightly into discs.

5. Bake in preheated oven for 10 to 12 minutes or until cookies look dry on top and are lightly browned on the bottom. Let cool on pan on a wire rack for 5 minutes, then transfer to the rack to cool completely.

Soft Banana Cookies

Thank you, bananas, for making homemade baked goods, like these old-fashioned-tasting cookies, so delicious, but also for making it so easy to get a day's supply of potassium.

Makes 24 cookies

Storage Tip

Store the cooled cookies in an airtight container in the refrigerator for up to 1 week or in the freezer for up to 3 months.

- Preheat oven to 350°F (180°C)
- 2 large baking sheets, lined with parchment paper

⅓ cup	coconut sugar	75 mL
1½ tbsp	psyllium husk	22 mL
½ cup	mashed very ripe banana	125 mL
6 tbsp	melted virgin coconut oil	90 mL
3 tbsp	water	45 mL
1 tsp	gluten-free vanilla extract	5 mL
½ cup	chickpea flour	125 mL
¼ cup	coconut flour	60 mL
1 tbsp	potato starch	15 mL
½ tsp	gluten-free baking powder	2 mL
¼ tsp	baking soda	1 mL
¼ tsp	ground nutmeg	1 mL
⅛ tsp	fine sea salt	1 mL

1. In a medium bowl, whisk together coconut sugar, psyllium, banana, coconut oil, water and vanilla. Let stand for 5 minutes to thicken.

2. In a large bowl, whisk together chickpea flour, coconut flour, potato starch, baking powder, baking soda, nutmeg and salt.

3. Add the banana mixture to the flour mixture and stir until just blended.

4. Drop dough by tablespoonfuls (15 mL) onto prepared baking sheets, spacing them 2 inches (5 cm) apart.

5. Bake, one sheet at a time, in preheated oven for 10 to 12 minutes or until just set at the center. Let cool on pan on a wire rack for 2 minutes, then transfer to the rack to cool completely.

Variations

Banana Chocolate Chip Cookies: Stir ½ cup (125 mL) miniature semisweet chocolate chips (vegan, gluten-free) into the batter at the end of step 2.

Toasted Coconut Banana Cookies: Stir ⅔ cup (150 mL) toasted unsweetened flaked coconut into the batter at the end of step 2.

Jam Thumbprints

Cookies that are actually beneficial for your gut? Yes! These cookies have a significant amount of potato starch, which is considered a "resistant starch" — a prebiotic that promotes the abundance of helpful bacteria and creates an environment where harmful bacteria do not fare well. A natural consequence of a better gut "ecosystem" is improved mineral absorption and better overall health.

Makes 24 cookies

Storage Tip

Store the cooled cookies in an airtight container in the refrigerator for up to 1 week or in the freezer for up to 3 months.

- Preheat oven to 350°F (180°C)
- 2 large baking sheets, lined with parchment paper

2/3 cup	coconut flour	150 mL
2/3 cup	potato starch	150 mL
2/3 cup	ground flax seeds (flaxseed meal)	150 mL
1/4 tsp	fine sea salt	1 mL
6 tbsp	coconut sugar	90 mL
2/3 cup	unsweetened applesauce	150 mL
1/2 cup	melted virgin coconut oil	125 mL
2 tsp	gluten-free vanilla extract	10 mL
1/4 cup	fruit-sweetened jam or preserves	60 mL

1. In a large bowl, whisk together coconut flour, potato starch, flax seeds and salt.

2. In a medium bowl, whisk together coconut sugar, applesauce, coconut oil and vanilla until well blended.

3. Add the applesauce mixture to the flour mixture and stir until just blended.

4. Roll dough into 1-inch (2.5 cm) balls. Place balls 2 inches (5 cm) apart on prepared baking sheets. Using your thumb, make a small indentation in the center of each ball. Spoon 1/4 tsp (1 mL) jam into each indentation. Cover loosely with foil or plastic wrap and refrigerate for 15 minutes.

5. Meanwhile, preheat oven to 350°F (180°C). Remove covering from one sheet of cookies (keep the other sheet covered in the refrigerator).

6. Bake, one sheet at a time, for 11 to 14 minutes or until just set at the edges (centers will be slightly soft). Let cool on pan on a wire rack for 5 minutes, then transfer to the rack to cool completely.

No-Oatmeal and Raisin Cookies

You would swear these raisin-flecked cookies have oatmeal in them if you hadn't made them yourself.

Storage Tip

Store the cooled cookies in an airtight container in the refrigerator for up to 1 week or in the freezer for up to 3 months.

- Preheat oven to 350°F (180°C)
- 2 large baking sheets, lined with parchment paper

⅓ cup	coconut sugar	75 mL
2 tbsp	ground flax seeds (flaxseed meal)	30 mL
½ tsp	baking soda	2 mL
¼ tsp	fine sea salt	1 mL
1 cup	smooth sunflower seed butter or tahini	250 mL
⅓ cup	well-stirred coconut milk (full-fat)	75 mL
½ cup	unsweetened flaked coconut	125 mL
½ cup	raisins	125 mL

1. In a medium bowl, stir together coconut sugar, flax seeds, baking soda, salt, sunflower seed butter and coconut milk until blended. Stir in coconut and raisins.

2. Drop dough by tablespoonfuls (15 mL) onto prepared baking sheets, spacing them 2 inches (5 cm) apart. Flatten slightly with your fingertips.

3. Bake, one sheet at a time, in preheated oven for 9 to 12 minutes or until just set at the edges (centers will be slightly soft). Let cool on pan on a wire rack for 10 minutes, then transfer to the rack to cool completely.

✳ Power Ingredient

Flax Seeds
Flax seeds are a good source of protein, with 1 to 2 grams per 1 tbsp (15 mL). For about 40 calories and 3 grams of fat, 1 tbsp (15 mL) of ground flax seeds offers 8 grams of fiber, omega-3 fatty acids and essential vitamins and minerals, including small amounts of potassium for a healthy heart and well-functioning muscles, and both iron and zinc to boost immunity.

Chocolate Chip Cookies

Dreams really do come true: these chocolate chip cookies prove it. Gone are the refined flours and sugars, and in their place are protein- and fiber-rich flours, deeply flavorful natural sugar, heart-healthy coconut oil and a result that is easily the best chocolate chip cookie you've ever tasted.

Tip

For this recipe, it is important to use coconut oil that is just softened, not completely melted.

Storage Tip

Store the cooled cookies in an airtight container in the refrigerator for up to 1 week or in the freezer for up to 3 months.

- Preheat oven to 350°F (180°C)
- Large baking sheet, lined with parchment paper

2 tbsp	psyllium husk	30 mL
1/3 cup	coconut water or water	75 mL
1/2 cup + 1 tbsp	chickpea flour	140 mL
1/3 cup	coconut flour	75 mL
4 tsp	potato starch	20 mL
1/2 tsp	baking soda	2 mL
1/4 tsp	fine sea salt	1 mL
1/4 tsp	ground cinnamon	1 mL
3/4 cup	coconut sugar	175 mL
1/2 cup	softened virgin coconut oil	125 mL
2 tsp	gluten-free vanilla extract	10 mL
1/2 cup	semisweet chocolate chips (vegan, gluten-free)	125 mL

1. In a small bowl or cup, combine psyllium and coconut water; let stand for 5 minutes to thicken.

2. In a medium bowl, whisk together chickpea flour, coconut flour, potato starch, baking soda, salt and cinnamon.

3. In a large bowl, using an electric mixer, beat coconut sugar and coconut oil on medium speed for 1 to 2 minutes or until blended and smooth. Scrape sides and bottom of bowl with a spatula. Add psyllium mixture and vanilla; beat for 1 minute, until blended and smooth.

4. Add the flour mixture to the coconut sugar mixture. With the mixer on low speed, beat just until incorporated. Stir in chocolate chips.

5. Roll dough into 14 equal balls. Place balls 2 inches (5 cm) apart on prepared baking sheet. Flatten each ball slightly with your palm.

6. Bake in preheated oven for 11 to 16 minutes or until just set at the edges (centers will be slightly soft). Let cool on pan on a wire rack for 5 minutes, then transfer to the rack to cool completely.

Chocolate Avocado Cookies

Avocado in chocolate cookies? You bet! It enriches the texture and adds a wealth of nutrients ranging from potassium to B vitamins. But perhaps most importantly, the resulting cookies are rich, delicious and very chocolaty.

Makes 30 cookies

Tip

Hass avocados (sometimes called Haas avocados) are dark-skinned avocados with a nutty, buttery flesh and a longer shelf life than other varieties, making them the most popular avocado in North America. To determine whether a Hass avocado is ripe, look for purple-black skin and gently press the top — a ripe one will give slightly.

Storage Tip

Store the cooled cookies in an airtight container in the refrigerator for up to 5 days or in the freezer for up to 3 months.

- Preheat oven to 350°F (180°C)
- 2 large baking sheets, lined with parchment paper

⅔ cup	unsweetened natural cocoa powder (see tip, page 274)	150 mL
½ cup	coconut flour	125 mL
⅓ cup	chickpea flour	75 mL
1 tsp	gluten-free baking powder	5 mL
½ tsp	fine sea salt	2 mL
¾ cup	coconut sugar	175 mL
⅓ cup	mashed ripe Hass avocado	75 mL
¼ cup	virgin coconut oil	60 mL
1 tsp	gluten-free vanilla extract	5 mL
½ cup	well-stirred coconut milk (full-fat)	125 mL
½ cup	miniature semisweet chocolate chips (vegan, gluten-free)	125 mL

1. In a medium bowl, whisk together cocoa powder, coconut flour, chickpea flour, baking powder and salt. Set aside.

2. In a large bowl, using an electric mixer, beat coconut sugar, avocado and coconut oil on medium speed until just blended. Increase speed to high and beat for 2 to 3 minutes or until light and fluffy. Beat in vanilla.

3. Add half the flour mixture to the avocado mixture. With the mixer on low speed, beat just until incorporated. Add coconut milk and the remaining flour mixture; beat until just blended. Stir in chocolate chips.

4. Drop dough by tablespoonfuls (15 mL) onto prepared baking sheets, spacing them 2 inches (5 cm) apart. Flatten slightly with your fingertips.

5. Bake, one sheet at a time, in preheated oven for 10 to 12 minutes or until just set at the edges (centers will be slightly soft). Let cool on pan on a wire rack for 5 minutes, then transfer to the rack to cool completely.

Coconut Macaroons

Bye-bye, sweetened condensed milk, eggs and table sugar, and hello to the most delicious, easiest to prepare macaroons ever. These beauties have everything a great macaroon should: crispy edges, a creamy center and deep coconut flavor.

Makes 24 cookies

Tips

For best results, do not use large-flake coconut in this recipe.

An equal amount of agave nectar or pure maple syrup can be used in place of the coconut nectar.

Storage Tip

Store the cooled cookies in an airtight container in the refrigerator for up to 5 days or in the freezer for up to 3 months.

- Preheat oven to 350°F (180°C)
- 2 large baking sheets, lined with parchment paper

1 cup	well-stirred coconut milk (full-fat)	250 mL
1/3 cup	coconut nectar	75 mL
2 tsp	gluten-free vanilla extract	10 mL
1/4 tsp	fine sea salt	1 mL
1/4 cup	potato starch	60 mL
3 cups	unsweetened flaked coconut	750 mL

1. In a medium bowl, whisk together coconut milk, coconut nectar, vanilla and salt until blended. Whisk in potato starch, a few teaspoons (10 to 15 mL) at a time, until blended and smooth. Stir in coconut.

2. Drop dough by tablespoonfuls (15 mL) onto prepared baking sheets, spacing them 2 inches (5 cm) apart.

3. Bake, one sheet at a time, in preheated oven for 20 to 24 minutes or until golden brown and firm to the touch. Let cool on pan on a wire rack for 10 minutes, then transfer to the rack to cool completely.

Coconut Biscotti

Be the hit of the party when you arrive with a platter of these crowd-pleasing biscotti. They have all of the taste and texture you expect from traditional biscotti, made better with coconut sugar, flour and oil.

Makes 36 cookies

Tips

Look for dried cranberries that are sweetened with fruit juice rather than sugar.

The biscotti will continue to harden as they cool after the second bake.

Storage Tip

Store the cooled biscotti in a cookie tin at room temperature for up to 5 days or freeze in an airtight container for up to 3 months.

Variation

Double Chocolate Biscotti: Reduce the chickpea flour to ³⁄₄ cup (175 mL), the coconut flour to 6 tbsp (90 mL) and the potato starch to 1¹⁄₂ tbsp (22 mL). Add ¹⁄₃ cup (75 mL) unsweetened natural cocoa powder to the flour mixture in step 2. Replace the dried fruit with an equal amount of miniature semisweet chocolate chips (vegan, gluten-free).

- Preheat oven to 350°F (180°C)
- Large baking sheet, lined with parchment paper

²⁄₃ cup	coconut sugar	150 mL
¹⁄₄ cup	psyllium husk	60 mL
¹⁄₂ cup	coconut water or water	125 mL
6 tbsp	melted virgin coconut oil	90 mL
2 tsp	gluten-free vanilla extract	10 mL
1 cup	chickpea flour	250 mL
¹⁄₂ cup	coconut flour	125 mL
2 tbsp	potato starch	30 mL
2 tsp	gluten-free baking powder	10 mL
¹⁄₄ tsp	fine sea salt	1 mL
¹⁄₂ cup	chopped dried fruit (apricots, raisins, cranberries)	125 mL

1. In a medium bowl, whisk together coconut sugar, psyllium, coconut water, coconut oil and vanilla until blended. Let stand for 5 minutes to thicken.

2. In a large bowl, whisk together chickpea flour, coconut flour, potato starch, baking powder and salt.

3. Add the coconut water mixture to the flour mixture and stir until just blended. Stir in dried fruit. Divide dough in half.

4. Place dough halves on prepared baking sheet and, using moistened hands, shape into two parallel 10- by 3-inch (25 by 7.5 cm) rectangles, spaced about 3 inches (7.5 cm) apart.

5. Bake in preheated oven for 23 to 26 minutes or until golden and center is set. Let cool on pan on a wire rack for 15 minutes. Reduce oven temperature to 250°F (120°C).

6. Cut rectangles crosswise into ¹⁄₂-inch (1 cm) slices. Place slices, cut side down, on baking sheet. Bake for 25 minutes. Let cool on pan for 1 minute, then transfer to wire racks to cool completely.

Buckeyes

Named for their resemblance to the nut of the Ohio buckeye tree, these confections are traditionally made from a mixture of peanut butter and powdered sugar, which is then partially dipped in chocolate. Here, I've replaced the high-allergen elements with coconut powerhouse ingredients, to delicious, nutritious effect.

Makes 24 pieces

Tips

If the sunflower butter is unsalted, add ⅛ tsp (0.5 mL) fine sea salt to the recipe.

You can replace the coconut nectar with an equal amount of coconut sugar, but combine the sugar with 1½ tbsp (22 mL) boiling water, stirring until most of the sugar is dissolved. Proceed as directed.

- Large baking sheet, lined with parchment paper

¾ cup	smooth sunflower seed butter (see tip, at left)	175 mL
¼ cup	coconut nectar	60 mL
½ cup	coconut flour	125 mL
½ cup	semisweet chocolate chips (vegan, gluten-free)	125 mL
1 tsp	coconut oil	5 mL

1. In a medium bowl, stir together sunflower seed butter and coconut nectar until blended. Add coconut flour, 1 tbsp (15 mL) at a time, stirring until a thick but still pliable dough forms.

2. Roll dough into 1-inch (2.5 cm) balls. Place balls on prepared baking sheet. Refrigerate for about 1 hour or until firm.

3. Place chocolate chips and coconut oil in a small, deep, microwave-safe bowl. Microwave on High for 30 seconds. Stir. Microwave in 15-second intervals, stirring after each, until mixture is melted and smooth.

4. Dip chilled balls, one at a time, in chocolate, coating one half of the ball. Return to prepared baking sheet, chocolate side down. Refrigerate for about 30 minutes or until chocolate is hardened.

Storage Tip

Store the chilled buckeyes in an airtight container in the refrigerator for up to 1 week or in the freezer for up to 3 months.

✳ Power Ingredient

Sunflower Seed Butter

Sunflower seed butter is more than an alternative to peanut butter; it is also a great addition to a healthy diet. It provides many nutrients, but its vitamin B_1, or thiamine, content, is especially notable. Thiamine activates enzymes within your cells, helping to drive the chemical reactions they need to function. Getting enough thiamine — which isn't always easy — helps you derive energy from food and produce nucleic acids, the building blocks that make up your DNA. Men need 1.2 milligrams of thiamine each day, according to the Linus Pauling Institute, and women need 1.1 mg. One tbsp (15 mL) of sunflower seed butter provides 0.4 mg!

No-Bake Lemon Coconut Bars

I have yet to meet anyone opposed to lemon desserts. If I did, I would offer them one of these bars to turn them around. The bright citrus flavor is all the more scrumptious in combination with coconut — flour, oil and flaked — and the prep is as easy as can be.

Makes 12 bars

Tips

Turmeric lends the filling a natural yellow color without affecting the flavor.

An equal amount of agave nectar can be used in place of the coconut nectar

- Food processor
- 8-inch (20 cm) square glass baking dish or metal baking pan, lined with parchment paper or foil
- Waxed paper

Crust

¾ cup	unsweetened flaked coconut	175 mL
¾ cup	packed pitted moist dates (such as Medjool)	175 mL
¼ cup	coconut flour	60 mL
1 tbsp	finely grated lemon zest	15 mL
⅛ tsp	fine sea salt	0.5 mL

Filling

2 tbsp	coconut flour	30 mL
Pinch	ground turmeric (optional)	Pinch
½ cup	melted virgin coconut oil	125 mL
⅓ cup	freshly squeezed lemon juice	75 mL
⅓ cup	coconut nectar	75 mL
	Additional coconut flour (optional)	

1. *Crust:* In food processor, pulse coconut until finely ground. Add half the dates and pulse until coarsely chopped. Add the remaining dates and pulse until all dates are finely chopped. Add coconut flour, lemon zest and salt; pulse until incorporated.

2. Transfer date mixture to prepared pan and, using a sheet of waxed paper, press evenly into bottom of pan.

Store the cut bars in an airtight container in the refrigerator for up to 1 week. Alternatively, wrap them in plastic wrap, then foil, completely enclosing them, and freeze for up to 3 months. Let thaw at room temperature for 4 to 6 hours before serving.

3. *Filling:* In a small bowl, whisk together coconut flour, turmeric (if using), coconut oil, lemon juice and coconut nectar until blended and smooth. Spoon and spread over crust.

4. Cover and refrigerate for about 6 hours or until chilled and filling is set. If desired, sprinkle top with a small amount of coconut flour (to resemble powdered sugar). Use liner to lift from pan. Cut into 12 bars.

✳ Power Ingredient

Turmeric

Turmeric — a bright yellow cousin of ginger and one of the primary ingredients in curry powder — has been used in Indian Ayurvedic medicine for millennia, and Western science is catching on. The active ingredient in turmeric is curcumin, a strong antioxidant that has been shown in test tube and animal studies to fend off cancer growth, amyloid plaque development and more. Turmeric has also shown promise for heart health: a 2012 study indicates that adding turmeric and other high-antioxidant spices to high-fat meals could help regulate triglyceride and insulin levels and protect the cardiovascular system.

Raspberry Crumble Bars

Lush with fresh raspberries, these bars taste like late summer. You can make them with blackberries too, but there's something about the sweet-tart taste of ruby raspberries that is irresistible.

<table>
<tr><td>Makes 12 bars</td></tr>
</table>

Tips

An equal amount of thawed frozen raspberries can be used in place of fresh.

Blueberries, blackberries or a combination of berries can be used in place of the raspberries.

Storage Tip

Store the cooled bars in an airtight container in the refrigerator for up to 1 week. Alternatively, wrap them in plastic wrap, then foil, completely enclosing them, and freeze for up to 3 months. Let thaw at room temperature for 4 to 6 hours before serving.

- Preheat oven to 350°F (180°C)
- Food processor
- Waxed paper
- 8-inch (20 cm) square metal baking pan, lined with parchment paper or foil

2 cups	raspberries	500 mL
3 tbsp	coconut sugar, divided	45 mL
2 tsp	potato starch	10 mL
1 tsp	finely grated lemon zest	5 mL
2 tsp	freshly squeezed lemon juice	10 mL
2/3 cup	raw sunflower seeds	150 mL
1/2 cup	unsweetened flaked coconut	125 mL
1/4 cup	coconut flour	60 mL
3/4 cup	packed pitted moist dates (such as Medjool)	175 mL
1/4 cup	melted virgin coconut oil	60 mL

1. In a large bowl, combine raspberries, 1 tbsp (15 mL) coconut sugar, potato starch and lemon juice. Gently toss to combine.

2. In food processor, combine sunflower seeds and coconut; pulse until finely ground. Add coconut flour, remaining coconut sugar and lemon zest; pulse one or two times to combine.

3. Add half the dates to the sunflower seed mixture and pulse until coarsely chopped. Add the remaining dates and pulse until all dates are finely chopped. Add coconut oil and pulse until incorporated.

4. Transfer half the date mixture to prepared pan and, using a sheet of waxed paper, press evenly into bottom of pan. Spoon and spread the berry mixture on top. Crumble the remaining date mixture evenly over the berries.

5. Bake in preheated oven for 35 to 40 minutes or until juices from berries are bubbling and topping appears dry and darker golden brown at the edges. Let cool completely in pan on a wire rack. Use liner to lift from pan. Cut into 12 bars.

Spiced Pumpkin Bars

These spiced bars are an easy and impressive alternative to pumpkin pie. No need to wait for the holidays, though: pumpkin, coconut and spice add up to a perfect bar cookie any time of year.

Tip

An equal amount of mashed cooked sweet potatoes can be used in place of the pumpkin.

Storage Tip

Store the cooled bars, loosely wrapped in foil or waxed paper, at room temperature for up to 2 days. Alternatively, wrap them in plastic wrap, then foil, completely enclosing them, and freeze for up to 3 months. Let thaw at room temperature for 4 to 6 hours before serving.

- Preheat oven to 350°F (180°C)
- 9-inch (23 cm) square metal baking pan, lined with parchment paper or foil

1 cup	coconut sugar	250 mL
3 tbsp	psyllium husk	45 mL
¾ cup	pumpkin purée (not pie filling)	175 mL
½ cup	melted virgin coconut oil	125 mL
⅓ cup	well-stirred coconut milk (full-fat)	75 mL
2 tsp	gluten-free vanilla extract	10 mL
½ cup	chickpea flour	125 mL
¼ cup	coconut flour	60 mL
2 tsp	pumpkin pie spice	10 mL
½ tsp	gluten-free baking powder	2 mL
¼ tsp	fine sea salt	1 mL

1. In a medium bowl, whisk together coconut sugar, psyllium, pumpkin, coconut oil, coconut milk and vanilla until well blended. Let stand for 5 minutes to thicken.

2. In a large bowl, whisk together chickpea flour, coconut flour, pumpkin pie spice, baking powder and salt.

3. Add the pumpkin mixture to the flour mixture and stir until just blended.

4. Spread batter evenly in prepared pan.

5. Bake in preheated oven for 40 to 45 minutes or until a toothpick inserted in the center comes out clean. Let cool completely in pan on a wire rack. Use liner to lift from pan. Cut into 12 bars.

Variation

Chocolate Chip Pumpkin Bars: Stir ½ cup (125 mL) miniature semisweet chocolate chips (vegan, gluten-free) into the batter at the end of step 3.

Butterscotch Blondies

Coconut sugar gives these blondies a distinctive butterscotch flavor that is the perfect foil for a scattering of dark chocolate chips.

Tip

An equal amount of tahini can be used in place of the sunflower seed butter.

Storage Tip

Store the cooled blondies, loosely wrapped in foil or waxed paper, at room temperature for up to 2 days. Alternatively, wrap them in plastic wrap, then foil, completely enclosing them, and freeze for up to 3 months. Let thaw at room temperature for 4 to 6 hours before serving.

- Preheat oven to 350°F (180°C)
- 9-inch (23 cm) square metal baking pan, lined with parchment paper or foil

½ cup	coconut sugar	125 mL
2 tbsp	psyllium husk	30 mL
½ cup	smooth sunflower seed butter	125 mL
¼ cup	well-stirred coconut milk (full-fat)	60 mL
¼ cup	melted virgin coconut oil	60 mL
2 tsp	gluten-free vanilla extract	10 mL
⅓ cup	chickpea flour	75 mL
¼ cup	coconut flour	60 mL
½ tsp	gluten-free baking powder	2 mL
⅛ tsp	fine sea salt	0.5 mL
⅓ cup	miniature semisweet chocolate chips (vegan, gluten-free)	75 mL

1. In a medium bowl, whisk together coconut sugar, psyllium, sunflower seed butter, coconut milk, coconut oil and vanilla until well blended. Let stand for 5 minutes to thicken.

2. In a large bowl, whisk together chickpea flour, coconut flour, baking powder and salt.

3. Add the sunflower seed butter mixture to the flour mixture and stir until just blended. Stir in chocolate chips.

4. Spread batter evenly in prepared pan.

5. Bake in preheated oven for 15 to 20 minutes or until a toothpick inserted in the center comes out clean. Let cool completely in pan on a wire rack. Use liner to lift from pan. Cut into 12 bars.

Coconut Black Bean Brownies

Black beans add instant richness to brownies, but no one (especially children!) will ever guess they are there. The beans also happen to be one of the healthiest foods around.

Makes 12 brownies

Tip

If you can only find a 19-oz (540 mL) can of beans, use about three-quarters of the can (about 1½ cups/ 375 mL drained).

Storage Tip

Store the cooled brownies in an airtight container in the refrigerator for up to 5 days or in the freezer for up to 3 months.

- Preheat oven to 350°F (180°C)
- Food processor or high-speed blender
- 12-cup muffin pan, greased with coconut oil

2 tbsp	psyllium husk	30 mL
⅔ cup	coconut water or water	150 mL
1	can (14 to 15 oz/398 to 425 mL) black beans, drained and rinsed	1
¾ cup	unsweetened natural cocoa powder (see tip, page 274)	175 mL
⅔ cup	coconut sugar	150 mL
¼ tsp	fine sea salt	1 mL
¼ cup	melted virgin coconut oil	60 mL
1 tsp	gluten-free vanilla extract	5 mL
1½ tsp	gluten-free baking powder	7 mL
⅓ cup	miniature semisweet chocolate chips (vegan, gluten-free)	75 mL

1. In a small cup or bowl, whisk together psyllium and coconut water. Let stand for 5 minutes to thicken.

2. In food processor, combine psyllium mixture, beans, cocoa powder, coconut sugar, salt, coconut oil and vanilla; process until completely smooth. Sprinkle with baking powder and process for 20 seconds or until combined.

3. Divide batter equally among prepared muffin cups. Sprinkle with chocolate chips.

4. Bake in preheated oven for 25 to 30 minutes or until tops are dry and edges start to pull away from the sides. Let cool completely in pan on a wire rack.

No-Bake Hemp Brownie Bites

Wonderful any time a chocolate craving strikes, these fudgy, dense, delicious treats — part cookie, part candy — fall into the "most requested" category.

Tips

An equal amount of sunflower seeds can be used in place of the hemp hearts.

Select natural cocoa powder rather than Dutch process. Natural cocoa powder has a deep, true chocolate flavor. The packaging should state whether it is Dutch process or not, but you can also tell by sight: if it is dark to almost black, it is Dutch process; natural cocoa powder is much lighter and is typically reddish brown in color.

Storage Tip

Store the brownie bites in an airtight container in the refrigerator for up to 1 week or in the freezer for up to 3 months.

- Food processor

1 cup	hemp hearts	250 mL
1 cup	packed unsweetened flaked coconut	250 mL
1 cup	packed chopped pitted dates	250 mL
⅔ cup	unsweetened natural cocoa powder (see tip, at left)	150 mL
¼ tsp	fine sea salt	1 mL
1 tbsp	melted virgin coconut oil	15 mL
	Additional hemp hearts or unsweetened flaked coconut (optional)	

1. In food processor, pulse hemp hearts and coconut until finely chopped. Add dates, cocoa powder, salt and oil; process until almost smooth, stopping once or twice to scrape sides of bowl.

2. Transfer hemp mixture to a medium bowl. Cover and refrigerate for about 2 hours or until firm enough to roll.

3. Roll hemp mixture into 1-inch (2.5 cm) balls. If desired, place additional hemp hearts on a large plate and roll balls to coat.

✳ Power Ingredient

Hemp Hearts
Hemp hearts (hulled hemp seeds) are super-seeds, without question. A mere 1½-tbsp (22 mL) serving contains 5 grams of easily digested protein, 86 milligrams of magnesium, 10% of the daily value of iron, 1245 milligrams of omega-3 fatty acids and 436 milligrams of omega-6 fatty acids. Hemp hearts contain a healthy anti-inflammatory 3:1 ratio of omega-6 to omega-3 fatty acids and have an especially beneficial type of omega-6 fat called gamma-linolenic acid (GLA), a direct building block of good anti-inflammatory hormones. They also contain vitamin E and are rich in other minerals, such as zinc and phosphorus.

Easy Chocolate Cake

Tender, not too sweet and super-chocolaty, this has everything you want in a go-to chocolate cake recipe. Antioxidant-rich coffee enhances the chocolate flavor, but you can use an equal amount of decaffeinated coffee or prepared coffee alternative.

Makes 8 servings

Tip

Select natural cocoa powder rather than Dutch process. Natural cocoa powder has a deep, true chocolate flavor. The packaging should state whether it is Dutch process or not, but you can also tell by sight: if it is dark to almost black, it is Dutch process; natural cocoa powder is much lighter and is typically reddish brown in color.

Storage Tip

Store the cooled cake, loosely wrapped in foil or waxed paper, at room temperature for up to 3 days. Alternatively, wrap it in plastic wrap, then foil, completely enclosing cake, and freeze for up to 6 months. Let thaw at room temperature for 4 to 6 hours before serving.

- Preheat oven to 350°F (180°C)
- 9-inch (23 cm) square metal baking pan, greased with coconut oil

3 tbsp	psyllium husk	45 mL
¾ cup	strong brewed coffee, cooled, or water	175 mL
1 cup	coconut sugar	250 mL
½ cup	melted virgin coconut oil	125 mL
¾ cup	well-stirred coconut milk (full-fat)	175 mL
2 tbsp	cider or white vinegar	30 mL
2 tsp	gluten-free vanilla extract	10 mL
⅔ cup	chickpea flour	150 mL
½ cup	unsweetened natural cocoa powder (see tip, at left)	125 mL
¼ cup	coconut flour	60 mL
1½ tbsp	potato starch	22 mL
1 tsp	gluten-free baking powder	5 mL
¾ tsp	baking soda	3 mL
½ tsp	fine sea salt	2 mL

1. In a medium bowl, whisk together psyllium husk and coffee. Whisk in coconut sugar, coconut oil, coconut milk, vinegar and vanilla; let stand for 5 minutes to thicken.

2. In a large bowl, whisk together chickpea flour, cocoa powder, coconut flour, potato starch, baking powder, baking soda and salt.

3. Add the coffee mixture to the flour mixture and stir until just blended.

4. Spread batter evenly in prepared pan.

5. Bake in preheated oven for 50 to 55 minutes or until a toothpick inserted in the center comes out with a few moist crumbs attached. Let cool in pan on a wire rack for 10 minutes, then invert cake onto rack to cool completely.

Gingerbread

Moist, dark and fragrant, this gingerbread is a modern twist on a seasonal classic. Dress it up or down — it's delectable any way you serve it.

Tip

......

Check your spices every 6 months to make sure they smell fragrant and robust. Replace any that are not up to snuff. Look for great prices by buying herbs and spices in bulk in the natural foods section of the grocery store.

- Preheat oven to 350°F (180°C)
- 9-inch (23 cm) round metal baking pan, greased with coconut oil

2 tbsp	psyllium husk	30 mL
1/2 cup	well-stirred coconut milk (full-fat)	125 mL
1/2 cup	coconut water or water	125 mL
1 tsp	cider or white vinegar	5 mL
2/3 cup	coconut sugar	150 mL
1/3 cup	melted virgin coconut oil	75 mL
1/2 cup + 1 tbsp	chickpea flour	140 mL
1/3 cup	coconut flour	75 mL
4 tsp	potato starch	20 mL
2 1/2 tsp	ground ginger	12 mL
1 tsp	ground cinnamon	5 mL
1/2 tsp	baking soda	2 mL
1/8 tsp	fine sea salt	0.5 mL
1/8 tsp	ground cloves	0.5 mL

1. In a medium bowl, whisk together psyllium, coconut milk, coconut water and vinegar. Whisk in coconut sugar and coconut oil; let stand for 5 minutes to thicken.

2. In a large bowl, whisk together chickpea flour, coconut flour, potato starch, ginger, cinnamon, baking soda, salt and cloves.

Store the cooled cake at room temperature in a cake keeper, or loosely wrapped in foil or plastic wrap, for up to 3 days. Alternatively, wrap it in plastic wrap, then foil, completely enclosing cake, and freeze for up to 3 months. Let thaw at room temperature for 4 to 6 hours before serving.

3. Add the coconut milk mixture to the flour mixture and stir until just blended.

4. Spread batter evenly in prepared pan.

5. Bake in preheated oven for 35 to 40 minutes or until a toothpick inserted in the center comes out with a few moist crumbs attached. Let cool in pan on a wire rack for 10 minutes, then invert cake onto rack to cool completely.

✳ Power Ingredient

Cloves

Cloves can easily claim the crowning title of super-spice based on their antioxidant levels alone: they have an oxygen radical absorbance capacity (ORAC value) of 290,000, which is through the roof (by comparison, pomegranate seeds and blueberries have scores of 10,500 and 4,669, respectively). Cloves are also brimming with manganese, more than almost any other food. Manganese is an important trace mineral for the body, activating multiple enzymes, helping with lipid metabolism (getting rid of fat) and keeping the nervous system stable (reducing irritability).

All-Natural Red Velvet Cupcakes

Traditional red velvet cake — a favorite dessert from the American South — gets its color from an ample dose of artificial red food coloring. Here, the deep red hue comes courtesy of vitamin-C-rich beets, which also contribute natural sweetness and moisture.

Makes 12 cupcakes

Tips

Tightly wrap 3 medium-large beets (greens removed) in foil. Roast in a 425°F (220°C) oven, directly on oven rack, for 45 to 60 minutes or until tender. Unwrap foil and let cool completely, then coarsely chop. Transfer to a food processor and purée until smooth. The beets can be roasted, peeled and puréed up to 3 days ahead. Store in an airtight container in the refrigerator.

A 15-oz (425 mL) can of whole beets, drained, can be used to create the purée.

If making the cupcakes ahead of time, do not frost until 1 to 2 hours before serving. The natural color of the beets can discolor the frosting if it's added too far in advance.

- Preheat oven to 350°F (180°C)
- 12-cup muffin tin, cups lined with paper or foil liners

1 cup	coconut sugar	250 mL
2 tbsp	psyllium husk	30 mL
1 cup	well-stirred coconut milk (full-fat)	250 mL
¾ cup	puréed beets (see tips, at left)	175 mL
⅓ cup	melted virgin coconut oil	75 mL
2 tsp	gluten-free vanilla extract	10 mL
½ cup	chickpea flour	125 mL
⅓ cup	coconut flour	75 mL
1½ tbsp	potato starch	22 mL
1½ tbsp	unsweetened natural cocoa powder (see tip, page 275)	22 mL
2 tsp	gluten-free baking powder	10 mL
¼ tsp	fine sea salt	1 mL
	Whipped Coconut Cream (page 299)	

1. In a medium bowl, whisk together coconut sugar, psyllium, coconut milk, beets, coconut oil and vanilla. Let stand for 5 minutes to thicken.

2. In a large bowl, whisk together chickpea flour, coconut flour, potato starch, cocoa powder, baking powder and salt.

3. Add the coconut milk mixture to the flour mixture and stir until just blended.

Store the unfrosted cupcakes in an airtight container in the refrigerator for up to 5 days. Alternatively, wrap them in plastic wrap, then foil, completely enclosing them, and freeze for up to 3 months. Let thaw at room temperature for 1 to 2 hours before serving.

4. Divide batter equally among prepared muffin cups.

5. Bake in preheated oven for 30 to 35 minutes or until a toothpick inserted in the center of a cupcake comes out clean, with a few crumbs clinging to it (centers may sink slightly). Let cool completely in pan on a wire rack.

6. Frost cupcakes with Whipped Coconut Cream.

❋ Power Ingredient

Beets

Our grandmothers were right: beets are great for us. A growing body of research indicates that antioxidant-rich beets can help reduce blood pressure and its associated risks, such as heart attacks and strokes. They contain a high content of nitrates, which produce a gas called nitric oxide in the blood that widens blood vessels and lowers blood pressure.

In addition, because they are loaded with folate, vitamins A and C, iron, potassium, manganese and fiber, beets are one of the best foods around for making your skin glow. Their powerful antioxidants stimulate cell production and repair, which can protect your skin from premature aging and wrinkles. Beets also thin bile, improving liver function and increasing detoxification, one of the biggest factors in boosting beauty from within.

Carrot Cupcakes with Whipped Lemon Coconut Cream

It's time to eat cupcakes for beauty's sake — just make sure they are these carrot cupcakes. Carrots have high levels of beta carotene, which acts as an antioxidant to help repair the cell damage that occurs through daily living. Vitamin A further protects the skin from sun damage, premature wrinkling, acne, dry skin, pigmentation, blemishes and uneven skin tone.

Makes 12 cupcakes

Tips

An equal amount of parsnips can be used in place of the carrots.

Other dried fruits can be used in place of the currants, or you can omit them altogether.

- Preheat oven to 350°F (180°C)
- 12-cup muffin tin, cups lined with paper or foil liners

²⁄₃ cup	coconut sugar	150 mL
2 tbsp	psyllium husk	30 mL
⅓ cup	well-stirred coconut milk (full-fat)	75 mL
⅓ cup	melted virgin coconut oil	75 mL
1 tsp	gluten-free vanilla extract	5 mL
1 tsp	white or cider vinegar	5 mL
⅓ cup	chickpea flour	75 mL
2½ tbsp	coconut flour	37 mL
2 tsp	potato starch	10 mL
¾ tsp	baking soda	3 mL
¼ tsp	gluten-free baking powder	1 mL
¼ tsp	ground cinnamon	1 mL
¼ tsp	ground ginger	1 mL
¼ tsp	fine sea salt	1 mL
1 cup	finely grated peeled carrots	250 mL
¼ cup	dried currants or raisins	60 mL
	Whipped Lemon Coconut Cream (variation, page 299)	

1. In a medium bowl, whisk together coconut sugar, psyllium, coconut milk, coconut oil, vanilla and vinegar. Let stand for 5 minutes to thicken.

2. In a large bowl, whisk together chickpea flour, coconut flour, potato starch, baking soda, baking powder, cinnamon, ginger and salt.

Store the unfrosted cupcakes in an airtight container in the refrigerator for up to 5 days. Alternatively, wrap them in plastic wrap, then foil, completely enclosing them, and freeze for up to 3 months. Let thaw at room temperature for 1 to 2 hours before serving.

3. Add the coconut milk mixture to the flour mixture and stir until just blended. Stir in carrots and currants.

4. Divide batter equally among prepared muffin cups.

5. Bake in preheated oven for 25 to 30 minutes or until a toothpick inserted in the center of a cupcake comes out clean, with a few crumbs clinging to it (centers may sink slightly). Let cool completely in pan on a wire rack.

6. Frost cupcakes with Whipped Lemon Coconut Cream.

Very Vanilla Cupcakes

Free of gluten, grains, nuts, seeds, eggs and dairy, these amazing treats might best be dubbed "Freedom Cupcakes." You can vary the flavor in myriad ways — using different extracts, citrus zests, chocolate chips . . . you name it — and no one will ever guess that these are "healthy," "alternative" or anything other than delicious.

Makes 12 cupcakes

Storage Tip

Store the unfrosted cupcakes in an airtight container in the refrigerator for up to 5 days. Alternatively, wrap them in plastic wrap, then foil, completely enclosing them, and freeze for up to 3 months. Let thaw at room temperature for 1 to 2 hours before serving.

- Preheat oven to 350°F (180°C)
- 12-cup muffin pan, cups lined with paper or foil liners

¾ cup	coconut sugar	175 mL
2 tbsp	psyllium husk	30 mL
½ cup	well-stirred coconut milk (full-fat)	125 mL
½ cup	coconut water or water	125 mL
⅓ cup	melted virgin coconut oil	75 mL
1 tbsp	gluten-free vanilla extract	15 mL
½ cup + 1 tbsp	chickpea flour	140 mL
⅓ cup	coconut flour	75 mL
4 tsp	potato starch	20 mL
1½ tsp	gluten-free baking powder	7 mL
½ tsp	fine sea salt	2 mL
	Whipped Vanilla Coconut Cream (variation, page 299)	

1. In a medium bowl, whisk together coconut sugar, psyllium, coconut milk, coconut water, coconut oil and vanilla. Let stand for 5 minutes to thicken.

2. In a large bowl, whisk together chickpea flour, coconut flour, potato starch, baking powder and salt.

3. Add the coconut milk mixture to the flour mixture and stir until just blended.

4. Divide batter equally among prepared muffin cups.

5. Bake in preheated oven for 24 to 28 minutes or until a toothpick inserted in the center of a cupcake comes out clean, with a few crumbs clinging to it (centers may sink slightly). Let cool completely in pan on a wire rack.

6. Frost cupcakes with Whipped Vanilla Coconut Cream.

Pies, Puddings and Other Desserts

Coconut Flour Pie Crust

Versatile and quick, this pie crust gives grain crusts a run for their money. Use it for all of your favorite sweet fillings, or omit the coconut sugar and use it for savory options.

Makes one 9-inch (23 cm) pie crust

Tip
......

If using a metal pie pan, decrease the parbaking time to 10 to 12 minutes and reduce the complete baking time to 21 to 25 minutes.

- Food processor
- 9-inch (23 cm) glass pie plate

1 tbsp	psyllium husk	15 mL
½ cup	cold water	125 mL
⅔ cup	chickpea flour	150 mL
⅓ cup	coconut flour	75 mL
¼ cup	potato starch	60 mL
2 tsp	coconut sugar	10 mL
¼ tsp	fine sea salt	1 mL
½ cup	virgin coconut oil, chilled, cut into small pieces	125 mL

1. In a small cup, whisk together psyllium and cold water until blended.

2. In food processor, combine chickpea flour, coconut flour, potato starch, coconut sugar and salt; pulse to blend. Add coconut oil and process until mixture resembles coarse crumbs. Sprinkle psyllium mixture over flour mixture and pulse until a slightly sticky dough forms.

3. Turn dough out onto a large sheet of parchment or waxed paper and gather into a ball. Place a second sheet of parchment or waxed paper on top. Using a rolling pin, roll dough out into a 10-inch (25 cm) circle. Remove top piece of parchment paper.

4. Invert pie plate on top of dough. Quickly flip both plate and dough over so that the dough rests in the plate. Gently peel away and discard parchment paper. Press dough into pie plate, patching it together, if necessary. Crimp and trim the edges as desired. Using a fork, prick the sides and bottom all over. Place in the freezer for 10 minutes.

5. Meanwhile, preheat oven to 350°F (180°C).

Tips

The pie recipes in this chapter call for either a parbaked or a baked crust. Make sure to note which is specified and follow the appropriate version of step 6, including letting the crust cool as instructed, before proceeding with the recipe.

This recipe is easily doubled; simply double the ingredients and divide the dough into two equal portions.

To Parbake

6. Bake for 12 to 14 minutes or until golden. Let cool slightly on a wire rack, then fill and bake as directed in the pie recipe.

To Bake Completely

7. Bake for 24 to 28 minutes or until golden brown and set at the edges. Let cool completely on a wire rack. Fill as desired.

Coconut Cream Pie

This glorious pie takes coconut to the max. Delighting in even the smallest slice ensures a few moments of bliss, as well as ample amounts of zinc, a mineral crucial to the strength and health of your immune system.

Storage Tip

Prepare the pie through step 2 and store, loosely wrapped in foil or waxed paper, in the refrigerator for up to 2 days.

½ cup	coconut sugar	125 mL
⅓ cup	potato starch	75 mL
2¾ cups	well-stirred coconut milk (full-fat)	675 mL
2 tbsp	virgin coconut oil	30 mL
¼ tsp	fine sea salt	1 mL
1 tsp	gluten-free vanilla extract	5 mL
1	baked Coconut Flour Pie Crust (page 284)	1
1½ cups	Whipped Coconut Cream (page 299)	375 mL
½ cup	unsweetened flaked coconut, toasted	125 mL

1. In a medium saucepan, over medium heat, stir together coconut sugar, potato starch, coconut milk and coconut oil. Cook, whisking, for 4 to 5 minutes or until mixture just begins to bubble. Reduce heat and simmer, stirring, for 4 to 5 minutes or until mixture is thickened. Remove from heat and whisk in salt and vanilla.

2. Pour filling into baked pie crust. Cover surface of filling with plastic wrap and refrigerate for at least 3 hours, until set, before serving.

3. Spread Whipped Coconut Cream over chilled pie filling. Sprinkle with toasted coconut.

Chocolate Cream Pie

Go ahead, savor a slice. The dark chocolate filling isn't just delectable and irresistible, it's also good for you!

Tip

Select natural cocoa powder rather than Dutch process. Natural cocoa powder has a deep, true chocolate flavor. The packaging should state whether it is Dutch process or not, but you can also tell by sight: if it is dark to almost black, it is Dutch process; natural cocoa powder is much lighter and is typically reddish-brown in color.

Storage Tip

Store the chilled pie, loosely wrapped in foil or waxed paper, in the refrigerator for up to 2 days.

2 tbsp	psyllium husk	30 mL
½ cup	coconut water or water	125 mL
⅔ cup	coconut sugar	150 mL
½ cup	unsweetened natural cocoa powder (see tip, at left)	125 mL
3 tbsp	potato starch	45 mL
1 tsp	instant espresso powder (optional)	5 mL
⅛ tsp	fine sea salt	0.5 mL
2 cups	well-stirred coconut milk (full-fat), divided	500 mL
½ cup	semisweet chocolate chips (vegan, gluten-free)	125 mL
1 tsp	gluten-free vanilla extract	5 mL
1	baked Coconut Flour Pie Crust (page 284)	1

1. In a small bowl or cup, combine psyllium and coconut water. Set aside.

2. In a large bowl, whisk together coconut sugar, cocoa powder, potato starch, espresso powder (if using) and salt. Whisk in ½ cup (125 mL) coconut milk until blended.

3. In a medium saucepan, bring the remaining coconut milk to a simmer over medium heat. Slowly whisk hot coconut milk into cocoa mixture.

4. Transfer cocoa mixture to saucepan and add chocolate chips. Cook over medium heat, whisking constantly, for 4 to 5 minutes or until thick and bubbly. Reduce heat and simmer, whisking, for 2 minutes. Remove from heat and whisk in psyllium mixture and vanilla.

5. Spread filling in baked pie crust. Cover surface of filling with plastic wrap and refrigerate for at least 3 hours, until chilled, before serving.

Banoffee Pie

Who would guess that such a brief and humble array of ingredients could produce such a supreme treat? The minimal effort required is a sweet bonus.

Storage Tip

Prepare the pie through step 2 and store, loosely wrapped in foil or waxed paper, in the refrigerator for up to 1 day. You can keep leftovers for up to 3 days; just remove the bananas before storing, then add freshly sliced bananas when ready to serve again.

- Food processor

3 cups	packed pitted moist dates (such as Medjool)	750 mL
1 cup	coconut water	250 mL
1 tsp	gluten-free vanilla extract	5 mL
1/8 tsp	fine sea salt	0.5 mL
1	baked Coconut Flour Pie Crust (page 284)	1
1 1/2 cups	Whipped Double Coconut Cream (variation, page 299), made with coconut nectar	375 mL
2	large bananas	2
1 tsp	freshly squeezed lemon juice	5 mL

1. In food processor, combine dates, coconut water, vanilla and salt; purée until creamy and smooth.

2. Spread filling in baked pie crust. Spread Whipped Double Coconut Cream evenly over filling. Refrigerate for at least 1 hour, until filling is firm, before serving.

3. Just before serving, slice bananas crosswise and arrange on top of pie. Brush with lemon juice to prevent browning.

Key Lime Pie

If ever a match was made in culinary heaven, it is lime and coconut. Every slice of this pie is loaded with fresh lime flavor, perfectly balanced by mellow coconut. Emerald green avocados lend bright color without any artificial ingredients.

Makes 8 servings

Tips

To toast sunflower seeds, place up to 3 tbsp (45 mL) seeds in a medium skillet set over medium heat. Cook, shaking the skillet, for 3 to 5 minutes or until seeds are fragrant. Let cool completely before use.

Hemp hearts can be used in place of the sunflower seeds. Toast them in the same manner as the sunflower seeds.

An equal amount of agave nectar can be used in place of the coconut nectar.

Storage Tip

Store the pie, loosely wrapped in foil or waxed paper, in the refrigerator for up to 3 days.

- Food processor
- 9-inch (23 cm) pie plate

Crust

½ cup	packed pitted moist dates (such as Medjool)	125 mL
1 cup	sunflower seeds, toasted (see tip, at left)	250 mL
½ cup	unsweetened flaked coconut	125 mL
Pinch	fine sea salt	Pinch
2 tbsp	virgin coconut oil	30 mL
½ tsp	gluten-free vanilla extract	2 mL

Filling

2	large ripe Hass avocados, cut into quarters	2
2 tsp	finely grated lime zest (Key lime or regular)	10 mL
¾ cup	freshly squeezed lime juice (Key lime or regular)	175 mL
⅓ cup	coconut nectar	75 mL
2 tbsp	coconut flour	30 mL
¼ tsp	fine sea salt	1 mL
1¼ cups	coconut cream	300 mL

1. *Crust:* In food processor, combine dates, sunflower seeds, coconut, salt, coconut oil and vanilla; process until a thick paste forms. Press mixture into bottom and sides of pie plate. Refrigerate while preparing filling. Clean bowl and blade of food processor.

2. *Filling:* In food processor, combine avocados, lime zest, lime juice and coconut nectar; purée until smooth. Add coconut flour, salt and coconut cream; purée until smooth.

3. Spread filling in prepared crust. Cover surface of filling with plastic wrap and refrigerate for at least 4 hours, until filling is firm, before serving.

Pumpkin Pie

Thanksgiving without pumpkin pie is almost unthinkable, and you can reap pumpkin's great health benefits at the same time.

- Preheat oven to 350°F (180°C)

¾ cup	coconut sugar	175 mL
2 tbsp	potato starch	30 mL
2½ tsp	pumpkin pie spice	12 mL
¼ tsp	fine sea salt	1 mL
2¼ cups	pumpkin purée (not pie filling)	550 mL
1 cup	well-stirred coconut milk (full-fat)	250 mL
2 tsp	gluten-free vanilla extract	10 mL
1	parbaked Coconut Flour Pie Crust (page 284)	1

1. In a large bowl, whisk together coconut sugar, potato starch, pumpkin pie spice, salt, pumpkin, coconut milk and vanilla until well blended.

2. Spread filling in parbaked pie crust.

3. Bake in preheated oven for 35 to 40 minutes or until center is set. Let cool completely on a wire rack. Serve at room temperature or refrigerate for up to 1 day, until ready to serve.

Caribbean Sweet Potato Pie

This version of sweet potato pie is enhanced by Caribbean flavors — coconut milk, lime, ginger and allspice — which add plenty of tropical appeal.

Tip

To make 1¾ cups (425 mL) sweet potato purée, you'll need 1⅓ lbs (675 g) sweet potatoes (about 2 large). Using a fork, prick sweet potatoes all over. Place on a large plate and microwave on High, turning every 5 minutes, for 15 to 20 minutes or until very soft. Immediately cut in half to release steam. When cool enough to handle, scoop flesh into a bowl and mash until smooth. Measure 1¾ cups (425 mL), reserving any extra for another use.

- Preheat oven to 350°F (180°C)

¾ cup	coconut sugar	175 mL
3 tbsp	potato starch	45 mL
1 tsp	ground allspice	5 mL
1 tsp	ground ginger	5 mL
¼ tsp	fine sea salt	1 mL
1¾ cups	cooked sweet potato purée (see tip, at left)	425 mL
1¼ cups	well-stirred coconut milk (full-fat)	300 mL
1 tsp	finely grated lime zest	5 mL
2 tbsp	freshly squeezed lime juice	30 mL
1	parbaked Coconut Flour Pie Crust (page 284)	1

1. In a large bowl, whisk together coconut sugar, potato starch, allspice, ginger, salt, sweet potato, coconut milk, lime zest and lime juice until well blended.

2. Spread filling in parbaked pie crust.

3. Bake in preheated oven for 50 to 55 minutes or until center is set. Let cool completely on a wire rack. Serve at room temperature or refrigerate for up to 1 day, until ready to serve.

Rhubarb Crumble

This no-hassle mix-and-bake dessert is at once old-fashioned and brand new. A generous dollop of whipped coconut cream on top elevates it from great to outstanding.

Makes 9 servings

Tips
....

Removing the foil halfway through baking allows the topping to become crisp and browned.

An equal amount of agave nectar or pure maple syrup can be used in place of the coconut nectar.

- Preheat oven to 375°F (190°C)
- 13- by 9-inch (33 by 23 cm) glass baking dish, sprayed with nonstick cooking spray

1¼ cups	unsweetened flaked coconut	300 mL
½ cup	coconut sugar	125 mL
⅓ cup	coconut flour	75 mL
1 tsp	ground cinnamon	5 mL
½ tsp	fine sea salt	2 mL
½ cup	melted virgin coconut oil	125 mL
2 tsp	gluten-free vanilla extract, divided	10 mL
1 tbsp	potato starch	15 mL
½ cup	unsweetened apple juice	125 mL
½ cup	coconut nectar or additional coconut sugar	125 mL
10 cups	fresh or frozen sliced rhubarb, thawed if frozen (½-inch/1 cm slices)	2.5 L
	Whipped Coconut Cream (page 299)	

1. In a medium bowl, whisk together coconut, coconut sugar, coconut flour, cinnamon and salt. Add coconut oil and half the vanilla; stir until crumbly.

2. In a large bowl, whisk together potato starch, apple juice, coconut nectar and the remaining vanilla. Add rhubarb and toss to coat.

3. Spoon rhubarb mixture into baking prepared dish and sprinkle with coconut mixture. Cover with foil.

4. Bake in preheated oven for 30 minutes. Remove foil and bake for 25 to 30 minutes or until browned and bubbling and rhubarb is tender. Let cool on a wire rack for 30 minutes.

5. Serve warm or at room temperature, topped with Whipped Coconut Cream.

Storage Tip

Store the cooled crumble, loosely wrapped in foil or waxed paper, in the refrigerator for up to 3 days.

Variations

Peach Crumble: Replace the rhubarb with an equal amount of sliced peeled peaches (fresh or thawed frozen). Decrease the coconut nectar by 1⁄4 cup (60 mL).

Apple Crumble: Replace the rhubarb with an equal amount of sliced peeled tart-sweet apples (such as Braeburn or Gala). Decrease the coconut nectar by 1⁄4 cup (60 mL).

* Power Ingredient

Rhubarb

Humble rhubarb is a great source of vitamin K and fiber, and a good source of vitamin C, calcium and potassium. But new research hints at an additional role for the celery-like plant: it could help lower cholesterol and improve arterial health. Additional studies also suggest that rhubarb may have various therapeutic benefits, ranging from laxative effects to the treatment of high blood pressure during pregnancy.

Baked Apples with Coconut, Pepitas and Cherries

Baked apple lovers, beware: this recipe ups the ante. Stuffed with cherries, pepitas and coconut, it may just become your go-to autumn dessert.

Makes 4 servings

Tips

Other varieties of dried fruit, such as cranberries, blueberries or raisins, may be used in place of the cherries.

Consider topping each apple with a dollop of coconut cream or plain coconut yogurt (store-bought or see recipe, page 49).

Storage Tip

Store the cooled apples, loosely covered in foil or plastic wrap, in the refrigerator for up to 1 day. Serve cold or warm in the microwave on Medium (70%) power for about 1 minute.

- Preheat oven to 350°F (180°C)
- 9-inch (23 cm) square glass baking dish or glass pie plate

4	tart-sweet apples (such as Braeburn, Gala or Fuji), cored	4
1/3 cup	dried cherries	75 mL
1/3 cup	chopped toasted green pumpkin seeds (pepitas)	75 mL
3 tbsp	coconut sugar	45 mL
1 1/2 tbsp	coconut flour	22 mL
1 tsp	ground cinnamon or ground cardamom	5 mL
4 tbsp	melted virgin coconut oil, divided	60 mL

1. Using a vegetable peeler, peel top inch (2.5 cm) of apples. Place apples, top side up, in baking dish.

2. In a small bowl, combine cherries, pumpkin seeds, coconut sugar, coconut flour, cinnamon and 2 tbsp (30 mL) coconut oil. Stuff mixture into apple cavities. Brush remaining coconut oil over each apple.

3. Bake in preheated oven, brushing occasionally with accumulated juices, for 45 to 55 minutes or until apples are tender.

4. Transfer apples to a plate and pour any pan juices over top.

❊ Power Ingredient

Cherries
Cherries are one of the best fruit sources of antioxidants, which help prevent many diseases associated with aging. They are rich in several plant compounds that have health benefits, including quercetin, a flavonoid with anticancer and heart-protecting qualities. Furthermore, their soluble fiber helps keep LDL ("bad") cholesterol levels low.

Coconut Milk Panna Cotta

If you think custard desserts are bland, this panna cotta is a must-make. Butterscotch-caramel notes from the coconut sugar and the refined flavor of vanilla are tied together by the mellow richness of coconut milk. The result? A finale with "wow."

Makes 4 servings

Tips

If using agar powder, reduce the amount used to 1 tsp (5 mL).

Coconut sugar is naturally dark brown, which will turn the panna cotta a very light tan color. For a white panna cotta, opt for an equal amount of blonde-colored natural cane sugar in place of the coconut sugar.

You can use seeds scraped from ½ vanilla bean in place of the vanilla extract. Add with the coconut milk in step 1.

Consider serving the panna cotta with fresh berries, such as blueberries, raspberries and/or blackberries.

Storage Tip

Store the panna cotta, loosely wrapped in foil or waxed paper, in the refrigerator for up to 2 days.

- Four 6-oz (175 mL) ramekins or custard cups

¼ cup	coconut sugar	60 mL
1 tbsp	agar flakes (see tip, at left)	15 mL
Pinch	fine sea salt	Pinch
2 cups	well-stirred coconut milk (full-fat)	500 mL
1 tsp	gluten-free vanilla extract	5 mL

1. In a medium saucepan, combine coconut sugar, agar flakes, salt and coconut milk. Let stand for 10 minutes.

2. Bring to a simmer over low heat, stirring occasionally. Continue to simmer, whisking occasionally, for 8 to 10 minutes or until agar has dissolved. Remove from heat and whisk in vanilla. Immediately pour into ramekins.

3. Cover loosely and refrigerate for at least 1 hour, until set and chilled.

✷ Power Ingredient

Agar
Agar is a vegetarian alternative to gelatin made from several varieties of seaweed. A good source of calcium and iron, agar contains no sugar, no fat and no carbohydrates, and is known for its ability to aid in digestion and remove toxins from the body. Agar absorbs glucose and is quickly digested, which may prevent the body from storing unnecessary fats and sugars. In addition to absorbing glucose, agar has been shown to absorb bile, which may help lower the amount of cholesterol absorbed by the body. Agar acts as a slight laxative, which may help certain digestive disorders, specifically liver sluggishness, constipation and slow motility. It is praised in China and Japan for its ability to reduce inflammation, calm the liver and suppress appetite.

Coconut Tapioca Pudding

Even if you typically insist on your pudding being completely smooth, you will swoon over this coconut tapioca pudding.

Makes 4 servings

Tip

Look for tapioca pearls at gourmet grocery or baking stores, online baking supply stores or Asian supermarkets.

Storage Tip

Store the cooled pudding, loosely covered with plastic wrap, in the refrigerator for up to 2 days.

⅓ cup	tapioca pearls	75 mL
1 cup	coconut water or water	250 mL
2 cups	well-stirred coconut milk (full-fat)	500 mL
¼ cup	coconut nectar or coconut sugar	60 mL
2 tsp	tapioca starch or potato starch	10 mL
2 tbsp	water	30 mL
¼ tsp	fine sea salt	1 mL
1 tsp	gluten-free vanilla extract	5 mL
2 tsp	chia seeds or poppy seeds (optional)	10 mL

1. In a large bowl, combine tapioca pearls and coconut water. Cover and let stand at room temperature for at least 4 hours or overnight.

2. In a medium saucepan, whisk together coconut milk and coconut nectar. Stir in tapioca pearl mixture. Cook, stirring, over medium heat until sugar is dissolved and mixture is just beginning to boil. Reduce heat and simmer, stirring constantly, for 10 to 12 minutes or until tapioca pearls are very tender.

3. In a small bowl, whisk together tapioca starch and water; stir into the pan. Cook, stirring, for 5 to 6 minutes or until slightly thickened. Remove from heat and stir in salt and vanilla.

4. Transfer pudding to a heatproof bowl or 4 individual serving dishes. Cover surface of pudding with plastic wrap and refrigerate for 3 to 4 hours or until chilled. Serve sprinkled with chia seeds, if desired.

> ✳ **Power Ingredient**
>
> *Tapioca*
> At first glance, tapioca — which is low in protein and has limited vitamins — has little to offer besides a few B vitamins. But take a closer look: tapioca has great amounts of iron and other minerals, such as calcium and manganese. It is also high in omega-3 and omega-6 fatty acids, both of which are critical for brain function.

Butterscotch Pudding

The true flavor of butterscotch is captured in this easy, creamy, coconutty pudding. Coconut sugar delivers the pudding's rich butterscotch flavor in one fell swoop.

Storage Tip

Store the cooled pudding, loosely covered with plastic wrap, in the refrigerator for up to 2 days.

½ cup	coconut sugar	125 mL
3 tbsp	potato starch	45 mL
⅛ tsp	fine sea salt	0.5 mL
2⅓ cups	well-stirred coconut milk (full-fat), divided	575 mL
2 tsp	gluten-free vanilla extract	10 mL

1. In a medium saucepan, whisk together coconut sugar, potato starch and salt. Whisk in ⅓ cup (75 mL) coconut milk until blended. Place saucepan over medium heat and cook, whisking, for 3 to 4 minutes or until sugar is dissolved.

2. Gradually whisk in the remaining coconut milk. Cook, whisking, for 2 to 4 minutes or until thickened. Remove from heat and whisk in vanilla.

3. Transfer pudding to a medium heatproof bowl or 4 individual serving dishes and let cool to room temperature. Serve at room temperature or cover surface of pudding with plastic wrap and refrigerate until cold.

Variations

Chocolate Pudding: Add ¼ cup (60 mL) unsweetened natural cocoa powder to the coconut sugar mixture in step 1. Increase the coconut milk to 2½ cups (625 mL).

Vanilla Pudding: Replace the coconut sugar with an equal amount of blonde-colored natural cane sugar.

Strawberry Coconut Mousse

This pretty-in-pink dessert is sweet with ripe strawberries and enriched with both coconut milk and coconut oil. With its juicy fruit, luxurious texture and delicate hue, it will please any dessert lover.

Makes 6 servings

Tip

Blueberries, peaches or apricots can be used in place of the strawberries.

Storage Tip

Store the mousse, loosely covered with plastic wrap, in the refrigerator for up to 2 days.

- Food processor or blender
- Six 6-oz (175 mL) ramekins or dessert glasses

¼ cup	potato starch	60 mL
⅛ tsp	fine sea salt	0.5 mL
1 cup	unsweetened apple juice	250 mL
⅓ cup	coconut nectar or agave nectar	75 mL
2½ cups	chopped strawberries	625 mL
1⅓ cups	well-stirred coconut milk (full-fat)	325 mL
¼ cup	melted virgin coconut oil	60 mL

1. In a medium saucepan, whisk together potato starch, salt, apple juice and coconut nectar. Bring to a simmer over medium heat, whisking often. Reduce heat and simmer, whisking constantly, for 30 seconds or until thickened (mixture will be very thick). Remove from heat and let cool for 10 minutes.

2. In food processor, combine apple juice mixture, strawberries, coconut milk and coconut oil; purée until creamy and smooth.

3. Divide mousse equally among ramekins. Cover and refrigerate for at least 4 hours, until chilled.

Whipped Coconut Cream

It's a beautiful thing when an alternative food surpasses the original. Case in point: this whipped coconut cream that is so much better than traditional dairy whipped cream. Although it is positively sublime as a topping for other desserts, it is a heavenly treat in itself when sweetened with a touch of coconut sugar or nectar, as in the variations below.

Makes about ¾ cup (175 mL)

Tips

Some brands of coconut milk now add emulsifiers to their products to prevent separation of the coconut fats and liquid. Making whipped coconut cream is not possible with these brands because the cream will not solidify properly when chilled. Be sure to check the ingredients on the coconut milk label; if emulsifiers are included on the list, opt for a different brand.

Flipping the can upside down places the solidified cream at the bottom and the milky coconut water on top; this makes it easier to pour off the liquid and scoop out the cream.

Storage Tip

Store any unused whipped coconut cream in an airtight container in the refrigerator for up to 2 weeks. Rewhip with an electric mixer before using.

- Electric mixer

1	can (14 oz/398 mL) coconut milk (full-fat)	1

1. Place the can of coconut milk in the refrigerator. Refrigerate for at least 24 hours.
2. Just before whipping the coconut cream, place a medium bowl (preferably metal) and the beaters from the electric mixer in the freezer for 5 minutes.
3. Remove can from refrigerator and flip upside down. Open can with a can opener and pour off liquid (store liquid in an airtight container in the refrigerator for another use). Scoop thick coconut cream into chilled bowl.
4. Whip the coconut cream with the electric mixer on high until soft peaks form. Use immediately.

Variations

Whipped Lemon Coconut Cream: Add 2 tsp (10 mL) coconut sugar, 1½ tsp (7 mL) finely grated lemon zest and 1 tbsp (15 mL) freshly squeezed lemon juice near the end of whipping in step 4.

Whipped Vanilla Coconut Cream: Add 2 tsp (10 mL) coconut sugar and 1 tsp (5 mL) vanilla extract near the end of whipping in step 4.

Whipped Double Coconut Cream: Add 1 tbsp (15 mL) coconut sugar or coconut nectar near the end of whipping in step 4.

Dates Stuffed with Lemon Coconut Cream

Evocative of cheesecake but so much easier, this minimalist dessert manages to be both everyday and upscale.

Makes 8 servings

Tip

Other varieties of moist, plump pitted dates may be used in place of the Medjool dates.

Storage Tip

Store the stuffed dates, loosely covered in foil or plastic wrap, in the refrigerator for up to 2 days.

8 tsp	chilled coconut cream (see page 18)	40 mL
¼ tsp	finely grated lemon zest	1 mL
2 tsp	freshly squeezed lemon juice	10 mL
8	large Medjool dates, pitted	8

1. In a small bowl, combine coconut cream, lemon zest and lemon juice until well blended.

2. Stuff each date with a heaping teaspoon (5 mL) of the coconut cream mixture. Refrigerate for at least 30 minutes, until filling is firm, before serving.

✳ Power Ingredient

Lemons

Lemons have a variety of health-enhancing properties and were even used by Romans as a cure-all for many poisons. The high vitamin C content of the juice helps prevent and treat infections and speed the healing of fevers, while the calcium in the peel (zest) benefits bone health. A lemon's antioxidants include limonene, an oil found in the peel that may help prevent breast and other cancers and lower "bad" blood cholesterol, and rutin, which has been found to strengthen veins and prevent fluid retention. Lemons also stimulate the taste buds and may be useful for people with a poor appetite.

Coconut Butter

Use this easy-to-make, frugal alternative to nut butter in any way you would the nutty spread. As you do, you'll reap the benefits of high fiber and protein.

Tip
....

The coconut butter will be solid once refrigerated. To make it spreadable, scoop out several spoonfuls and microwave on High for 5 to 10 seconds or until softened.

Storage Tip
....

Refrigerate the coconut butter in an airtight container for up to 3 months.

- Food processor

8 oz	unsweetened flaked coconut (2 cups/500 mL)	250 g
⅛ tsp	fine sea salt	0.5 mL
2 tbsp	virgin coconut oil	30 mL
1 tsp	gluten-free vanilla extract (optional)	5 mL

1. In food processor, combine coconut, salt, coconut oil and vanilla (if using); process for 1 minute, then scrape down the sides of the bowl.

2. Continue to process in 30-second intervals, stopping to scrape sides of bowl each time. After 3 minutes, the coconut will appear finely chopped. After 5 to 8 minutes, the mixture will be grainy and somewhat paste-like. After 10 to 12 minutes, the mixture will be creamy and the consistency of peanut butter.

Coconut Butter Bark

You can use any variety of chopped dried fruit in this gorgeous, delectable treat, but cherries are my fruit of choice because they are one of the best fruit sources of antioxidants.

Makes 16 pieces

Tips

When lining the pan, allow the parchment paper to hang over the sides so you can easily remove the bark once it is set.

An equal amount of agave nectar or pure maple syrup can be used in place of the coconut nectar.

Storage Tip

Refrigerate the bark in an airtight container for up to 2 months.

- 8- by 4-inch (20 by 10 cm) loaf pan, lined with parchment paper

1¼ cups	coconut butter (store-bought or see recipe, page 301)	300 mL
1 tbsp	coconut nectar	15 mL
½ cup	dried cherries	125 mL
⅓ cup	raw or lightly toasted green pumpkin seeds (pepitas)	75 mL

1. In a small saucepan, melt coconut butter over low heat, stirring constantly. Remove from heat and stir in coconut nectar.

2. Pour mixture into prepared pan. Sprinkle with cherries and pumpkin seeds.

3. Refrigerate for at least 1 hour, until set. Remove from pan and cut into pieces.

Variations

Chocolate Coconut Butter Bark: Omit the coconut nectar. Add ⅓ cup (75 mL) semisweet chocolate chips (vegan, gluten-free) to the coconut butter in step 1, heating and stirring until melted.

Butterscotch Bark: Omit the coconut nectar. Add 2½ tbsp (37 mL) coconut sugar to the coconut butter in step 1, heating and stirring until melted. Remove from heat and stir in 1 tsp (5 mL) gluten-free vanilla extract.

Lemon Apricot Bark: Add 2 tsp (10 mL) finely grated lemon zest and 1 tbsp (15 mL) freshly squeezed lemon juice with the coconut nectar. Replace the dried cherries with chopped dried apricots.

Coconut Ice Cream

Here's to perfect ice cream that supports great health. The creaminess in this interpretation is exclusively coconut milk. Perhaps a second serving is in order!

Tip

An equal amount of agave nectar or pure maple syrup can be used in place of the coconut nectar.

- Ice cream maker

2¼ cups	well-stirred coconut milk (full-fat)	550 mL
½ cup	coconut nectar	125 mL
1 tsp	gluten-free vanilla extract	5 mL
⅛ tsp	fine sea salt	0.5 mL

1. In a medium bowl, whisk together coconut milk, coconut nectar, vanilla and salt until well blended. Cover and refrigerate for at least 4 hours or until cold.

2. Pour into ice cream maker and freeze according to manufacturer's instructions.

3. Spoon into an airtight container, cover and freeze for at least 4 hours, until firm, or for up to 1 week.

Variation

Toasted Coconut Ice Cream: Add ½ cup (125 mL) toasted unsweetened flaked coconut to the ice cream maker along with the coconut milk mixture in step 2.

Roasted Banana Coconut Ice Cream

At last: ice cream that is as healthful as it is decadent! Bananas are the only sweetener — roasting them intensifies their sweetness multifold — and coconut milk is the only "cream." Together they offer fiber, heart-healthy fat, vitamins B_6 and C and manganese in each spoonful.

Makes 6 servings

Tip

For best results, use bananas that are ripe but firm or semi-firm. If they are soft and mushy, they will break down too much during roasting.

- Preheat oven to 400°F (200°C)
- 9-inch (23 cm) square metal baking pan, greased with coconut oil
- Blender or food processor
- Ice cream maker

3	large bananas, sliced crosswise	3
1 tbsp	melted virgin coconut oil	15 mL
1¾ cups	well-stirred coconut milk (full-fat), divided	425 mL
⅛ tsp	fine sea salt	0.5 mL

1. Arrange bananas in a single layer on prepared pan and drizzle with coconut oil. Bake in preheated oven for 15 to 20 minutes, tossing once or twice, until browned and somewhat syrupy. Transfer to a wire rack and let cool completely in pan.

2. In blender, combine cooled bananas, coconut milk and salt; process until smooth.

3. Transfer to a bowl, cover and refrigerate for at least 4 hours or until cold.

4. Pour into ice cream maker and freeze according to manufacturer's instructions.

5. Spoon into an airtight container, cover and freeze for at least 4 hours, until firm, or for up to 1 week.

Variation

Chocolate Roasted Banana Ice Cream: Add ¼ cup (60 mL) unsweetened natural cocoa powder and 2 tbsp (30 mL) coconut sugar in step 2.

Instant Strawberry Ice Cream

Who wouldn't covet strawberry ice cream made in less than 5 minutes with a blender?

Makes 4 servings

Tip
......

Although this recipe can be made in either a blender or food processor, the former is preferable, as it will produce a creamier dessert.

- Blender or food processor

3½ cups	frozen strawberries, thawed for 10 minutes	875 mL
⅓ cup	coconut nectar or agave nectar	75 mL
½ cup	well-stirred coconut milk (full-fat), chilled	125 mL
1 tbsp	freshly squeezed lemon juice	15 mL

1. In blender, combine strawberries and coconut nectar; process until coarsely chopped. Add coconut milk and lemon juice; pulse until smooth and creamy, scraping down the sides once or twice.

2. Serve immediately in small dessert dishes.

Variation

Use an equal amount of frozen blueberries or chopped frozen peaches, apricots, mangos, bananas or pineapple in place of the strawberries. Let fruit thaw for 10 minutes before using, to achieve an ice cream–like texture.

Chocolate Gelato

This gelato, made decadently rich with coconut milk and cocoa powder in place of dairy and chocolate, is a triumph.

Tip
......

Select natural cocoa powder rather than Dutch process. Natural cocoa powder has a deep, true chocolate flavor. The packaging should state whether it is Dutch process or not, but you can also tell by sight: if it is dark to almost black, it is Dutch process; natural cocoa powder is much lighter and is typically reddish brown in color.

- Ice cream maker

2/3 cup	unsweetened natural cocoa powder (see tip, at left)	150 mL
3 1/2 cups	well-stirred coconut milk (full-fat), divided	875 mL
1 tsp	gluten-free vanilla extract	5 mL
3/4 cup	coconut sugar	175 mL
2 tbsp	potato starch	30 mL
1/8 tsp	fine sea salt	0.5 mL

1. In a large bowl, whisk together cocoa powder, 2/3 cup (150 mL) coconut milk and vanilla to make a smooth paste.

2. In a medium saucepan, whisk together coconut sugar, potato starch, salt and the remaining coconut milk. Bring to a simmer over medium heat, whisking gently. Reduce heat and simmer, whisking constantly, for 2 to 3 minutes or until mixture begins to thicken.

3. Pour the hot coconut milk mixture over the cocoa paste, whisking until blended and smooth. Cover and refrigerate for at least 4 hours or until cold.

4. Pour into ice cream maker and freeze according to manufacturer's instructions.

5. Spoon into an airtight container, cover and freeze for at least 4 hours, until firm, or for up to 1 week.

Lemon Blueberry Cream Pops

Why restrict delectable blueberries to muffins and pies? Here, they shine in cool, creamy ice pops guaranteed to thrill your palate.

Tip

You can use 4-oz (125 mL) paper cups as ice-pop molds. Place them on a baking sheet, then fill until almost full. Cover with foil, then make a small slit to insert ice-pop sticks or small bamboo skewers and freeze as directed.

Variation

Peaches and Cream Pops: Substitute chopped peeled peaches (fresh or thawed frozen) for the blueberries and orange juice (preferably freshly squeezed) for the apple juice.

- Blender
- 8-serving ice-pop mold

1 cup	fresh or thawed frozen blueberries	250 mL
2/3 cup	unsweetened apple juice	150 mL
2/3 cup	well-stirred coconut milk (full-fat)	150 mL
1 tbsp	freshly squeezed lemon juice	15 mL

1. In blender, combine blueberries, apple juice, coconut milk and lemon juice; purée until smooth.
2. Pour mixture into ice-pop molds, insert sticks and freeze for 4 to 6 hours, until solid, or for up to 1 week. If necessary, briefly dip bases of mold in hot water to loosen and unmold.

✳ Power Ingredient

Blueberries

Blueberries are a fruit favorite, as well they should be. They are high in vitamin C and fiber, and appear to help urinary tract infections. Their carotene, in the form of lutein and zeaxanthin, helps keep eyes healthy, and they are a good source of anthocyanins, which can help prevent heart disease and memory loss. A study from the University of Reading and the Peninsula medical school in England suggests that blueberries can even reverse age-related memory loss, thanks to an abundance of antioxidants called flavonoids.

Deep purple blueberries are the richest of all fruits in antioxidant compounds. Multiple scientific studies indicate that the compound pterostilbene, found in the berries, helps lower cholesterol and may help prevent diabetes and some cancers.

Cucumber Coconut Water Spa Pops

One of these faintly sweet ice pops is an easy way to get the benefits of a spa for pennies. Along with refreshing flavor, the cucumbers in each pop offer revitalization to your system.

Makes 6 pops

Tips

You can use 4-oz (125 mL) paper cups as ice-pop molds. Place them on a baking sheet, then fill until almost full. Cover with foil, then make a small slit to insert ice-pop sticks or small bamboo skewers and freeze as directed.

An equal amount of agave nectar can be used in place of the coconut nectar.

- Blender
- 6-serving ice-pop mold

1 cup	coarsely chopped peeled seedless cucumber	250 mL
2 cups	coconut water	500 mL
2 tbsp	freshly squeezed lemon or lime juice	30 mL
1 tbsp	coconut nectar	15 mL

1. In blender, combine cucumber, coconut water, lemon juice and coconut nectar; purée until smooth.

2. Pour mixture into ice-pop molds, insert sticks and freeze for 4 to 6 hours, until solid, or for up to 1 week. If necessary, briefly dip bases of mold in hot water to loosen and unmold.

✳ Power Ingredient

Cucumbers
The cucumber is a type of melon and comes from the same family as watermelon, zucchini and other squash. Cucumbers are 95% water, keeping the body hydrated while helping it eliminate toxins. They still pack a lot of nutrition. The flesh of cucumbers is a very good source of folate and vitamins A and C. In fact, cucumbers have most of the vitamins the body needs in a single day.

References

Abujazia, Mouna Abdelrahman, Norliza Muhammad, Ahmad Nazrun Shuid, and Ima Nirwana Soelaiman. 2012. "The Effects of Virgin Coconut Oil on Bone Oxidative Status in Ovariectomised Rat." *Evidence-Based Complementary & Alternative Medicine (Ecam)*: 1–6.

"ALSUntangled 15: Coconut Oil." 2012. *Amyotrophic Lateral Sclerosis* 13, no. 3: 328–30.

Bowden, Jonny. 2007. *The Healthiest Foods on Earth.* Gloucester, MA: Fair Winds.

"Coconut Oil: Supervillain or Superfood?" 2014. *Harvard Heart Letter* 24, no. 5: 7.

"Coconut Oil Inhibits Caries." 2012. *British Dental Journal* 213, no. 6: 269.

Dayrit, Fabian M., Ian Ken D. Dimzon, Melodina F. Valde, Jaclyn Elizabeth R. Santos, Mark Joseph M. Garrovillas, and Blanca J. Villarino. 2011. "Quality Characteristics of Virgin Coconut Oil: Comparisons with Refined Coconut Oil." *Pure and Applied Chemistry* 83, no. 9: 1789–99.

"Diving into the Science on Coconut Water and Health." 2010. *Environmental Nutrition* 33, no. 7: 7.

Fife, Bruce. 2004a. *The Coconut Oil Miracle.* New York: Avery.

———. 2004b. "Nature's Miracle Oil." *Macrobiotics Today* 44, no. 5: 16–19.

Fonseca, Aluísio M., Francisco Jose Q. Monte, Maria da Conceição F. de Oliveira, Marcos C. de Mattos, Geoffrey A. Cordell, Raimundo Braz-Filho, and Telma L. G. Lemos. 2009. "Coconut water (*Cocos nucifera L.*) — A new biocatalyst system for organic synthesis." *Journal of Molecular Catalysis B: Enzymatic* 57, no. 1–4: 78–82.

Gunn, Bee F., Luc Baudouin, and Kenneth M. Olsen. 2011. "Independent Origins of Cultivated Coconut (*Cocos nucifera L.*) in the Old World Tropics." *Plos ONE* 6, no. 6: 1–8.

Hayatullina, Zil, Norliza Muhammad, Norazlina Mohamed, and Ima-Nirwana Soelaiman. 2012. "Virgin Coconut Oil Supplementation Prevents Bone Loss in Osteoporosis Rat Model." *Evidence-Based Complementary & Alternative Medicine (Ecam)*: 1–8.

Intahphuak, S., Parirat Khonsung, and Ampai Panthong. 2010. "Anti-Inflammatory, Analgesic, and Antipyretic Activities of Virgin Coconut Oil." *Pharmaceutical Biology* 48, no. 2: 151–57.

Iyer, Mohan N. Harihara, Babul C. Sarmah, Madan K. Tamuli, Anubrata Das, and Dhireswar Kalita. 2012. "Effect of Dietary Sunflower Oil and Coconut Oil on Adipose Tissue Gene Expression, Fatty Acid Composition and Serum Lipid Profile of Grower Pigs." *Archives of Animal Nutrition* 66, no. 4: 271–82.

Kadey, Matthew G. 2010. "Coconut Water: The Inside Story." *Vegetarian Times*, no. 374: 15.

Lau, Beatrice Y., Val Andrew Fajardo, Lauren McMeekin, Sandra M. Sacco, Wendy E. Ward, Brian D. Roy, Sandra J. Peters, and Paul J. LeBlanc. 2010. "Influence of High-Fat Diet from Differential Dietary Sources on Bone Mineral Density, Bone Strength, and Bone Fatty Acid Composition in Rats." *Applied Physiology, Nutrition & Metabolism* 35, no. 5: 598–606.

Marina, A.M., Y.B. Che Man, and I. Amin. 2009. "Virgin Coconut Oil: Emerging Functional Food Oil." *Trends in Food Science & Technology* 20, no. 10: 481–87.

Marina, A.M., Y.B. Che Man, S.A. Nazimah, and I. Amin. 2009. "Antioxidant Capacity and Phenolic Acids of Virgin Coconut Oil." *International Journal of Food Sciences and Nutrition* 60 Suppl 2: 114–123.

Murasaki-Aliberti, Nathalia da C., Rodrigo M.S. Da Silva, Jorge A.W. Gut, and Carmen C. Tadini. 2009. "Thermal Inactivation of Polyphenoloxidase and Peroxidase in Green Coconut (*Cocos nucifera*) Water." *International Journal of Food Science & Technology* 44, no. 12: 2662–68.

Nafar, Firoozeh, and Karen M. Mearow. 2014. "Coconut Oil Attenuates the Effects of Amyloid-ß on Cortical Neurons in Vitro." *Journal of Alzheimer's Disease* 39, no. 2: 233–37.

Nandakumaran, Moorkath, Elisaveth Angelaki, Nasser Al-Azemi, Hameed Al-Sarraf, and Eyad Al-Saleh. 2011. "Influence of Coconut Oil Administration on Some Hematologic and Metabolic Parameters in Pregnant Rats." *Journal of Maternal-Fetal and Neonatal Medicine* 24, no. 10: 1254–58.

Nasirullah, Rizwan Shariff, Umesha Shankara Shetty, and Reddy Sunki Yella. 2010. "Development of Chemically Interesterified Healthy Coconut Oil Blends." *International Journal of Food Science & Technology* 45, no. 7: 1395–1402.

Nevin, K.G., and T. Rajamohan. 2006. "Virgin Coconut Oil Supplemented Diet Increases the Antioxidant Status in Rats." *Food Chemistry* 99, no. 2: 260–66.

Nurul-Iman, Badlishah Sham, Yusof Kamisah, Kamsiah Jaarin, and Hj Mohd Saad Qodriyah. 2013. "Virgin Coconut Oil Prevents Blood Pressure Elevation and Improves Endothelial Functions in Rats Fed with Repeatedly Heated Palm Oil." *Evidence-Based Complementary & Alternative Medicine (Ecam)*: 1–7.

Schaffner, Carl P. 1985. "In Defense of Coconuts." *Natural History* 94, no. 8: 4.

Trinidad, Trinidad P., Aida C. Mallillin, Divinagracia H. Valdez, Anacleta S. Loyola, Faridah C. Askali-Mercado, Joan C. Castillo, Rosario R. Encabo, Dina B. Masa, Angelica S. Maglaya, and Modesto T. Chua. 2006. "Dietary Fiber from Coconut Flour: A Functional Food." *Innovative Food Science & Emerging Technologies* 7, no. 4: 309–17.

Turner, Lisa. 2011. "Off the Shelf. Coo-coo for Coconut." *Better Nutrition* 73, no. 4: 56–60.

Vysakh, A., M. Ratheesh, T.P. Rajmohanan, C. Pramod, S. Premlal, B. Girish Kumar, and P.I. Sibi. 2014. "Polyphenolics Isolated from Virgin Coconut Oil Inhibits Adjuvant Induced Arthritis in Rats Through Antioxidant and Anti-Inflammatory Action." *International Immunopharmacology* 20, no. 1: 124–130.

Willett, Walter C. 2011. "Coconut Oil." *Harvard Health Letter* 36, no. 7: 7.

Yong, Jean W.H., Liya Ge, Yan Fei Ng, and Swee Ngin Tan. 2009. "The Chemical Composition and Biological Properties of Coconut (*Cocos nucifera L.*) Water." *Molecules* 14, no. 12: 5144–64.

Library and Archives Canada Cataloguing in Publication

Saulsbury, Camilla V., author
    The complete coconut cookbook : 200 gluten-free, grain-free and nut-free vegan recipes using coconut flour, oil, sugar and more / Camilla V. Saulsbury.

Includes index.
ISBN 978-0-7788-0488-8 (pbk.)

    1. Cooking (Coconut). 2. Cookbooks. I. Title.

TX814.2.C63S29 2014   641.6'461   C2014-904232-9

Index